Union V

Union Warriors at Sunset

The Lives of Twenty Commanders After the War

ALLIE STUART POVALL

McFarland & Company, Inc., Publishers
Jefferson, North Carolina

All photographs are from the Library of Congress.

LIBRARY OF CONGRESS CATALOGUING-IN-PUBLICATION DATA

Names: Povall, Allie Stuart, 1941– author.
Title: Union warriors at sunset : the lives of twenty commanders
after the war / Allie Stuart Povall.
Other titles: Lives and careers of eighteen generals and two admirals
Description: Jefferson, North Carolina : McFarland & Company, Inc., Publishers, 2022 |
Includes bibliographical references and index.
Identifiers: LCCN 2022049743 | ISBN 9781476690506 (paperback : acid free paper) ∞
ISBN 9781476649870 (ebook)
Subjects: LCSH: United States—History—Civil War, 1861-1865—Veterans—Biography. |
United States—History—1865—Biography. | Generals—United States—
Biography. | Admirals—United States—Biography. | Veterans—United States—
Biography. | United States. Army—Biography. | BISAC: HISTORY / United States
/ Civil War Period (1850-1877) | HISTORY / Military / United States
Classification: LCC E467 .P85 2022 | DDC 973.7092/2   dc23/eng/20221025
LC record available at https://lccn.loc.gov/2022049743

BRITISH LIBRARY CATALOGUING DATA ARE AVAILABLE

ISBN (print) 978-1-4766-9050-6
ISBN (ebook) 978-1-4766-4987-0

On the cover: President Ulysses S. Grant,
half-length portrait, seated, facing right, between 1869
and 1885, printed later, Library of Congress

Printed in the United States of America

McFarland & Company, Inc., Publishers
Box 611, Jefferson, North Carolina 28640
www.mcfarlandpub.com

To four women
who have made a difference in my life:
For Janet, who is my love and my rock,
and in loving memory of
Emily Povall Lucas, my aunt and my godmother,
who gave me unconditional love when I needed it most,
and in memory of Margie Riddle Bearss and Clara Beall Watson,
two high school teachers who showed me the way.

Table of Contents

Introduction

This book is a companion to my work on Confederate commanders: *Rebels in Repose: Confederate Commanders After the War.* The Union commanders I cover—the "Holy Trinity" of Sheridan, Sherman and Grant; plus fifteen other generals; and two admirals—came from all over what the United States then comprised. One—George Thomas—even came from secessionist Virginia, and his service for the Union cost him his biological family, a wound he carried with him for the rest of his life. At the start of the war, Admiral David Farragut was stationed in Norfolk, which he had made his home for many years. He and his wife lost all of their friends there, a loss that deeply wounded them for the rest of their lives.

Many of these commanders were West Point graduates, but some were not. William Tecumseh Sherman was, but when the war started, he had been out of the army for several years, working as a banker and then as a putative lawyer in Kansas, both unsuccessfully. Indeed, both banks for which he worked went under, and he later told the unemployed Grant that West Point and the army did not prepare a man for a civilian career. In their cases, that was an understatement of leviathan proportions.

The Union's greatest general, at least in my opinion, Ulysses S. Grant, had also been out of the army for a number of years. He was a dismal failure at everything he attempted after leaving the army: farming, mostly, but also real estate, and he had to sell firewood on St. Louis street corners to feed his family and had to sell his pocket watch to buy them Christmas presents. When the war broke out, he was a clerk in his brothers' leather goods store in Galena, Illinois. Grant would, of course, go on to serve two terms as president of the United States after the war, a meteoric rise if ever there was one. Another general—Dan Sickles—was a successful, albeit controversial, politician. He shot and killed his wife's lover, the son of Francis Scott Key who wrote "The Star-Spangled Banner." Another— Joshua Lawrence Chamberlin, the hero of Gettysburg—was a college professor at Bowdoin College in Maine, and he would serve four terms as governor after the war. Other Union officers served in the "old army" with Southern friends who would fight for the Confederacy but with whom the Union commanders would, in many cases—Grant with Longstreet, for example—renew those friendships after the war.

Inclusion in this book is, at the margins, unquestionably arbitrary. There are commanders who are not in this book about whom I could have written, and as it is at law, there are hard cases on either side of the line, which is anything but bright. Nevertheless I have attempted to include men whose record of achievement during the war was high as well as those with interesting postwar lives, such as Lew Wallace, whose wartime record was not particularly distinguished but who wrote *Ben Hur* after the war. That novel is one of the best-selling of all time, and it has been made into a movie three times. In selecting my subjects, I hope that I have been fair, but some readers will undoubtedly feel that I have omitted worthy commanders. To them, in advance, I apologize.

I used myriad sources for this work, many secondary and many primary, including the memoirs of those who wrote them. I also relied on *Battles and Leaders of the Civil War*, which contains firsthand articles that originally appeared in *Century Magazine*. These articles covered specific Civil War battles and were written by many of the generals who fought them. *Battles* helped me understand not only the battles but also how the commanders perceived those conflicts and how they perceived themselves. Some used that medium to attack those who, they thought, had been unfair to them in their own articles. These clashes were not anomalous. The literary conflicts were so bad on the Confederate side that they have been termed "the Battle of the Books," a second civil war—it was not very civil—among many of the Confederate commanders.

I wrote this book out of—I won't say "idle"—curiosity. What these men did with their lives after the war has always interested me, and finally, relatively late in life, I got around to exploring this phase of their lives. This book is the result of that inquiry and the resulting research.

CHAPTER ONE

George Gordon Meade

"Old Snapping Turtle," "Old Four Eyes"

Prior to the Civil War

George Gordon Meade was born on December 31, 1815, in Cadiz, Spain, where his father was a wealthy merchant. Meade's father died, however, in 1828, and George, who wanted to be a lawyer, instead entered West Point in 1831 on an appointment by President Andrew Jackson, to whom his well-placed family was connected. Meade's intention was to secure an education as an engineer, serve the required one year and then resign to enter the engineering profession as a civilian. He was thus an indifferent student, especially with respect to discipline and demerits, but, based upon his academic performance, he managed to finish nineteenth out of fifty-six cadets in his class.

In spite of his academic performance, Meade did not receive an appointment to the engineering corps but instead joined the artillery. When his one-year commitment was up, he resigned and entered the practice of engineering as a railroad surveyor. The depression of 1837 ended railroad construction, and Meade suddenly found himself out of work. But once again, his family intervened and secured

MAJ. GEN. GEORGE G. MEADE

George Gordon Meade (c. 1863).

3

for him a position in the U.S. Topographical Bureau. Meade undertook various surveying projects for the bureau, until he finally determined that the bureau was a dead end. His brother-in-law Henry A. Wise was a congressman from Virginia, and Wise obtained Meade's old commission for him in the army. In 1840, Meade married Margaret Sergeant, daughter of a prominent Whig politician and congressman, John Sergeant, who had once been a candidate for vice president. Once again, Meade had established political connections that would benefit him later.

Then came that prerequisite course for the Civil War, the Mexican-American War, which would produce twenty luminaries who would serve in both the Union and the Confederate armies. During that war Meade served on the staff of General Zachary Taylor, and, as a staff officer, he thus saw no actual combat, but he did meet future luminaries Ulysses "Sam" Grant, James Longstreet, Jefferson Davis, Robert E. Lee, P.G.T. Beauregard and Joseph E. Johnston, all names he would encounter again in the cataclysmic struggle to come. During the Mexican War, Meade developed a reputation as a man with a short fuse. He also developed a hatred for the press, which had attacked Taylor for his perceived inaction. Both of these predilections would inform his actions during the Civil War.

After the Mexican War, Meade went to work overseeing the construction of lighthouses. He was at this point in his life a "tall, lean, hatchet-faced aristocrat with an aquiline nose."[1] Working out of his old hometown, Philadelphia, Meade and Margaret maintained an active social life among the aristocrats along the Northeast coast, and this led to connections with the business elite who had contracts with the federal government. Then followed an assignment in Detroit, which allowed him to avoid the assignments that were the bane of the pre–Civil War junior officer: lonely, boring duty in the forts of the western frontier. The Meades loved Detroit, and by the end of that sinecure, his marriage to Margaret had produced seven children.

Then came the election of Abraham Lincoln and the secession of Southern states. Besides Henry J. Wise, another of Margaret's sisters had married into a wealthy Southern family. Meade was thus not unsympathetic to the South, but he was a Philadelphia blueblood, and it was to the North that his real sympathies lay. Moreover, he was a professional soldier who had taken the oath of allegiance to the United States. Meade decided to stay with the Union.[2]

The Civil War

With the rolling thunder of P.G.T. Beauregard's guns in Charleston Harbor, war came to the United States. Notwithstanding the North's need for professional soldiers, Meade remained in Detroit for several months, champing at the bit for a field command. Finally, Margaret pulled strings with her congressman father, and Meade secured a promotion to brigadier general in command of a brigade of Pennsylvania volunteers. Assigned to General George Brinton McClellan's Army of the Potomac, Meade, like that army, did nothing for the remainder of 1861.

Finally, in the spring of 1862, McClellan began the Peninsula Campaign, whose objective was to capture Richmond. Pressing steadily against the army of Confederate general Joseph E. Johnston, McClellan moved cautiously up the peninsula toward Richmond, until its church steeples were in sight. Then, Johnston was wounded, Robert E. Lee took over, and everything changed. In a series of battles known as the Seven Days, Lee, much to Meade's disgust, drove McClellan's numerically superior Union Army back down the peninsula. Meade saw combat in five battles, and in the last one, Gaines Mill, he was wounded in his arm and back. Meade then retired to Philadelphia to recover from his wounds. The Philadelphia newspapers complimented his bravery and acumen as a leader of men.

Meade returned for the debacle at Second Bull Run and covered John Pope's ignominious retreat toward Washington. At this point it was said of Meade that he was "completely lacking in charisma and the ability to inspire his men." He "looked like … a burned-out college professor. His thin bearded face and balding head gave the impression that he was serious, almost sad. Possessing a broad, high forehead and a hawk-like nose, Meade was referred to as a 'damned google-eyed old snapping turtle' by his troops. To many, this epithet would have been an insult, but it did not seem to bother Meade."[3]

Lee then invaded Maryland, and Lincoln and Edwin Stanton brought the sluggish McClellan back to replace the inept John Pope. McClellan followed Lee into Maryland, and after a series of engagements, he faced off with Lee along Antietam Creek near Sharpsburg. It was during this campaign that Meade won the sobriquet "Old Snapping Turtle," when he struck a soldier with the flat of his sword for eating a peach from a tree that Meade had ordered the soldier to guard. Meade called the rascal a "mercenary villain" and threatened to cut off the man's head.[4]

Then followed the famous Lost Order, in which a Union soldier found a copy of Lee's campaign plan wrapped around some cigars. The order revealed that Lee had split his army. McClellan read the order and exclaimed that if he couldn't "whip Bobbie Lee," he would go home. Perhaps he should have gone home. He dilly-dallied for eighteen hours, which allowed Lee to reconstitute his army along Antietam Creek. Thus ensued the bloodiest day of the Civil War.

The Union line ran from north to south along the east side of

Antietam Creek, and Meade's brigade was at the north end. He and his brigade saw extensive combat that first morning, and one of his soldiers wrote that he had seen Meade astride his horse as bullets whistled by his head and splattered on the ground around him.

Once again, the Old Snapping Turtle struck. He found a soldier cowering in terror at the rear of his brigade and struck him with the flat of his terrible swift sword, exclaiming, "I'll move him." And he did.[5]

The bloody battle ended in a tactical draw but a strategic victory for McClellan and the Army of the Potomac, as Lee withdrew from Maryland following the battle. Lincoln and Stanton, again chagrined by McClellan's lethargy in pursuing the retreating Bobbie Lee, replaced McClellan with Ambrose Burnside. Burnside quickly moved on Lee and caught him at Fredericksburg in December. It was a fatal "catch." Burnside launched his army against Lee's fortified positions along Marye's Heights and watched as the Confederates slaughtered his men. In all, Burnside lost 12,700 men to Lee's 5,300, and Meade lost 1,800 of his 5,000 men. Meade, however, received a promotion to major general and command of a corps.[6]

Lincoln pulled the plug on Burnside and replaced him with Joseph "Fighting Joe" Hooker, who formulated a brilliant plan for a spring campaign in northern Virginia. Hooker split his army, with three corps left at Fredericksburg to hold Lee there, and three other corps crossing the Rappahannock above Fredericksburg to move against Lee's left flank. Hooker outnumbered Lee two to one, and his plan was perfect. Its execution would be far less than perfect. Hooker, like McClellan before him, was confident: "I can march this army to New Orleans," he boasted. "My plans are perfect, and when I start to carry them out, may God have mercy on General Lee, for I will have none."[7]

God, unfortunately for Hooker and Lincoln, did indeed have mercy on General Lee, who split *his* army and sent Stonewall Jackson around Hooker's right flank. Jackson slammed into Hooker's exposed flank, rolled it up like a cheap rug and drove Hooker and his army back across the Rappahannock. That night, Jackson was shot by his own men. He died a few days later.

Meade's corps saw no combat, but it did, once again, cover the retreating army's rear. A group of subordinate generals—Meade was not one of them—moved to have Hooker replaced. The ever-aggressive Lee undertook his second invasion of the North, and when Hooker failed to attack his supply line, as urged by Lincoln and Stanton, they relieved him with a very reluctant Meade. What would follow would be Meade's day in the sun, at a small Pennsylvania town named Gettysburg.

The story of Gettysburg is well-known and will not be covered in detail here. Meade, in the aftermath of savage Confederate attacks on the first of three days of combat, reconstituted his army along Cemetery

Ridge. There he withstood a series of vicious Confederate assaults on the second day, and on the third, repulsed the legions of Confederate general George Pickett, whose name would forever be enshrined in Confederate lore and legend as the author of "Pickett's Charge." On the fourth day, the two armies rested, and then, on the fifth day, Lee began his sad retreat back into Virginia, crossing the raging Potomac on pontoons erected by his engineers in the middle of the night. Lincoln, Stanton and Henry Halleck, Lincoln's chief of staff, had vehemently urged Meade to pursue and destroy Lee's army before it could cross, but Meade did not. That failure was the genesis of criticism that would dog Meade the rest of his life.

Meade again demonstrated the basis for his "Old Snapping Turtle" moniker when, in August 1863, he had five deserters shot. He called the executions "sanguinary."[8]

The remainder of 1863 saw only skirmishes as Lee and Meade pirouetted, each trying to gain an advantage on the other. Meade feared that his lack of success would lead to his relief by Lincoln, but that did not occur. Lincoln had other plans for Meade, and the North. His plan was to be executed by one man: Ulysses S. Grant, victorious leader of the armies of the west. Grant would now assume command of all Union armies, east and west, north and south.

When Grant arrived in the east, he did not take a seat in Washington to command from an armchair. Instead, he made his headquarters with the Army of the Potomac. Meade then offered to resign and allow Grant to place his own man in command of that army. Grant refused and, in fact, placed his headquarters tent next to Meade's. The two would work in tandem for the remainder of the war.[9]

In spite of vicious attacks by other Union generals—led by the roguish Dan Sickles—on Meade for his performance at Gettysburg, Meade soldiered on under Grant's direction. That year—1864—saw Grant initiate the "Overland Campaign," which engendered bloody battles at the Wilderness, Spotsylvania Courthouse and a particularly bloody one at Cold Harbor, where Grant foolishly launched his army in a Fredericksburg-type assault on Lee's entrenched army. The slaughter was terrible, and Grant would regret that assault for the rest of his life.

One significant incident took place during the Battle of Spotsylvania Courthouse, when Meade's army became ensnarled in traffic with General Philip Sheridan's cavalry. Meade jumped Sheridan, and Sheridan, whose philosophy with respect to the use of cavalry differed dramatically from Meade's, engaged Meade in a shouting match. That conflict laid the foundation for enmity between the two men that would last for the remainder of Meade's life.[10]

Another incident further illustrates the saturnine nature of Meade's personality. A journalist named Edward Cropsey—reported as "Crapsey" in some journals—wrote an article for the *Philadelphia Inquirer* that, for the most part, was favorable to Philadelphia's hometown hero, Meade. Cropsey had trailed Grant in the west and now shadowed him in the east. Cropsey concluded his article with this: "History will record, but newspapers cannot, that on one eventful night during the present campaign GRANT's presence saved the army, and the nation too; not that General MEADE was on the point to commit a blunder unwittingly, but his devotion to his country made him loath to risk her last army on what he deemed a chance. Grant assumed responsibility and we are still On to Richmond."[11]

Cropsey had crossed the wrong man. The Old Snapping Turtle had the reporter placed backward on a mule and forced to wear a sign that read, "LIBELER OF THE PRESS." Cropsey was then drummed out of camp to the tune of "The Rogue's March."[12] The old adage *never pick a fight with a man who buys ink by the barrel* applied, and the Northern press went after Meade like piranhas. One reporter wrote that Meade was "as leprous with moral cowardice as the brute that kicks a helpless cripple in the street, or beats his wife at home."[13] From then on eastern newspaper coverage was focused exclusively on Grant and Sheridan; Meade became a media pariah.

Grant flanked Lee after Cold Harbor, crossed the James and eventually bottled up Lee at Petersburg, where, in a harbinger of another great conflict to come, the two sides dug in, and a long conflict involving mostly trench warfare ensued. There would be numerous battles and skirmishes over the next eleven months, but several, in particular, stand out. First was the Crater, Ambrose Burnside's ambitious plan to tunnel under the Confederate lines, plant explosives and then blow a gap in the Confederate lines through which his charging troops would spell the end to Lee's defense of Richmond. Meade thought the plan was nonsense but eventually acquiesced, as did Grant. The explosion went off as planned, and two divisions, the second consisting of Black troops, rushed toward the gap. The explosion, however, had created a crater into which the troops poured, and the Confederates shot them like ducks in a barrel. Meade's army lost over 4,000 men, and Meade wanted to court-martial Burnside. Instead, at Grant's request, relieved Burnside of his command.[14]

Finally, after a bitterly cold and wet northern Virginia winter, spring came and with it two important battles. First up was Five Forks, at which Sheridan broke Lee's line while Confederate generals George Pickett and Fitzhugh Lee enjoyed a shad bake hosted by General Thomas Rosser.[15] Sheridan would, on that basis, claim responsibility for ending the siege at Petersburg, but it was actually an unnamed assault up and down the line on the next day that spelled doom for Lee's army. Meade once again bitterly resented Sheridan's grab for glory.

One other issue nettled Meade during this time. Sheridan and William Tecumseh Sherman, commanding the Army of Tennessee in the Deep South, had received promotions to major general in the regular army. Meade had not, although he was their senior in rank. Meade leaned on Grant until Grant, tired of hearing about it, intervened with Lincoln and got Meade's promotion approved and backdated so that he was once again senior to Sherman and Sheridan.[16]

Lee retreated west and suffered a crushing defeat at Sayler's Creek, and Sheridan finally cut him off at Appomattox. Lee surrendered to Grant on April 9, 1865, in the living room of Wilmer McLean's house, and the war was effectively over, although Sherman would still need to obtain the surrender of General Joseph Johnston in North Carolina. Besides Grant, eleven Union officers attended the surrender. Meade did not.

Two days after the surrender, Meade crossed the lines to visit Robert E. Lee, his old comrade from the Mexican War. Lee was not at his headquarters, but soon Meade and his entourage "saw some men riding toward them. One of them had a gray beard and was wearing a blue military coat and a gray hat. It was Lee, followed by some of his staff." Meade greeted Lee, who at first did not recognize his old adversary, but then asked, "But what are you doing with all that gray in your beard?" "You have to answer for most of it!" Meade replied. Meade then introduced his staff officers, some of whom were in a state of disbelief that they were actually shaking the hand of Robert E. Lee. Meade and Lee then moved away from the others and talked. After that conversation, Lee and his staff rode away into the fog that covered the northern Virginia countryside and into the mists of history and legend.[17]

Meade would later meet with Lee in Richmond and urge him to take the oath of allegiance to the United States, but Lee declined, choosing instead to wait until he could see what the Union's policy toward the defeated South would be. The two men discussed the "Negro question," and then Meade departed, feeling bad for Lee's "diminished position." The two old adversaries would never see each other again.

The final event of the war was the "Grand Review" in Washington. It was a two-day spectacle, with Meade leading the Army of the Potomac down Pennsylvania Avenue on the first day, and Sherman leading the Army of Tennessee the second day. Following this parade, George Gordon Meade returned to his beloved Margaret in Philadelphia.

Postwar

With the war ended, many of the North's generals returned home. Meade was no exception: he returned to Margaret in Philadelphia, where the citizenry had raised money to buy the Meades a house. Meade was, however, a career army officer, so his military career did not end with the conclusion of the Civil War. President Andrew Johnson divided the country into five military districts, and Meade was given the largest, the Department of the Atlantic, which ran from Maine through South Carolina. His headquarters, fortuitously, was in Philadelphia, and his district included three former Confederate states, Virginia and the two Carolinas. Meade visited the three states and compiled a report on the economic and political situation extant in those defeated Southern states.

In March 1866, Meade joined Sherman and George Thomas in St. Louis as a member of a board to make selections for general officers in the regular army. While there, he received orders to deal with one of the most bizarre episodes in American history: the Fenian invasion of Canada.

The Fenians were an Irish liberation organization whose purpose was to force the British to free Ireland. They intended to do this by invading Canada and using its northern provinces as bases from which to attack Britain, forcing the British to liberate their homeland. The Fenians' name came from Ireland's pre–Christian warriors, and this modern bunch sought to be warriors in that ancient tradition. As historian Tom Huntington states with pellucidity, "Perhaps it sounded more realistic in 1865."[18]

The Irish were a formidable political, social and military force in the United States. Some 175,000 had fought for the North in the Civil War, and they—or any portion of them—constituted a significant military outfit. The Fenian leader was hard-fighting, hard-drinking Thomas W. Sweeney, a veteran of the Mexican War, Indian Wars and the Civil War, as well as a drunken brawl with two Union brigadier generals, which got him court-martialed but subsequently acquitted. One-armed, twice-wounded "Fighting Tom" was the brains—to the extent there were any—behind the invasion-of-Canada scheme, and to accomplish his mission, he recruited Northern and Southern Irish veterans alike to further the Fenian cause. In addition, the Fenians approached Secretary of State William Seward in an effort to secure financing for their cause, offering the secretary a means of punishing Great Britain for its "flirtations" with the South during the War.[19] Seward, however, evinced no interest.

Nevertheless, Sweeney had recruited around ten thousand men, and his followers even had a song:

> We are the Fenian Brotherhood, skilled in the art of war,
> And we're going to fight for Ireland, the land that we adore,
> Many battles have we won, along with the boys in blue,
> And we'll go and capture Canada for we've nothing else to do.

Apparently, that was indeed the case.

Sweeney's followers were a fractious, combustible lot. A group of about 300 Fenians—not commanded by Sweeney—began assembling in Eastport, Maine,[20] and other Maine border towns in preparation for an invasion of Campobello Island, later to be the summer home of Franklin Delano Roosevelt. By April 1866 they were conducting raids into Canada. U.S. Customs agents seized a shipload of putative Fenian arms on April 17. Still, the Fenians, some armed only with pistols, stayed in Maine and menaced Maine's Canadian neighbors with an occasional but mostly harmless sortie across the border.

Maine was in Meade's Atlantic District, so Grant, now general of the army, ordered Meade to Maine with all deliberate speed to break up the liberation army.[21] Along the way he picked up a force of about 160 soldiers and some artillery and arrived in Eastport on April 19, 1866. Meade impounded Fenian weapons and took them to Fort Stevens. He then warned the Fenians that any further incursions into Canada would result in their arrest. That took the wind out of the Fenian sails, and they began breaking up and heading south.[22] A few of them conducted desultory raids into Canada during which they set fires to some "woodpiles" and a warehouse. Thus ended the Campobello Island invasion.

Sweeney, however, was not so easily deterred. By June he assembled a force of some 800 men in the Buffalo, New York, area and crossed the Niagara River to launch his invasion. The Irish toughs ran into a hastily assembled volunteer militia, who tried to stop the invaders at the Canadian town of Ridgeway. Sweeney's vastly superior force of veterans chewed the militiamen up, killing nine of them. The invasion was on. Or was it?

It was not. Sweeney and the Fenian leadership quickly decided that they had taken on more than they could handle and began withdrawing, right into the waiting arms of the United States Army, which had been placed in position on the U.S. side of the Niagara River by a gunboat, the USS *Michigan,* and a steam tug, the USS *Harrison.* Although the Fenians had committed a violation of the Federal Neutrality Act, Meade chose not to prosecute them and instead ordered them paroled on the condition that they not bear arms on U.S. soil again. Meade also provided transportation home for those Fenians who could not afford a train ticket. Thus ended—with a mournful sigh—the New York aspect of the Fenian invasion of Canada.

But there was more. By now some seven thousand Fenians had assembled all along the Canadian border between Buffalo and St. Albans, Maine. Meade, therefore, moved along that border, arresting the "Irish Liberation Army" leaders as he went. Disheartened, the Fenians accepted Meade's offer of free transportation home. The second and final chapter of the Fenian invasion book was closed, and Meade returned home to Philadelphia.[23]

On August 31, 1866, President Andrew Johnson reorganized the departmental structure put in place in the immediate aftermath of the war and assigned Meade responsibility for the Department of the East, with responsibility for the former Confederate states of Georgia, Alabama and Florida.[24] Meade's view was that if the North tried to punish every Southerner who had participated in the war, they would have to punish every male, and the ensuing bloodshed would be greater than that shed in the war. He acted, therefore, as a benevolent dictator, with the authority— exercised only once—to remove elected public officials.

Subsequently, in December 1867, he took command of the Northern District of the South, which included five Southern states: Georgia, Florida, Alabama, South Carolina and North Carolina.[25] The Southern states were in the process of adopting new constitutions, a prerequisite for reentering the Union. To supervise this process, Meade moved to Atlanta, and it was here that he removed two elected Georgia officials: the governor and the treasurer, who refused to provide funding for a constitutional convention.[26] Georgia, after adopting a constitution that passed Congressional Reconstruction muster, reentered the Union in July 1868.

But then came an incident in Columbus, Georgia, that rattled the Reconstruction cage: the Ashburn Murder. Ashburn was a North Carolina unionist who led the local freedman organization in Columbus, Georgia. A mob killed him on the night of March 30, 1868. Meade sent William Mills, a detective, to investigate, and the War Department followed with a detective named Reed, also to investigate. Although Mills arrested ten men, the investigation unraveled, and the ten were freed. Nothing ever came of the investigations, and there was, therefore, no punishment.[27]

Next was an incident on September 19, 1868, when, in Camilla, Georgia, four hundred or so freedmen came to town for a Republican rally, anathema to the local Southerners, and a gunfight between the freedmen and the local whites ensued. Once again, Meade sent Mills, and once again, nothing came of it.

While in Atlanta, Meade won acclaim when he led the restoration of the local Episcopal Church with funds solicited in the North. He engaged in social activities with Atlanta's leaders and won their confidence and cooperation. It was for Meade a happy time.[28]

But there was trouble on the horizon for the former commander of the Army of the Potomac. When Grant became president, he named William T. Sherman to succeed him as a full general in command of the United States Army. That left Sherman's old position as a lieutenant general open, and Meade, next in seniority, wanted that position. He went to Washington and met with President Grant, his old commander, with whom he had enjoyed a warm relationship during the war. Meade made his case for promotion to lieutenant general in Sherman's aftermath. Grant listened without comment and with a somber demeanor and expressionless face. Meade left. Grant promoted Sheridan, several months Meade's junior, to Sherman's old position and rank.[29] Meade was crushed. He wrote to Margaret that "the blow has been struck and our worst fears realized ... you can imagine the force of this blow"[30] He would never become a lieutenant general, and that fact would haunt him for the remainder of his days.

Sherman, now a full general and general-in-chief of the army, ordered Meade to return to Philadelphia as head of the Department of the Atlantic. He did, and he would never depart that city again. During those years he served as a commissioner of Fairmont Park and was instrumental in developing and executing plans for landscaping and pathways there. He also worked tirelessly for the orphans' home. Meade and Margaret lived in the house purchased for them by the citizens of Philadelphia in the aftermath of Meade's triumph at Gettysburg. In addition, they spent their summers at a country home about ten miles from town.

Time marched on, and the Old Snapping Turtle, a career soldier who would never complain publicly about the crushing blow inflicted by Grant, soldiered on through the largely uneventful years. In 1869, he suffered a savage attack of pneumonia, and though written off by many Philadelphians, Meade rallied and survived.

Then, on October 31, 1872, Meade and Margaret were taking their daily walk when Meade complained of a pain in his side. On November 6, six days after the onset of the debilitating pain, George Gordon Meade, the hero of Gettysburg, died and passed into history. But first there had to be a funeral to honor the hero. It would be one for the ages.[31]

The funeral took place on November 12, and some fifty thousand people filled the streets.[32] President Grant and General of the Army Sherman arrived. Four generals, including, strangely, Philip Sheridan, Meade's detested nemesis, served as pallbearers. The *Philadelphia Enquirer* spoke glowingly of the fifty-six-year-old general, and an Episcopal bishop predicted that Meade's name would live in history as a result of all he had accomplished as a military figure. As historian Huntington points out, however, "predicting the future apparently was not the bishop's strong suit."[33] They buried Meade in Laurel Hill Cemetery. The epigraph on his tombstone reads, "He did his work bravely and is at rest."[34]

"After his death, Philadelphia collected $100,000 as a gift to his heirs. The City further honored him with a statue in Fairmont Park. That would have pleased the tough old soldier."[35]

So what, then, is Meade's legacy?

For the most part, it is a mixed bag. Meade got lost after Gettysburg in the dust of the U.S. Grant arrival and assumption of overall command. Historians in the years after the war—persuaded perhaps by the sour grapes of Daniel Sickles and his coterie of Gettysburg Meade negativists—relegated the sour, taciturn "Old Snapping Turtle" to the Union general scrapheap. Of all of the Union officers who wrote and spoke about Meade after the war, only two rose to his defense—Andrew Atkins Humphreys, his chief of staff—and Theodore Lyman, his aide and good friend. It was, however, not enough, and Meade, from the Civil War forward, got lost in the mists of history.

Even today, many Civil War buffs believe that Grant relieved Meade after Gettysburg, but, of course, that is not the case. Meade, as we have seen, continued to command the Army of the Potomac, although there is—and always will be—debate about who *actually* commanded that army. And his encounters with the press, never salutary, generated bad press for him after the Cropsey/Crapsey incident and other less dramatic encounters that did not help his public relations cause.

Lincoln said of Meade, with whom he had once expressed his dissatisfaction to Henry Halleck: "Not only a brave and skillful officer, but a true man."[36] Let that, then, be his epitaph.

CHAPTER TWO

George Brinton McClellan

"Young Napoleon, Little Mac"

Just as Meade's performance at and after Gettysburg engendered controversy, George Brinton McClellan's performance throughout his tenure as commanding general of the Army of the Potomac made him one of the most controversial of Civil War Union generals. Unlike Meade, criticism of whom arose out of one battle—Gettysburg—McClellan's performance in *two* campaigns created the controversy that continues to swirl about the general to this day.

Beginnings

Born in Philadelphia on December 3, 1826, George Brinton McClellan, like Meade, joined a socially prominent family. His father, also George—a graduate of Yale College who had also earned a medical degree from the University of Pennsylvania—and his mother, Elizabeth Brinton, came from old mainline Philadelphia families, although the McClellans did not enjoy the wealth of their social peers. George Senior was an ophthalmologist, but in those days, physicians did not enjoy the income that they would later. Nevertheless, young George enjoyed a "privileged upbringing," attending outstanding private schools and enjoying the aid of a tutor. At age eleven, George entered a preparatory school, and two years later, at the tender age of thirteen, matriculated at the University of Pennsylvania.[1] Then, after another two years, he had almost completed the curriculum there, and his father "engineered" an appointment for him to West Point.[2]

At fifteen, McClellan was actually too young for the Academy, but his father wrote the secretary of war in the spring of 1843 and then wrote President Tyler to try to secure a West Point appointment for young George. Based upon young George's academic record and his "athletic five foot eight inch frame," West Point officials waived the age requirement and admitted him six months shy of his sixteenth birthday. He was, it was said, a near genius.[3]

McClellan excelled at West Point and finished second out of fifty-nine cadets. Chagrined because he was not first, McClellan nevertheless had excelled in a brilliant West Point class—the class of 1846—that would produce twenty Civil War generals. At West Point, McClellan's best friends were Southerners, and he would always believe that those friendships gave him an insight into the Southern mind that other Northerners lacked. Not finishing first led him to form a belief that life was unfair and that "a long struggle in this world is all that life consists of."[4]

Based upon his West Point performance, and unlike George Meade, McClellan received his commission in the prestigious engineering branch, but his heart by the time he graduated was in the campaigns of Napoleon and Napoleonic tactics. He fancied himself a "young Napoleon," although he never called himself that. On the other hand, he did not discourage those who did.[5] The class of 1846 graduated right into the teeth of the Mexican War, and those who received orders into that conflict were pleased, as it gave them an opportunity for immediate combat experience and for brevet—temporary—promotions. McClellan was no exception, and based upon his outstanding service in that conflict, received two brevet promotions.

Next up were three years on the faculty at West Point. Subsequently, he received assignments to various engineering positions and an appointment as a member of a commission appointed to visit and study the Crimean War. In his free time he designed a saddle based on a Hungarian model that the army adopted for its cavalry units and that would remain the standard cavalry saddle until the horse cavalry passed into the dustbin of history. McClellan also invented the so-called shelter tent, which would become known as the "pup tent."[6]

He married Ellen Marcy, the daughter of one of his commanding officers, and he underwent a religious conversion that firmly grounded him in "strict Calvinism and predestination."[7] With promotions slow and peacetime duty stultifying, McClellan, as did many junior officers of that era, resigned from the army in 1857 and, like Meade, entered the railroad business with the Illinois Central, where he met one of the railroad's attorneys, Abraham Lincoln, with whom McClellan was singularly unimpressed. That feeling would one day be mutual.[8]

The Civil War

When the war came, McClellan received a major general's commission in the Ohio volunteers and took command of all troops in the state of Ohio. Subsequently, he received the same rank in the regular army

MAJOR GEN: M?CLELLAN.

George Brinton McClellan (1861–1864).

and assumed command of three states: Ohio, Illinois and Indiana. It was during this period that he developed the habit of carping about his superiors and his "enemies" in the chain of command. At one point he hired the detective Allan Pinkerton not to spy on the Confederates but to spy on his perceived enemies on the Union side.

McClellan first led troops in combat in what was to become West Virginia, where he defeated the Confederates three times and drove them out of the future Union state. That performance cemented his reputation as *the* rising star of the Union Army and led to his promotion to command what he would christen the Army of the Potomac and his relief of the aging General Winfield Scott as commander of *all* Union forces. He was thirty-four years old. Still, in spite of his success, McClellan continued to hurl insults at his superiors, especially Edwin Stanton, the secretary of war, whom McClellan detested, and Lincoln himself, whom McClellan called "an idiot." Once, Lincoln called unannounced at McClellan's Washington house but found that McClellan was not home. So he waited. And waited. Finally, McClellan returned, brushed by Lincoln and went directly to his room. Lincoln sent a servant to tell McClellan that he wanted to see him. The servant returned to tell the president that McClellan said to tell the president that he had gone to bed.[9]

Still, in spite of his various personality disorders, McClellan managed to whip the feckless Army of the Potomac—badly defeated at First Bull Run—into a fighting force. He reorganized his army, cashiered incompetent officers, drilled his troops and fed and clothed them, which, all combined, led his men to love Little Mac.[10] That adulation, combined with highly favorable press coverage, engendered in McClellan a belief that he was the Union messiah.

Although Lincoln and Stanton, in the fall of 1861, wanted McClellan to launch an immediate invasion of northern Virginia that would capture Richmond, McClellan was having none of that. Winter then set in and it was too late to undertake such a campaign. The spring of 1862 came, and finally, Lincoln had enough: he ordered McClellan and his army of 150,000 men to either move or McClellan to resign. McClellan moved, undertaking on March 4, 1862, an amphibious invasion of the Virginia peninsula, all the while carping about his enemies in Washington: Henry Halleck, Edwin Stanton and even Lincoln himself.

After landing his vastly superior army on the tip of the peninsula, McClellan slowly—ponderously, most historians say—moved his army up the peninsula. His glacial pace allowed the Confederates time to constitute their forces on the peninsula, and finally, at Seven Pines, Confederate forces under General Joseph E. Johnston attacked. The battle was a tactical draw, but Johnston was wounded, and Robert E. Lee took command of what he named the Army of Northern Virginia. Lee attacked, and he attacked, and he attacked. In a series of battles known as the Seven Days, he drove McClellan's numerically superior army—Lee had 65,000 men, and McClellan 127,000—back down the peninsula; all the while McClellan begged Washington for more troops. McClellan wrote of the Confederates to his wife: "The rascals are very strong and outnumber me considerably … but I will yet succeed, notwithstanding all they do & leave undone in Washington."[11] Of Lincoln, McClellan wrote to his wife, "Honest A has again fallen into the hands of my enemies & and is no longer a cordial friend of mine!"[12]

McClellan evacuated his army from the peninsula and returned it to Washington, where Lincoln relieved him as commander of the Army of the Potomac, replacing him with John Pope. McClellan then refused to send more than one division to reinforce Pope, whom McClellan disliked, exacerbating Pope's Second Bull Run disaster. In the aftermath of that catastrophe, Lincoln, dismayed by Pope's desultory performance, replaced him with McClellan.

After Second Bull Run, Lee invaded Maryland, and McClellan shadowed him, once again convinced that Lee's army consisted of over 110,000 men and that Joe Johnston, now recovered from his Seven Pines wound, was on McClellan's heels with an army of 150,000. Another of Mills's estimates put Lee's army at 190,000 and created out of whole cloth another Confederate army of 250,000 ready to march on Washington. McClellan bit like a hungry mule. It was what he wanted to hear. It was the Peninsula Campaign in spades.[13]

Then came the famous "Lost Order," which revealed to McClellan that Lee had split his army into four parts, and McClellan uttered his famous line about whipping Bobbie Lee or going home. The actual numbers of the two armies were 71,500 for McClellan and about 40,000 for Lee, but Lee's troops were scattered all over western Maryland. With the Lost Order, McClellan had a grand opportunity to smash Lee once and for all, if he would move and move quickly. If. He did not, Lee reconstituted his army along Antietam Creek, and the bloody Battle of Antietam ensued. There, a full frontal assault by McClellan would have destroyed the Army of Northern Virginia in a half day, but McClellan, safely headquartered miles behind the front, instead attacked piecemeal from north to south, and Lee was able to use interior roads and lines of communication to move troops and counter McClellan's attacks. The battle ended when Ambrose Burnside finally crossed the easily fordable Antietam Creek—after repeated, bloody attempts to cross what would forever be known as "Burnside's Bridge"—but was attacked and repulsed by A.P. Hill's division coming up from Harper's Ferry. Lee subsequently withdrew his army back across the Potomac, and once again, McClellan did nothing to follow or attack him.

Lincoln then relieved McClellan, and for Little Napoleon, the war was effectively over, although it would not end for another two and a half years.[14]

A Napoleon Without an Army

In Trenton, a Democratic Party stronghold, McClellan received a hero's welcome. Then he and Ellen moved to a Fifth Avenue hotel in New York City, where this time the welcome was tumultuous. The McClellans' hotel stay was not for long: a group of wealthy Democrats gave him "a handsome fully-furnished four-story brick house on West 31st Street, one of Manhattan's most desirable residential areas."[15] Many of his wealthy friends were Democratic Party "copperheads": poisonous snakes who opposed the war. These "snakes" constituted the conservative wing of the Democratic Party. McClellan, too, wanted peace, and if it took victory to attain his primary goal—preservation of the Union—then so be it. He had no wish to abolish slavery. The Copperheads had a slogan: "The Constitution as it is, the Union as it was."[16]

It was the winter of 1862–1863, and McClellan, who never saw a conspiracy that he did not embrace, was convinced that Stanton et al. were having "government agents" read his mail, so he developed a code for his telegrams. That December, Burnside replicated Lee's headlong assaults at Malvern Hill that Lee would again employ at Gettysburg and hurled his legions into Lee's entrenched troops along Marye's Heights overlooking Fredericksburg. The results were, of course, predictable: Burnside got burned. Badly.

The Army of the Potomac was once again in disarray: it was the winter of Lincoln's discontent, and it was the army's "Valley Forge" winter. As McClellan's political popularity grew, Lincoln began to consider whether to have him relieve Henry Halleck as general-in-chief. The Committee on the Conduct of the War called him to testify, and McClellan wrote to Ellen: "I have many—very many—bitter enemies and they are making their last grand attack.... I am in battle and must fight it out." He considered the committee "the most accomplished set of villains and blackguards that were ever collected together."

The appearance went well for him, however. He moved seamlessly from testifying into his report of his fifteen months in command of the Army of the Potomac. It was not unexpectedly a self-serving defense of all that he had done and not done. Also unsurprisingly, the "report" was more of a memoir than a command and battle report, and McClellan was not shy about placing the blame for his less-than-sanguinary results on those whom he perceived as his enemies in Washington.[17] Secretary of War Stanton and General-in-Chief Halleck were reluctant to publish McClellan's 756-page treatise, so it sat for a while. Finally, Congress stepped in and authorized publication of a third of it, omitting supporting "reports" of McClellan's subordinates, as well as Allan Pinkerton's inflated reports of enemy army sizes.

Again, not surprisingly, this general without a command began con-templating his retirement from the army. McClellan was told that he was a strong candidate for the presidency of the New Jersey Railroad, and he drafted his letter to Lincoln resigning his major general's commission. A problem arose, however: he did not get the $5,000-a-year job, and his major general's salary of $6,000 a year looked better and better. Then, Democratic Party friends devised a plan for him to participate in the liq-uidation of a railroad, and he netted nearly $20,000 from this financial legerdemain.[18]

Joseph "Fighting Joe" Hooker and the Army of the Potomac got whacked at Chancellorsville, and once again there was a cry for McClellan to relieve Hooker. That opportunity seemed to come when Hooker, pressed by Lincoln and Halleck, offered his resignation in the mistaken belief that it would be rejected. It was not, however, and Lincoln handed over com-mand of the Army of the Potomac not to Little Mac but to George Gordon Meade. Never one to stay quiet—at least for long—McClellan began writ-ing articles—anonymously—for a weekly called the *Round Table*, in which he, in two of the articles, posited his strategy for winning the war in north-ern Virginia.

As McClellan's political stock began to rise in connection with the Democratic Party nomination for the presidency, Republicans began shooting at him. First, there was the old charge that he had been on a gun-boat downriver during the battle at Malvern Hill, which he denied. Then, there was another charge that he had the entire Maryland Legislature arrested in 1861. He acknowledged that he had but that he had acted pur-suant to orders. And then finally, the most serious allegation: he and Lee had met on the battlefield at Antietam, and McClellan had agreed to allow Lee and the Army of Northern Virginia to escape unmolested across the Potomac, "clearing the way for a compromise peace settlement preserv-ing slavery." Republican news rags had a field day with that one, but the Joint Committee on the Conduct of the War revealed that it had already investigated the charge and found that it was made by a madman from Maryland.[19]

Horace Greeley, one of his most prominent critics, said that as bad as Burnside, McDowell and Hooker were, they were no worse than McClel-lan. In short, he said, "I hate McClellan." On June 15, 1864, McClellan spoke at the dedication of a monument to honor the Civil War dead. Here he chose to set forth his platform for the presidency: the Union's purpose in prosecuting the war was to preserve the Union and the Constitution and nothing more. McClellan's opponents—Secretary of War Stanton in particular—were incensed. Stanton ordered the West Point officers who had invited McClellan to be transferred. Moreover, there was evidence that Stanton was subjecting McClellan and other leading Democrats to "constant War Department surveillance."[20]

On July 11, Jubal A. Early came up out of the Shenandoah Valley of Virginia to menace Washington—he actually came within sight of the Capitol dome—engendering a furor among Washingtonians and indeed, throughout the North. Once again, there arose a cacophony in support of McClellan's return to command. Grant, now general-in-chief of the U.S. Army, had earlier said that he was willing to use "McClellan in some capacity," but nothing came of it, and Grant gave Philip Sheridan command of the Army of the Shenandoah. McClellan remained a general without a command.[21]

Then, in August, the Democrats gave McClellan the nomination for president, and the campaign against his erstwhile critic and adversary, Lincoln, was on. But fate intervened: Atlanta fell to Sherman, and the entire mood in the North shifted 180 degrees. The campaign then sank to mudslinging and muckraking, and Allan Pinkerton, McClellan's old private eye, convinced McClellan once again that Stanton was using detectives to follow McClellan and that the detectives were informing Stanton of every person with whom McClellan came into contact. And again, Little Mac resorted to the use of codes in all of his correspondence.

The election came, and the army turned against McClellan. In a precursor to the general election, men of the 60th Massachusetts, stationed in Indianapolis to guard Confederate prisoners, voted prior to the election overwhelmingly for Lincoln. "Some of the boys voted twenty-five times each," a soldier reported. McClellan's problem with the army was the same as it was with the general electorate: Republicans tarred him with the peace platform, and in light of all of the losses suffered by the army, to turn and accept peace at this point seemed a blasphemy. Moreover, the North had accepted the abolition of slavery as a hard-and-fast objective. McClellan had not. The result was preordained: Lincoln drubbed Little Mac in the Electoral College, 212 to 21.[22]

McClellan was only thirty-nine years old, and he now faced retirement from both the army and, at a minimum, *national* politics. He submitted his resignation from the army to Lincoln, who accepted it without comment, which was hurtful to Little Mac. McClellan next received an offer of the presidency of Morris and Essex Railroad in New Jersey, but ultimately, its owners decided that he was too controversial, and he did not get the position, which was also painful for him. He then considered offering "his sword" to Czar Alexander of Russia or to the French puppet Maximilian in Mexico. Instead, he decided on a "self-imposed exile in Europe," which his wealthy friends made possible.[23]

He and his family departed New York on January 25, 1865. In Europe, McClellan found what he was looking for: acceptance as a military hero and a great American general, which was not inconsistent with his own view. Lee and Johnston surrendered, and McClellan said that he hoped for a "magnanimous and merciful course towards a fallen foe." Then, he learned of Lincoln's assassination, which "filled him with 'unmingled horror & regret,' he wrote. 'How strange it is that the military death of the rebellion should have been followed with such tragic quickness by the atrocious murder of Mr. Lincoln! Now I cannot but forget all that had been unpleasant between us, & remember only the brighter parts of our intercourse.'"[24]

The McClellan family stayed in Rome most of the spring of 1865, and they loved the city with its "historical wonders and artistic treasures." McClellan thought it "the most interesting place in the world." They summered that year in Switzerland, and he began work on his memoirs, turning down "attractive job offers" that his American benefactors procured for him. Ellen was pregnant with their second child, and, in accordance with Victorian custom, they kept that matter private.

Winter brought a stay in Dresden, and for the next two years, they wintered in the south of France and summered in Switzerland. After the birth of their son, Ellen suffered poor health, and they moved from one spa to another so that she could take the waters. The nature of Ellen's illness is unknown. McClellan was pleased to meet the great chief of staff of the Prussian army, Helumuth von Moltke, who "flattered him with the observation that his Peninsula campaign of 1862 would surely have ended the Civil War had he not been 'shamefully' treated by the Lincoln government, no doubt based upon McClellan's report of that campaign." He also met a French veteran of the Napoleonic wars and delighted in the old man's stories of those campaigns.

The elections of 1868 approached—the Republicans nominated Grant—and there was some interest among Democrats in again running McClellan for president; however, he was not interested, and "a newspaper remarked [that] 'the party would only ensure a Republican victory by running the man who didn't take Richmond against the man who did.'"[25] In September of that year, a homesick McClellan returned home to an offer from the newly formed University of California of its presidency, which he declined, preferring instead to remain in the New York-New Jersey area.

Then followed a tour of duty as engineer of the New York City Department of Docks and then another as president of the Atlanta and Great Western Railroad at $15,000 a year, which made him a "modestly wealthy" man. McClellan then built a house on Orange Mountain in New Jersey, the first home that the McClellans acquired . In 1873, he formed his own firm of consulting engineers and accountants to represent Europeans involved in investing in American railroads. In October 1873, he returned to Europe to "introduce" his firm to investors and banks. On that trip he spent five months in Egypt, where his old friend Charles P. Stone—who had been sacrificed on Edwin Stanton's army altar of shame—was chief of staff to the khedive of Egypt.[26]

Eighteen seventy-six came and with it, another presidential election. Grant was gone, and the field was wide open. Samuel J. Tilden was the Democratic candidate, and Rutherford B. Hayes, a wounded Civil War general, ran on the Republican ticket. Tilden won the popular vote, but the Republicans cut a deal with Southern electors to secure their vote in return for an end to Radical Reconstruction, and Hayes took office for what would be two terms.

McClellan was not through with politics, however. The New Jersey Democratic Party nominated him for governor in the fall of 1877, and he won the general election that November. McClellan was able to exercise the duties of that office from his home, Maywood, as he traveled to Trenton only one day a week. Then, on the heels of that office and his daughter's coming-out party in New York, came another trip to Europe in 1881. That trip brought the bad news that the warehouse in which he had stored the manuscript of his memoirs had burned and that his memoirs had been destroyed.

After returning to the United States, McClellan began writing his memoirs again. His engineering/accounting firm did well, and he sat on the boards of several companies. His wealth grew, and the family spent their winters in New York City and their summers either on Orange Mountain or in the White Mountains of New Hampshire or on Mount Desert Isle, Maine.

In 1884 he supported Grover Cleveland for president, and when Cleveland, a Democrat, won, McClellan waited expectantly for an appointment to serve as secretary of war, but to his deep disappointment, the appointment never came. In May 1885, he wrote an article for *Battles and Leaders of the Civil War*[27] in which he once again blamed the failure of the Peninsula Campaign on the administration and in particular, and not surprisingly, on Secretary of War Edwin Stanton, whom he loathed. He wrote of meetings with Lincoln and Stanton and gave his recollection of the facts arising out of those meetings, as well as his interpretation of those facts. Of course, neither Lincoln nor Stanton was alive to rebut McClellan's inflammatory allegations.

McClellan's final journey was to retrace an earlier trip made by him and Randolph Marcy, who accompanied him now to the Red River country in Texas, followed by a railroad trip to Denver, Salt Lake City and San Francisco. "In his journal he noted the pleasure it gave him when at every stopover old soldiers called to pay their respects." In mid–September "he was back at Maywood to mark, as he did every year, the anniversary of the Battle of Antietam."[28]

October came and with it an attack of angina pectoris. McClellan seemed to recover from the attack, but on October 28, there were more chest pains. At 3:00 a.m. the next morning, he said, "I feel easy now. Thank you." And then he died, only fifty-eight years old. Of all of the former commanders of the Army of the Potomac, only John Pope remained. Messages of condolence arrived by the hundreds in Orange, from President Cleveland and other national leaders, from generals who had fought with him and against him, from men who had served in the ranks of the Army of the Potomac. The country had lost "one of her purest and most patriotic sons," August Belmont said. P.G.T. Beauregard described the great esteem he felt for General McClellan "as a man and soldier," and Joe Johnston mourned "a dear friend whom I have so long loved and admired."[29]

Lengthy obituaries recounted and evaluated the events of McClellan's crowded life. In the opinion of the *New York Evening Post*, "Probably no soldier who did so little fighting has ever had his qualities as a commander so minutely and we may add, so fiercely discussed." There was universal recognition of his role in organizing the Army of the Potomac. The *New York Times* thought his failures were due less to circumstances than to temperament. "His error was in expecting and requiring a degree of perfection in preparation and of absolute safeguard against the possibility of failure, such as the highest generalship would not, under the circumstances, have exacted." The *New York World* was unrepentantly partisan to the end: "No General who fought in the war from its outbreak to its close was ever actuated by nobler sentiments and purer and more patriotic motives. Yet no soldier was ever more unjustly dealt with or more harshly, cruelly and unfairly criticized."[30]

Then followed a simple service at Madison Square Presbyterian Church on a muzzy Manhattan day. Joe Johnston, his Peninsula Campaign adversary, served as a pallbearer, as did Winfield Scott Hancock, the hero of Gettysburg, and other Union generals. After the funeral service, McClellan was taken to Trenton and buried in a family plot overlooking the Delaware River. His epitaph in the *New York World* was simply this: "History will do him justice." There remains, however, to this day a serious question as to whether history has indeed done justice to this controversial Union general.

The ambiguity of George McClellan's Civil War service admits both praise and criticism. He forged a powerful weapon of war, the Army of the Potomac, yet wielded it weakly. He roused both the admiration of his troops and the ire of his superiors. He parried Lee's thrust into the

North but was himself checked at the gates of Richmond. Indeed, McClellan's legacy defies any easy categorization and simple judgment. Perhaps Ulysses S. Grant expressed it best when asked after the war to evaluate McClellan as a general. "McClellan," he replied, "is to me one of the mysteries of the war."[31]

CHAPTER THREE

David Glasgow Farragut

Beginnings

Like fellow Union warrior George Gordon Meade, David Glasgow Farragut had roots in Spain, or at least in a Spanish province, Minorca, a Mediterranean island off the east coast of the Iberian Peninsula. But unlike Meade, who was merely born in Cadiz, Spain, and whose parents were American, Farragut's ancestral roots were in Spain. He was of distinguished Spanish lineage, and one of his ancestors, Don Pedro Farragut, was a hero of the Moorish wars who had helped drive the Moors from Spain.[1] David Glasgow Farragut was actually named at birth

James Glasgow, but he would later change his first name to David.[2]

His father, George, was a roundabout who had once served in the Russian navy and in 1776, after traveling to Charleston, South Carolina, offered his services to the American colonies in their revolt against Great Britain.[3] He received an appointment as a first lieutenant in South Carolina's nascent navy and subsequently engaged in land operations with South Carolina general Francis Marion, famously known as "the Swamp Fox." George Farragut also fought with Nathaniel Green at Cowpens against General Cornwallis. In the War of 1812, Farragut,

David Glasgow Farragut (1860–1865).

a confirmed soldier of fortune, fought for the last time with Andrew Jackson at New Orleans.[4]

In 1795, George was serving as a major in the east Tennessee militia when he met and subsequently married Elizabeth Shine. He bought land near Knoxville, Tennessee, and farmed and operated a ferry across the Holston River, operations occasionally punctuated by military expeditions against the Cherokee and Creek Indians. George and Elizabeth's first child, a son named William, was born there, followed four years later—in 1801—by James (David). Two more children—a daughter, Nancy, and a son, George—were born later.[5]

Father George moved his family to New Orleans shortly after James's birth and was there when Commodore David Porter came to take command of the New Orleans naval establishment. Commodore Porter was accompanied by his father, the venerable David Porter, Sr., who had first been appointed to a command in the navy by George Washington. The elder Porter loved to fish in Lake Pontchartrain, and one hot day, the old man passed out in his boat of sunstroke. George, who was fishing nearby, rescued the eighty-four-year-old Porter and took him home to wife Elizabeth, who cared for Porter until his death. Shortly after Porter's death, Elizabeth caught yellow fever and died, leaving George with five young children. In appreciation of George and Elizabeth's care of his father, Commodore David Porter offered to take charge of and care for the young James. Eventually, Porter adopted him. Thus James's life at that point took a decidedly nautical turn.[6]

Three years later, Porter secured an appointment as a midshipman for young James, then only nine years old. There was at that time no Naval Academy, so the path to an officer's commission took the hopeful candidates through the rigors of a midshipman's life and duties. Those duties were whatever an officer said they were, and whatever he was told to do, the midshipman had better do it quickly. The War of 1812 came, and while James's biological father was fighting with Andrew Jackson, James accompanied his adoptive father when he took command of the frigate *Essex*. It was said the little fellow

> moved gracefully, yet his actions were resolute. He was neither as dark as a Spaniard nor as light as an Irishman, but rather a striking combination of both, with dark brown hair and hazel eyes. His face had already begun to take on the features of his later portraits—the thin lips, high cheekbones, and the long angular nose known in those days as aquiline. Porter must have felt a sense of pride when he came onboard *Essex* and spotted his foster son decked out in a full-dress uniform—blue coat with tails embossed with gold-laced diamonds on the standing collar, white breeches, shiny shoes with buckles, a gold-laced cocked hat, and a short-curved sword just like a lieutenant.[7]

The *Essex* roamed the Atlantic and the Caribbean and then sailed around the horn to the Pacific, the first American ship to sail in those waters. Again, the *Essex* attacked British shipping. But two British warships caught up with the *Essex* and sank her in the Battle of Valparaiso. Farragut saw firsthand the results of a sea battle: dead and wounded men, body parts strewn about the deck, and he saw how to command a ship in combat.

Following the War of 1812, Farragut served on various ships as he moved up the midshipman ladder toward a commission. He saw how good commanders took care of their men and how bad commanders operated as martinets. Finally, in 1822, he received his commission as a lieutenant. Stationed in Norfolk, he married Susan Marchant in 1824. Assignments to various ships followed, diminished by Farragut's failing eyesight, and the navy was overrun with officers, so sea billets were difficult to find. Those without them were placed on leave at half pay. Finally, in 1838, he received orders to the famed *Constellation*, and later that year took his first command, of the sloop *Erie*. While in command of the *Erie*, he watched a French fleet destroy what seemed to be an impregnable fortress near Veracruz. It was a lesson that registered with him, and it was a lesson that would serve him well in a future war.[8]

His wife Susan died in 1840, and the next year Farragut received the much-coveted promotion to commander. Once again, he moved up the command ladder until he ran out of ships and took "awaiting orders" status in Norfolk, where he met and married Virginia Dorcas Loyall, who came from a prominent and prosperous old Virginia family. The Mexican War arrived in 1846, and Farragut took command of the USS *Saratoga*, which was relegated to blockade duty. Subsequently he served in shore commands, including one in San Francisco, where he created the Mare Island Shipyard. Promoted to captain, the highest rank in the navy, in 1855, he then began a long relationship with the USS *Brooklyn* in 1858, a ship that would sail with him into nautical history, lore and legend.[9]

The momentous winter of 1861–1862 found Farragut once again awaiting orders in Norfolk. The great cataclysm loomed, and Farragut faced an emotional dilemma, which was this: Norfolk was his hometown and Virginia his state. He had been born in Tennessee and lived in New Orleans. His two sisters also lived in New Orleans, so his ties to the South were substantial. But he had taken an oath to serve and defend the United States, and he had done so for fifty-nine years. Accordingly, Farragut decided to honor his oath. As word spread through Norfolk of his decision, anger quickly followed. Virginia seceded from the Union in the aftermath of Fort Sumter. Accordingly, in the middle of the night, Farragut and his family fled Norfolk and went to New York.

One of the planks of the North's war planning was the so-called "Anaconda Plan," which called for the blockade of all Confederate ports to choke off supplies to the nascent country. This would be a huge undertaking for an undermanned, under-shipped navy, but there was more: even if that blockade were successful, supplies would continue to flow into the eastern Confederacy from its states on the west side of the Mississippi. Something had to be done to sever this link and close the Mississippi to that traffic. That would require the capture of New Orleans and the Confederate citadel at Vicksburg. Farragut was the man assigned to do that.[10]

Farragut boldly sailed his fleet up the Mississippi, shelled the two forts protecting New Orleans into submission and then, working in tandem with a Union Army of eighteen thousand men under the command of Benjamin Butler, took the city without firing a shot. Mary Boykin Chesnut, the Confederate diarist, wrote in her unflinching style, "New Orleans is gone, and with it the Confederacy."[11] Farragut emerged from the New Orleans campaign "a national hero [and] … his name quickly became a household word throughout the country."[12]

He now faced the Confederate Gibraltar at Vicksburg, which would also require army assistance. That assistance would be provided by the two imposing Union generals of the western theater, William Tecumseh Sherman and Ulysses S. Grant. Those two generals did not arrive at Vicksburg until the next year, and Farragut's foster brother, David Dixon Porter, whose fleet was above Vicksburg, ran the gauntlet south, met Grant's army, which was on the western side of the river, and ferried them across to Bruinsburg, Mississippi. From there Grant moved east to Jackson then looped back to Vicksburg, to which he laid siege. The Gibraltar of the Confederacy fell to Grant, Farragut and Porter on July 4, 1863. With the concomitant Union victory at Gettysburg, the fall of Vicksburg spelled doom for the Confederacy. Farragut, now a rear admiral, once again emerged a hero. He was called the "American Viking."[13]

With the final panel of the Confederate triptych—Mobile—looming, Farragut needed a rest, so he left the Mississippi River to David Dixon Porter and, with three ships—the *Hartford*, the *Richmond* and the *Brooklyn*—sailed north to New York.[14] There he was greeted as a hero of the first magnitude. The country was in a better mood than it had been in a long time.

A month earlier a Confederate army under General Robert E. Lee had been badly defeated in [the] three-day battle at Gettysburg, Pennsylvania, and General George Meade's successful Union army had chased Lee all the way back into Virginia. As a result of this stunning victory, New Yorkers were especially anxious to welcome home a true hero of the war. The Northern press had been reporting on Farragut's activities up and down the river for over a year, and many people wanted a glimpse at him.[15]

Secretary of the Navy Gideon Welles invited Farragut to Washington "whenever he felt like traveling," and "eighty-one of New York City's leading citizens signed a letter exalting Farragut…. In it they exclaimed, 'The whole country, but especially this commercial metropolis, owes you a large debt of gratitude.' The Chamber of Commerce called the passing of the lower river forts and the capture of New Orleans 'one of the most celebrated victories of any time.'" A New York newspaper "said that he had earned a name for himself equal to 'the naval commanders of any nation.'"[16]

On September 11, Farragut took Secretary Welles up on visiting Washington and enjoyed a dinner party that Welles gave for him. He did not see President Lincoln, but Lincoln said, "General Meade, after defeating Lee at Gettysburg, failed to follow up his advantage," giving rise to Lincoln's observation that the navy trained their men better than the army. "Welles recorded in his diary that [Lincoln] thought there had not been … so good an appointment in either branch of the service as Farragut."[17]

In January 1864, Farragut sailed south for Mobile, guarded by three forts, a narrow entrance mined with what were then known as "torpedoes." The port was guarded by the imposing CSS *Tennessee*, "the finest and most dangerous ironclad built in the South." Operating with the *Tennessee* were three other ironclads and three wooden ships.[18] All in all, taking Mobile would be a daunting task.

Farragut did not move against Mobile until August, as he awaited the arrival of ironclads and troops to help him with the assault. On August 5, he struck. Trouble came almost immediately when the lead monitor, *Tecumseh*, hit a mine and sank in two minutes.[19] Then the *Brooklyn*, leading the large ships and its commanding officer having watched the demise of *Tecumseh*, began to slow and drift toward the minefield.[20] Farragut would later say that he asked God what to do, and God told him to "go on."[21] He ordered that *Hartford* turn to port directly into the minefield in order to get around *Brooklyn*. As *Hartford* passed *Brooklyn*, Lieutenant John C. Watson on *Hartford* shouted—another account has Drayton shouting it, and still another has Farragut shouting it—over to *Brooklyn* and asked its commanding officer, Captain Alden, what was wrong. Alden replied, "Torpedoes!" Then came one of the most famous moments in all of the United States Navy's illustrious history. Farragut, according to Watson and upon hearing Alden's response, shouted, "Damn the torpedoes! Full speed ahead, Drayton! Hard a starboard! Ring four bells!" He then shouted to Jouett on *Tecumseh* to reverse his engines and swing *Hartford's* bow left to port to get around *Brooklyn*, and after *Hartford* began turning, he shouted, "Jouett, full speed!"[22] The turn took *Hartford* dead center into the minefield, and the other ships followed. Farragut now risked his entire squadron, but, notwithstanding *Tecumseh*'s loss, he was betting that the mines had been in the water too long and would prove defective.[23] Under those circumstances, he was willing to take the risk, and although his men could hear the mines banging along the ships' sides as they passed through the minefield, none exploded, and Farragut successfully led his squadron into Mobile Bay.

The actual words that Farragut spoke are, like so many other famous sayings, subject to controversy. Historian Chester C. Hearn believes that the version set forth above is correct.[24] On the other hand, James P. Duffy sets forth the colloquy as follows: Farragut shouted, "Damn the torpedoes!" Then, to *Hartford*'s captain, he shouted, "Four bells, Captain Drayton!" And then to Jouett, lashed alongside *Hartford*, he shouted, "Go ahead, Jouett, full speed!"[25] Farragut biographer Charles Lee Lewis sets it forth as follows: "Damn the torpedoes!" Then to Drayton, "Four bells, Captain Drayton, go ahead!" Then to the captain of the *Metacomet*, "Jouett, full speed!"[26] There are also versions that have him shouting "Damn the torpedoes! Full *steam* ahead!" Watson's version—he was closest to Farragut—is likely the most accurate, but "time [has] eroded Farragut's orders to simply, 'Damn the torpedoes, full speed ahead.' It became a naval battle cry that has stirred sailors on to battle for over a hundred years."[27]

Tennessee next came at Farragut's wooden ships, whose shells ricocheted harmlessly off the ironclad. *Tennessee* was commanded by Admiral Franklin "Buck" Buchanan, an old friend of Farragut's. Buchanan had commanded the *Merrimac* in its famous battle with the Union *Monitor*, but, under relentless fire from the Union fleet, he was wounded, and the commanding officer, Captain Johnson, raised the white flag. The Battle of Mobile Bay was over.

In one of those footnotes to the battle that lend color to it, Farragut invited the wounded Buchanan to come aboard the *Hartford* for medical attention. Buchanan refused to board the *Hartford* because of inexplicable hostility toward Farragut and thus was transferred to another Union ship for treatment. Farragut was hurt by Buchanan's unexpected and unexplained response to his kind invitation.[28]

On September 3, President Lincoln "tendered national thanks to Admiral Farragut" for his performance in Mobile Bay. With that victory and others at Vicksburg, Gettysburg and Atlanta, doom, as Mary Boykin Chesnut had prophesized, now hung over the Confederacy like the gun smoke that overhung Mobile Bay in the aftermath of Farragut's triumph. And that battle also spelled the end of something else: the age of wooden ships. Although *Tennessee* had been defeated, it was defeated in large part by the ironclads in Farragut's fleet. From that signal victory forward, the age of iron and then steel ships had arrived. And finally, Farragut's commands at sea had ended. He was sixty-three years old and in poor health. It was time to go ashore.[29]

Once again, he returned triumphantly to New York City, and after extensive ceremonies celebrating his heroic stature, he went home to Hastings-on-Hudson. On December 21, 1864, Farragut received another promotion, this time to the newly created rank of vice admiral. The Merchants Committee of New York City gave him $50,000 to purchase a house in the city.[30]

With the arrival of 1865, for the Farraguts, the war was over.

Postwar

That year—1865—would be a whirlwind. Besides the promotion, Farragut spent time in Washington, at one point attending the opera with President Lincoln and at all times going to dinner parties held throughout the city for him.[31] Secretary Welles then appointed Farragut to head a navy board formed to consider and recommend officers for promotion. This assignment was not to his liking, but ever the dutiful navy officer, Farragut soldiered on.[32]

He also continued the social whirl of Washington, and his friend, the commanding officer of the *Hartford*, Captain Drayton, "took special pains to warn Mrs. Farragut that 'because I am away she must not permit him to run wild, and get back to the late hours which through constant lecturing I thought to have somewhat broken.'"[33] He sat on the front row for Lincoln's second inauguration and then, with Virginia, headed back to Norfolk to visit old friends. That trip led to his entry into Richmond when it fell.

> Here [in Norfolk] at noon on April 3, the Admiral heard of the evacuation of Richmond, and he and Brigadier-General George H. Gordon left immediately by steamer for the Virginia capital. Landing at Varina on the James River below Richmond, they arrived on horseback in the city the morning of the 4th. Order had been restored by General Weitzel's troops but there was yet some confusion, the smoke still rising from the ruins of the areas which had been devastated by fire. They rode to the Capitol, where General Wetzel had his headquarters in the Senate Chamber. "The door opened, and a smooth-faced man, with a keen eye and a firm, quick, resolute step, entered," according to war correspondent Charles C. Coffin. "He wore a plain blue blouse, with three stars on the collar. It was the old hero who opened the way to New Orleans, and who fought the battle of the Mobile from the masthead of his vessel—Admiral Farragut.... It was a pleasure to take the brave Admiral's hand, answer his eager questions as to what Grant had done. Being latest of all present from Petersburg, I could give him the desired information. Thank God it is about over! said he."[34]

But the trip also ended unsatisfactorily when the couple's old friends in Norfolk shunned them. They left Norfolk, never to return, following Lincoln's assassination, and after seeing Andrew Johnson installed as president, the couple departed for Hastings-on-Hudson. On November 5, 1865, Farragut "purchased the elegant brownstone home ... at 133 East 36th Street in New York City."[35] There they would spend the rest of 1865,[36] the hero at rest:

> As an uneducated orphan trained under the eye of Captain David Porter, he had risen from virtual obscurity to become the most famous and respected admiral in the Civil War—and as a modest man, he had not prepared himself for the notoriety that followed.[37]

Farragut's next honor came on July 25, 1866, when Congress established a new rank for Farragut: like the other two admiral ranks he had occupied, this one was without precedent in America's history.[38] The position carried with it an annual salary of $10,000, and Farragut, now 65 years old, "passed into history as the first full admiral in the United States Navy."[39]

> Farragut's star was then in the ascendant. That summer a portrait of him by William Page was exhibited in the Somerville Gallery in New York. It represented him as "lashed to the rigging of the *Hartford* in Mobile Bay" and was praised as a masterly work. The portrait was painted from life. In the artist's studio ... the Admiral himself showing Page with a small piece of rope just how the quartermaster made him fast to the futtock shrouds. This portrait was purchased by a committee of citizens, and on December 2, 1869 it was given to the Grand Duke Alexis at the Academy of Design in New York for presentation to Czar Alexander II of Russia.[40]

The evening of July 25, 1865, Secretary Welles "and the admiral rode to the home of General Grant to extend their congratulations, for Grant had been elevated to full general by the same legislation."[41]

> The public praised the decision, and when Johnson toured the country to promote his Reconstruction policies, he carried with him a retinue including Farragut, Grant, several distinguished officers, three cabinet members, and many others. Everywhere he stopped, huge crowds assembled to cheer Farragut and Grant. The general received the most attention, as the Radical Republicans were already manipulating him for partisan designs. On went the tour, from New York to St. Louis, with dozens of stops in between. In large cities like Cleveland and Chicago, the opposition attempted to portray the president as perpetually drunk, but only Grant overindulged, so much so that at Cleveland Mrs. Farragut found him to be so "stupidly communicative" that his friends spirited him off to Detroit "to conceal his shame."[42]

Then came the grand tour of Europe, when, on June 7, 1867, Farragut assumed command of the navy's European Squadron aboard his flagship, the USS *Franklin*, a four-thousand-ton frigate carrying 750 men and thirty-nine guns. The commanding officer of the *Franklin* was Alexander M. Pennock, who was the husband of Mrs. Farragut's first cousin. The surgeon was J.M. Foltz, who had been Farragut's surgeon during the New Orleans campaign. Farragut had served on the ship's named predecessor, *Franklin*, as a midshipman.

Farragut held a reception aboard that ship on June 18, 1867. "In attendance were the president, his cabinet, and hundreds of friends, wives, and daughters of his wealthy New York patrons."[43] In response to this affair, President Johnson granted Farragut a waiver of the navy rule that prohibited "wives from cruising with their husbands on men-of-war." Captain Pennock's wife was also allowed to sail with her husband.[44]

The tour began at Cherbourg on July 14, 1866, after the Atlantic crossing, and it would last until November 1868. In Europe the tour would be characterized by "endless receptions, lavish banquets, and festivities ashore." The *Franklin* used enough gunpowder in returning salutes to fight through another war, and they visited every port in Europe, from St. Petersburg to Portugal and from Italy to England. Farragut's only rest occurred between ports, and without Captain Drayton to watch him, the admiral overindulged.[45]

The Farraguts met and dined with royalty, military officials and political leaders in every country that they visited.[46] Farragut was a true American military hero, and he drew crowds wherever he went. Back home, in keeping with his heroic stature, Democrats considered running him against Grant in the presidential election of 1868, but Farragut, from his flagship off Malta, "wisely declined." He "knew his limitations and never developed an interest in politics."[47]

Along the way, Admiral and Mrs. Farragut met, and in some cases, dined with, King Christian IX of Denmark, the king of Portugal, the queen of Spain, King Victor Emmanuel of Italy, the Emperor Louis Napoleon of France, Pope Pius IX and, finally, Queen Victoria and the Prince of Wales, who would later become King Edward VII. In a colloquy with the King of Portugal, the King asked, "you wrote a history of the late war, I believe?' Farragut replied that he had not turned author yet. The American minister, said, however, 'Admiral Farragut, your majesty, has *made* the history of the war.'"[48]

The *Franklin* and the Farraguts returned to New York on November 10, 1868. Johnson had just lost the presidential election to Grant, and the Radical Republicans, who had taken charge of Congress in the elections of 1866, now had a clear field upon which to run in implementing Radical— also known as "Congressional"—Reconstruction. Secretary Welles, who refused to serve under Grant, urged Farragut to accept the secretary of the navy position if it were offered. It was not.

The Farraguts attended Grant's inauguration on March 4, 1869, but did not attend the ball that evening, which, Secretary Welles wrote, "developed into disgraceful affairs with intoxication."[49] The admiral then watched as Grant filled up his administration with political hacks and business cronies who knew nothing about the subject matter areas over which they were to exercise control. Secretary of the navy, for example, was to be "Adolph E. Borie of Philadelphia, a man who knew nothing about the navy but who had amassed a fortune by shrewdly profiteering during the Civil War." Grant's predilection for appointing cronies would eventually be his undoing and would, for history, stain the great general's name with shame.

One of Grant's strange arrangements was to offset Borie's ineptitude by appointing Farragut's foster brother, David Dixon Porter, to actually run the navy. This bizarre arrangement resulted in a junior admiral— Porter was a vice admiral—having administrative authority over a full admiral, Farragut. Porter then appointed Commodore James Alden as chief of the Bureau of Navigation. It was Alden, of course, who had commanded the *Brooklyn* at Mobile and whose trepidation with the torpedoes led Farragut to damn them. Later, when Farragut wrote his report of the battle, he stated that *Hartford,* and not *Brooklyn,* led the column of Union ships into the bay. While technically, *Brooklyn* had led the way, she, under Alden's command, faltered at *the* critical moment, requiring that *Hartford,* under Captain Drayton and at Farragut's command, take the lead, which she did. Alden had never forgotten what he considered to be that slight.

Alden then undertook a series of moves designed to harass and insult Farragut. Alden changed, for example, Farragut's pennant from a blue field with four white stars to "one with stripes of red and white." Another move was to make Farragut port admiral of New York, which Farragut politely declined "out of 'self-respect and regard for the Navy.'" Finally, however, Borie resigned, and the new secretary "gradually ousted Porter and began restoring the department's lost dignity. The change, however, came too late to alleviate the strain on Farragut."[50]

Farragut and Virginia then took a train cross-country to San Francisco and Mare Island, the shipyard that Farragut had started and supervised in the years before the war. The admiral enjoyed the visit and renewing old acquaintances, but he took a cold and became ill, so that by the time that the couple reached Chicago on the way home, Farragut had suffered "a life-threatening heart attack. For a few days the doctor doubted if Farragut would recover, but the admiral called upon his reserve vitality and finished the journey to New York." The attack had torpedoed his health and from that point on, his health began to decline. Then came another shock: Porter now claimed publicly that he was the architect of the attack that led to the surrender—to Farragut—of New Orleans. Farragut left unanswered Porter's contention.

In January 1870, Farragut visited Portland, Maine, where he encountered a number of his former officers, including Commander Schley, who had, in 1863, commanded the *Monongahela* during the run past Port Hudson. Schley, who would later gain fame in the Spanish-American War, told Farragut how well he looked, especially in light of his illness. But Farragut told him, "I am not a well man." And he was not.

He visited Portsmouth, New Hampshire, that summer, and in full dress uniform, as they approached the harbor, "he glanced at his blue pennant floating from the masthead and solemnly declared, 'it would be well if I died now, in harness.'"[51] Nevertheless he enjoyed his visit to the yard, and one day he walked upon the wooden deck of the old sailing sloop *Dale*. After taking one last look, he returned to shore, remarking, "That is the last time I shall ever tread the deck of a man-of-war."

"On Sunday, August 14, 1870, a soft breeze blew in from the Atlantic, eight bells struck at noon, and 'the spirit of the great Admiral put out to sea.'"[52] Farragut's Portsmouth funeral drew a large crowd, but it did not draw Grant or Porter. Farragut had not supported Grant for president in 1868, and Grant, therefore, refused to attend his funeral.

The admiral had intended that he be buried at Annapolis, but his wife, Virginia, under pressure from her New York friends and "civic leaders," agreed to have his remains reinterred at Woodlawn Cemetery in the Bronx, after temporary interment in a vault near the church in Portsmouth. It was a fitting farewell for Farragut: Grant and his cabinet attended that service following the public outcry that resulted from his failure to attend Farragut's Portsmouth funeral. The governor of New York and his staff also attended.

"Ten thousand soldiers and sailors, the New York Fire Brigade, and thousands of citizens turned out on September 30 as *Brooklyn* pulled to the wharf. From West and Canal Streets the long procession began its march up Broadway to the Harlem railway at 47th Street, passing draped public buildings while bells tolled and minute guns fire. A cold, heavy rain poured from the skies, drenching everyone and everything. Half of the procession turned away and sought shelter."

At the cemetery, General George Gordon Meade "saluted the first admiral of the navy and said, 'I believe that the Admiral was more beloved than any other commander of the late war, either Army or Navy.'" George Dewey, soon to become—after Farragut and Porter—the third admiral of the navy and who had served under Farragut as executive officer on board one of Farragut's ships, the USS *Mississippi*, said that as he confronted the problems of entering Manila Bay, then finding and attacking the Spanish fleet, he famously asked himself, "What would Farragut do?" Dewey then steamed into the bay, found the Spanish fleet at Cavite, attacked it and virtually destroyed it. That is. Indeed, exactly what Farragut would have done.[53]

CHAPTER FOUR

Philip Henry Sheridan

"Little Phil"

Beginnings

Abraham Lincoln said that Philip Sheridan was "a little chap, with [a] long body, short legs, not enough neck to hang him, and such long arms that if his ankles itch, he can scratch them without stooping," and also said that Sheridan was "a swarthy non-descript individual" with a bullet-shaped head.[1] Philip A. Sheridan was, in addition, a tough little Irishman—he was five feet, five inches tall; during the war, he weighed about 130 pounds—and that toughness would manifest itself time and again throughout his, by today's standards, relatively short life.

No one knows for certain where Sheridan was born. Perhaps harboring at some point presidential aspirations, Sheridan claimed variously to have been born in Boston, Albany and New York, and his mother said in 1888 that he was born in Somerset, Ohio. Some say that he was born on a ship between Ireland and America, and Sheridan biographer Eric J. Wittenberg, among others, posits that he was born in Ireland, where a plaque marks the house in which he purportedly was born.

Philip Henry Sheridan (1862–1864).

39

A neighbor there, who drove the family to Dublin to begin their long journey to America, stated that Philip's mother, Mary, held Philip in her arms during that ride. So the jury remains out on that question, but what we do know for certain is that the future general was the third of six children and that his older sister, Rosa, died at sea during the voyage to America.

Sheridan's father worked on a construction crew building roads and canals and was away much of the time, so his mother, Mary, was both Sheridan's caretaker and role model. The boy attended Somerset's one-room school, run by an Irishman named Patrick McNanly, assisted by a hard-drinking Virginian named Thorn, and both liberally applied the cane. Thorn's beatings were the genesis of Sheridan's lifelong hatred of the South—a hatred that would be exacerbated by some of his experiences at West Point—and both men's beatings caused him to play what he said in his memoirs was "hookey."[2] The boy was combative and a good street fighter, and his looks were decidedly "simian."[3]

Sheridan left school at age fourteen and worked in a succession of dry goods stores, moving up from a clerk who stocked goods to bookkeeper and chief clerk at Finck and Dittoe's. The Mexican War came along when Sheridan was fifteen, and it engendered a strong desire in him to attend West Point and to become an army officer. Through his work at Finck and Dittoe's he met a congressman named Thomas Ritchey, and through the congressman's efforts, Sheridan secured an appointment to West Point in 1848.

At West Point, Sheridan remained the pugilistic, hot-tempered Irishman that he had always been, his temperament exacerbated by the strict West Point regimen, the more than three hundred rules that governed every aspect of cadet lives and hazing by his West Point betters. At one point, after a scolding from a cadet superior from Virginia, Sheridan lowered his bayonet and aimed it at the Virginian's stomach, exclaiming, "God damn you, sir, I'll run you through." After the Virginian reported him, Sheridan attacked him with his fists that night. Those incidents garnered the little Irishman a year's suspension from the Academy. He returned in 1852, and his senior year came within eleven demerits of automatic dismissal. But he did graduate, finishing thirty-fourth out of about fifty cadets in his class. The exact number varies with the source. The superintendent Sheridan's senior year was Colonel Robert E. Lee, who, many years later, would have a fateful encounter with his former student.

After graduation, Sheridan fought Indians along the Rio Grande, then transferred to California, where he relieved future adversary John Bell Hood. Future comrade George Crook was there, and they cemented the friendship they had formed at West Point. From California, Sheridan moved on to Oregon, where he took an Indian mistress.

The Civil War began, and Sheridan languished in Oregon before finally receiving orders to St. Louis. There he became associated with General Henry Halleck, who was impressed by the tough little Irishman. When, in the aftermath of the bloody battle at Shiloh, Halleck relieved Grant and took command of Grant's army, Sheridan accompanied him south. He then moved into the cavalry, in which he had no experience. In Corinth, Mississippi, Sheridan renewed an acquaintance with William Tecumseh Sherman. The two men both had a predilection for profanity and thus got along well.[4]

Bravery at a skirmish near Booneville, Mississippi, brought a promotion to brigadier general and also brought a horse that he named Rienzi, which would gallop into legend with Sheridan. Several more skirmishes followed, including one with Confederate colonel William C. Faulkner, great-grandfather of the author of the same name. Promotion to major general came and with it command of a division. Sheridan's rise in rank had been meteoric: he had moved from captain to major general in six months.

Next up was an encounter with Bragg at Chickamauga, where Sheridan's division, under attack by James Longstreet's corps, "dissolved into a mob of fugitives." Sheridan managed, however, to rally many of his men and to join George Thomas on Horseshoe Ridge, where Thomas, the "Rock of Chickamauga," made the fabled stand that saved William Rosecrans's army. Subsequently, Grant took command of the Army of Tennessee, which was bottled up in Chattanooga, and fought his way out at battles such as Missionary Ridge, where Sheridan's men achieved an improbable victory against a well-entrenched, elevated foe.

President Lincoln ordered Grant east to take command of all Union armies, and Grant took the mercurial Sheridan with him to command the cavalry wing of Meade's Army of the Potomac. This appointment gave rise to his conflicts with Meade about the manner in which Meade used his cavalry: screening and guarding supplies. Sheridan, on the other hand, wanted to be a separate, independent fighting force, and following a traffic snafu during the Battle of Spotsylvania Courthouse, the two engaged in a shouting match. Grant did just what Sheridan wanted and, overruling Meade, cut Sheridan loose for a long sortie that took his cavalry to the gates of Richmond and caused the death of Confederate cavalry icon J.E.B. Stuart.

After the Union debacle at Cold Harbor, Sheridan's cavalry days were over. Grant dispatched him west to take command of the Army of the Shenandoah with two objectives: destroy Jubal A. Early and his army and render Virginia's breadbasket useless as a source of supplies for Lee's army. Sheridan burned the Valley and destroyed Early's army in a series of battles. He returned to Meade's Army of the Potomac, then entrenched at Petersburg opposite Lee's Army of Northern Virginia. The war had reached its endgame, and Sheridan rapidly pushed it toward its inexorable denouement. At Five Forks, he broke through Lee's lines and rolled up his right flank, which, coupled with a breakthrough assault the next day, forced Lee to abandon Petersburg and head west. On April 3, at Sayler's Creek, the little Irishman inflicted a defeat on Lee that prompted him to exclaim, "My God! Has the army been dissolved?"[5]

Finally, in one of the more famous colloquies of the war, Sheridan told Grant that "if the thing is pressed, I think Lee will surrender." Lincoln then told Grant, "Let the thing be pressed."[6] It was pressed. Sheridan cut Lee off at Appomattox, and Lee, finally cornered, was brought to bay. He surrendered on April 9, 1865.

Sheridan accompanied Grant to the surrender in Wilmer McLean's living room, but he behaved in a way that brought discredit to the little Irishman. Earlier that day he had sent two notes to Lee complaining that Lee's troops were firing on his men during the armistice leading up to Lee's surrender. At the surrender he suddenly and abrasively demanded that Lee return the notes. Lee did, but that incident would cost Sheridan his participation in the Grand Review that would take place late in May. Confederate general John B. Gordon said of Sheridan, "His style of conversation and general bearing, while never discourteous, were far less agreeable and pleasing than … those of any other officer in the Union Army whom it was my fortune to meet. There was an absence of that delicacy and consideration which was exhibited by other Union officers."[7]

Then came the actual surrender of the Army of Northern Virginia commanded by General John Brown Gordon to the Union troops, commanded by General Joshua Chamberlain. "The Cavalry Corps was pointedly excluded from the April 12 surrender ceremony. Sheridan's lack of 'delicacy' during his encounters with Gordon and Lee at Appomattox was surely one reason, but the Rebels' smoldering resentment of Sheridan's hard-riding troopers was probably the primary one."

The Union's battles with the Army of Northern Virginia and with Early's little force in the Shenandoah Valley were over. It was time for Sheridan to move on.

Postwar

Lee's surrender did not, of course, end the war. There was still Joseph E. Johnston's army in North Carolina with which to deal, as well as Kirby Smith's Confederate army beyond the Mississippi River. Sheridan received orders to deal with the former and then the latter. He started south with infantry and his cavalry corps, but Johnston surrendered before Sheridan could join Sherman. Grant then sent Sheridan to take on Kirby Smith, but again, Smith surrendered before Sheridan could get there. On the way to Texas, as Sheridan approached the Mississippi River, he and his staff saw shady-looking characters rowing across the river with two horses in tow. Some of the Union troops pursued, and while they did not catch the men in the boat, those men cut the horses loose and escaped. It turned out to be Sheridan's old adversary Jubal A. Early, who was on his way to Texas to join Confederate troops who had not surrendered. Old Jube shortly wrote a note to Sheridan demanding payment for the two horses, which Sheridan's men had captured. Sheridan obviously ignored the demand. He thought Early was delusional in his desire to avoid capture.[8]

1865–1868

Sheridan went on to Texas, where he positioned his army of 52,000 troops along the Rio Grande and forced the French, who had taken over the country while the United States was engaged in the Civil War, to evacuate their 40,000 troops, who had propped up the puppet regime of Austrian Archduke Ferdinand Maximilian. The Mexicans then captured and executed Maximilian on June 19, 1867.

In the states of the Confederacy, former Confederates quickly took control of state governments, putting into law Black codes in all of the secessionist states except Tennessee. President Andrew Johnson, however, "turned a blind eye" to the encroachments on Black freedom of the former Confederates. Violence against the former slaves mounted. Texas, indeed, descended into anarchy and violence against Blacks. Sheridan, in Galveston, after observing the chaos, said, "If I owned Hell and Texas, I would rent out Texas and live in Hell."[9]

Instead, Sheridan, charged with responsibility for Texas and Louisiana, went to New Orleans, through which he had passed on this way to Texas. While he had been gone, whites, on July 30, 1866, attacked Blacks attending a meeting to elect delegates to a constitutional convention, with as many as forty Blacks killed and 140 or so wounded. Brigadier General William Sherman said, "It was a riot. It was an absolute massacre by the police, which wasn't exceeded in murderous cruelty by that of Fort Pillow."[10] The white mob in New Orleans had attacked with clubs, knives and pistols and had attacked not only the people in the constitutional convention but random people on the streets. Sheridan sympathized with the Southern Black freedman, but Louisiana danced to the tune played by the Southern Democrats, the party of the ante bellum South.

In the November elections of 1866, Radical Republicans gained a veto-proof majority in Congress and, unlike Johnson, did not turn a blind eye to violence in the South. Thus, on March 2, 1867, Radical—or

Congressional—Reconstruction began. Reconstruction Act Number One created five military districts over states that had rejected the Fourteenth Amendment. Sheridan took command of the Fifth District, which, likely to fuel his resentment given his feelings about Texas, consisted of Louisiana and Texas.

When the ten states comprising the five districts did not ratify the Fourteenth Amendment and did little or nothing to implement the First Reconstruction Act, Congress followed up with the Second Reconstruction Act, which empowered the military commanders to conduct elections of delegates to a constitutional convention. The Second Act also disenfranchised former Confederate officials and Union Army officers who had aligned with the Confederacy. Others could vote if they swore loyalty to the Union. The monster provision was that Blacks could vote. Finally, Congress passed the Third Reconstruction Act, which permitted the military commanders over the military districts to remove elected officials.

Sheridan, before the end of March, promulgated General Order Number One, establishing his authority over all Fifth District government affairs, including the power to remove officials. Without hesitation and in light of the previous year's slaughter of Blacks in New Orleans, he went after elected officials who had participated, either actively or passively, in the attack. He nailed the New Orleans judge and two elected officials who had been in his crosshairs since then, and he subsequently removed the mayor, the Louisiana attorney general and a district judge. Of the five district commanders, only Sheridan at this point removed elected civilian officials, and he was not done yet. Subsequently he fired most of the elected officials in New Orleans and ultimately removed the governors of Texas and Louisiana. These moves angered President Johnson, and Johnson began aiming his presidential guns at Sheridan.

Sheridan refused to allow a procession when the remains of Confederate general Albert Sidney Johnston landed in Galveston on the way to Austin for interment. Citizens marched anyway, and Sheridan removed the mayor for failing to stop the procession. The South fought back. Some citizens of Brownsville fired upon Union soldiers. All over the South, murders of freedmen, Union sympathizers and soldiers increased. Sheridan continued to remove elected officials and recommended the imposition of martial law. Johnson finally had enough: in August 1867 he removed Sheridan, saying that "Sheridan's administration of the Fifth Military District has, in fact, been one of absolute tyranny, without reference to the principles of our government or the nature of our free institutions ... a resort to authority not granted by law."[11]

Despite everything, Sheridan had successfully overseen the registration of tens of thousands of black voters in Louisiana and Texas—indisputably his greatest achievement. He had punished the most odious instances of official corruption and misconduct.... He had attempted to protect loyal and Unionists and blacks from the violence that permeated the Fifth Military District. He had made a maximum effort to carry out his mission, as he perceived it.[12]

Sheridan would later say, "I was not loath to go." Texas, and presumably Louisiana now, were likely still worse than hell.

With Little Phil's ride on the unruly Fifth District mule over, he quickly received orders from Grant to assume command of the Department of the Missouri, with headquarters at Fort Leavenworth, Kansas. The district included all of the land situated from the Mississippi River to the Rocky Mountains. A new and different set of challenges awaited him there.

1868–1871

Sheridan reported to Fort Leavenworth and immediately took six months' leave to Somerset. He then went to Washington, D.C., where he worked with Sherman and Grant on a new Army Code of Regulations and new Articles of War. Sheridan enjoyed the social life in Washington. As Sherman said to his wife, "I am pushing Sheridan as hard as I can to work, but he don't [sic] want to hurry through. He enjoys the parties." In March 1868, Little Phil returned to Fort Leavenworth, where there was trouble brewing on the Southern Plains.

Comanches and Kiowas were raiding in Texas, and Sioux, Cheyenne and Arapahos were active in Kansas, Oklahoma and Colorado. It fell to Sheridan to stop the raids. His problem—*one* of his problems—was that he had only 2,600 troops to patrol over 1,200 miles, while the tribes in his jurisdiction had 6,000 warriors. When two punitive expeditions in September 1868 failed, Sheridan resolved to implement the tactics that had made him successful in the Shenandoah Valley: a winter campaign aimed at food, livestock and village destruction. He implemented that plan with brutal effectiveness and, in so doing, during the winter of 1868–1869, in killing snow and rain, broke the power of the Southern Plains tribes, sending them starving onto reservations.

One of his subordinates was the flamboyant Colonel George Armstrong Custer, of whom Sheridan, after the winter campaign, said, "If there is any poetry or romance in war, he could develop it."[13] Custer and his Seventh Cavalry attacked a camp of sleeping Cheyenne and killed 310 men, women and children. Custer then hauled fifty-three squaws back to Sheridan. The eastern newspapers blasted Sheridan and Sherman for allowing Custer to execute the brutal slaughter, but Sherman, Sheridan's immediate superior, had Sheridan's back.

Then, a Cheyenne chief told Sheridan that he was a "good Indian," to which Sheridan replied, "The only good Indians I ever saw were dead." That phrase would subsequently be corrupted to "The only good Indian is a dead Indian." Sheridan would later deny that he ever said it, but a subordinate, Lieutenant Charles Nordstrom, who was present, said that Sheridan had indeed said precisely that.[14]

Grant won the presidency in November 1868 and invited Sheridan to attend his inauguration on March 2, 1869. Sherman became commanding general of the army, and Sheridan took Sherman's place as commander of the Department of Missouri, Dakota and the Platte. That move brought him a promotion to lieutenant general, the second-ranking officer in the army, outranking his former superior, George Meade, much to the latter's sorrow. Sheridan moved his headquarters from St. Louis to Chicago, where he transformed himself from the fighting lion of the plains to the social lion of Chicago.

Sheridan bought a house on Michigan Avenue and took dance lessons arranged by Mrs. George Pullman, wife of the inventor of the Pullman coach. His classmates included Pullman, Marshall Field and Robert Todd Lincoln, and he learned to waltz and polka. While trout fishing in Wisconsin, an elderly farmer asked Sheridan to point out the "famous general." Sheridan replied that it was he, and the farmer said, "How could such a little man with such a low voice as yourn [sic] command a big army?" He met the English Earl of Dunraven, who described Sheridan as a "delightful man with the one peculiarity of using the most astounding swear words quite calmly and dispassionately in ordinary conversation."[15]

With his promotion, Sheridan's last field command was history, but controversy arising out of his command's treatment of the Indians continued to brew. One of his subordinates—Major Eugene Baker—and the Second Cavalry raided the wrong village and killed 173 peaceful Piegan Indians living there under a safe conduct pass, including over 53 women and children. The chief came out to the waiting soldiers to show them the pass, but they shot him dead and attacked the village anyway. Baker's men then burned the village and took 140 prisoners and several hundred horses. A Boston abolitionist wrote, "I know of only three savages on the northern plains—Colonel Baker, General Custer and at the head of them all, General Sheridan." Pilloried in the East but praised in the West, Sheridan and the army, metaphorically, circled the wagons, and Sheridan, now through his subordinates, fought on, all the while excoriating the eastern press, which pursued and bayed after him like a pack of wild dogs.[16]

In Europe, the Franco-Prussian War was underway, and Sheridan, having just fought a hard war in America, was anxious to see how the Europeans did it. Upon application to Grant, the president authorized the mercurial Sheridan to Europe as an observer. He and his aide General

James W. Forsyth were to be the guests of the king of Prussia, who, Sheridan and Grant both thought, would win the war. Grant's authorization was as follows:

> Lieutenant General Ph. H. Sheridan, of the United States Army, is authorized to visit Europe, to return at his own leisure, unless otherwise ordered. He is recommended to the good offices of all representatives of this Government whom he may meet abroad.
>
> To citizens and representatives of other Governments I introduce General Sheridan as one of the most skillful, brave and deserving soldiers developed by the great struggle through which the United States Government has just passed. Attention paid him will be appreciated by the country he has served so faithfully and efficiently.

Sheridan and Forsyth sailed for England and then on to Berlin, from which they took a train to the front lines, or at least almost to the front lines. They made the last part of the trip in a hay wagon, arriving on August 17, 1870. There, the king, William I, and his "Iron Chancellor," Count Otto von Bismarck, who was using the war as a lever to unite the various German kingdoms and principalities and would then wrestle two such provinces away from France, Alsace and Lorraine, met the American general. Bismarck described Sheridan as "a small, corpulent gentleman of about forty-five, with a dark mustache and a thick tuft, who spoke the Yankee dialect."[17]

Sheridan watched two battles in which the Prussians were victorious, including the famous Prussian victory at Sedan, and followed the Prussian army for about two months. That army, under the command of Helmut Von Moltke, thoroughly whipped the French in every battle, and Napoleon III surrendered to Bismarck after Sedan, but his national guard valiantly fought on. Von Moltke drove the French into Paris, which the Prussians surrounded and to which they then laid siege, pounding the city with their huge Krupp siege guns and starving its inhabitants, in four months, into submission. The war cost the two combatants 320,000 dead and France the two aforementioned provinces, and it resulted in the unification of Germany, thus laying the seeds for a far greater conflict to come some forty years in the future. Sheridan accompanied the Prussians on their triumphal entrance into Paris.

Sheridan told Bismarck and the king that while the Prussian infantry was the finest in the world, they did not know how to use their cavalry, having sacrificed it in a frontal assault on a heavily defended French position. Sheridan compared the manner in which the Prussians used their cavalry to that of his old adversary, George Meade. Meade's grandson learned of what Sheridan had said and, following in his grandfather's footsteps, heaped scorn on Sheridan for thinking his cavalry "the best on earth."[18]

Sheridan was contemptuous of the French, whom he said were disorganized, fought poorly and lacked "élan."[19] After two months, he had enough, concluding that there was nothing to be learned from the Prussians or the French but much that the Prussians and the French could learn from him. He did tell Bismarck that the way to gouge peace from an adversary was to wage total warfare against the civilian population and through the cries of the oppressed people, force the adversary to surrender.

After leaving France, Sheridan toured Belgium, Austria and Turkey and then went on to Italy and Greece. In Italy he hunted deer on King Victor Emmanuel's private preserve, killing eleven. Finally, he visited Turkey, where he saw the sultan in a procession, preceded by "the mysterious, veiled ladies of his harem." Sheridan: "Now and then a pretty face was seen, rarely a beautiful one." Then, in an amazing case of the pot calling the kettle black, he said, "many were plump, even to corpulence, and these were the closest veiled, being considered the greatest beauties I presume, since with the Turk, obesity is the chief element of comeliness."[20] In a strange coincidence, Sheridan's old adversary James Longstreet, who had famously told Custer that he did not deal with Yankee subordinates, would be appointed ambassador to Turkey in 1880. Longstreet's thoughts with respect to the sultan's harem are not recorded.[21]

Sheridan stayed ten months in Europe, visiting Eastern Europe, dining with the Belgium king and queen and visiting England, Ireland and Scotland. Then, on May 24, 1871, he returned home, but there was more pleasure awaiting him in the United States. That autumn, he took charge of a hunting expedition to the western plains, featuring a "glittering assembly of press moguls and business tycoons," including "James Gordon Bennett, publisher of the *New York Herald*; Charles Wilson, publisher of the *Chicago Evening Journal*; Anson Stager, president of Western Electric;" and an army colonel named Daniel Rucker, who would later play an important role in Sheridan's life. Leonard Jerome, a New York financier, also was on the trip. He would one day be the grandfather of Winston Churchill. The group, supported by sixteen wagons, ate heartily, drank heavily and shot virtually anything that could walk or fly, from buffalo, assisted by William Cody, to elk, antelope and wild turkey. They slaughtered over six hundred buffalo, an act outrageous today, but in Sheridan's day and in his mind, killing six hundred buffalo was nothing. Others slaughtered them in the thousands. Moreover, Sheridan, as noted, thought killing *all* of the buffalo would starve the Indians and force them onto reservations. There, dependent on the largesse of the United States, incompetent bureaucrats and unscrupulous vendors, they would live on the hard, mean edge of starvation.[22]

Sheridan returned to Chicago following the hunt, even more corpulent after the astonishing amount of food and drink consumed on the plains. Then, on October 8, 1871, came an event that stunned the nation. It was the great Chicago fire, and Sheridan was there not only to see it but to help stop it, and he would also help deal with its aftermath. While there is no evidence to support the tale that the fire started when Mrs. O'Leary's cow kicked over a lantern, there is no question that the fire started near Patrick O'Leary's barn. It was dry and windy, and the fire raced through Chicago like the horses that stampeded through its streets trying to escape the conflagration. Sheridan took charge and helped direct the destruction of buildings to set up fire breaks, then, subsequently, arranged through the army, with the full support of President Grant and Commanding General Sherman, rations and tents for the homeless. The fire did not destroy Sheridan's home, but it did destroy his papers, which were in his office that was consumed by the fire. Sheridan, after the fire, deployed troops to stop the looting. Sadly, the fire took Sheridan's horse Breckenridge, captured at Missionary Ridge.[23]

Unknown at the time, the fire had—for Sheridan—the salutary effect of sending Colonel Daniel Rucker, a member of the hunting party, his wife and his daughter Irene, then in her teens, into Sheridan's house as fire refugees. Irene would subsequently play a prominent role in Little Phil's life.

1872–1884

Impressed by the autumn 1871 hunt, Grant asked Sheridan to organize another hunt in January 1872, to honor the Russian czar's son, Grand Duke Alexis. The czar had supported the Union during the war, and the hunt would be Grant's payback. Sheridan took it on with the efficiency of the general that he was, organizing a small army to support the expedition, including twenty Sioux Indians and once again utilizing William—now "Buffalo Bill"—Cody. Also on the hunt would be the army's famous cavalryman, Lieutenant Colonel George Armstrong Custer, the "flamboyant war hero and Indian fighter," who had once shot his own horse while riding alongside a buffalo that he was trying to shoot with his revolver.[24]

Sheridan ordered the department commanders of the Platte and the Missouri to support the operation. His aide Colonel Forsythe was responsible for "mess arrangements," and the commander of the Platte "converted Omaha barracks into a supply depot for the hunt." Another general, John Pope, "monitored the southern buffalo herds' movements and telegraphed Sheridan with daily updates…. Hundreds of army personnel were assigned to making sure the grand duke was well fed and entertained—and that he killed a buffalo."[25]

He killed two, and the hunting party killed "thirty or forty." They left the carcasses strewn about the prairie, the dead buffalo a symbol of the problem that would engender trouble on those same plains in the days to come. But in the meantime, there was an event that would forever change the life of Bill Cody, who had earlier been invited by the publisher James Gordon Bennett to come to New York. Sheridan now encouraged Cody to go, and Cody, apprehensive, finally decided to do so. He stopped along the way in Chicago and boarded with the two Sheridan brothers, then went on to the city.

To his surprise, Cody liked New York and loved the theater. And after more scouting in the West, Cody was invited back to New York in 1872 by Ned Buntline, who had written dime novels about "Buffalo Bill" Cody; Buntline wanted him to appear in his play, "Scouts of the Prairie." It was the beginning of Cody's show business career, culminating in the Wild West Show and his tenure as the reigning celebrity of his era.[26]

The savage slaughter of the buffalo by white hunters continued unchecked. In 1872 and 1873, 1,250,000 hides went east to tanneries, and by the end of 1874, it was estimated that 4,873,730 buffalo had been slaughtered, only 150,000 by the Indians. The going rate for a buffalo hide in the east was $3.50. The math was simple, the butchery horrible. One hunter, Josiah W. Movar, killed 21,000 in three years. Sheridan continued to urge elimination of the buffalo as a source of food for the Indians. Only then, he argued, could the Indians be forced onto the reservations. Sheridan had the backing of Secretary of the Interior Columbus Delano to make the Indians dependents of the government. The killing raged on.[27]

The problem—*one* of the problems—was that the Indians were starving on the reservations. The government did not keep its promise to feed the tribes there, so finally, in desperation, the tribes would begin hunting and raiding off the reservations. The raids by Comanches, Kiowas and Cheyenne began in 1872 and took place throughout 1873 and continued into 1874, when, on June 27, about 700 Indians from four different tribes surrounded and attacked twenty-nine buffalo hunters—one of them a young man named Bat Masterson—at a place called Adobe Walls. The fight extended over several hours, and the hunters, armed with the .50-caliber Sharps buffalo rifles, fought the Indians to a standstill, killing thirteen, wounding an unknown number and losing three of their own men. The Indians withdrew. This was, however, the opening salvo of what would be known as the Red River War, and Sheridan once again would be the architect of the army's campaign, ordered by Sherman to make the Indians "knuckle under" at once.[28]

"At once" demanded a summer campaign, antithetical to the winter campaigns designed and implemented enthusiastically by the architect of the campaigns against both Indians and Shenandoah Valley dwellers. But Sheridan complied, and for the remainder of 1874 and into 1875, Sheridan's army of 2,700 pursued and repeatedly attacked a 1,200-man raiding party, until finally the Indians gave up and returned to their reservations. The Red River Campaign effectively broke the power of the Indians of the Southern Plains. Trouble, however, similar in its making, was brewing with the Sioux on the Northern Plains.

An interesting footnote to the Red River Campaign is that one of Sheridan's subordinates was Colonel Ranald Mackenzie, a highly regarded young officer prized by his superiors for his—among other desirable qualities—ruthlessness, which, as Sheridan biographer Joseph Wheelan notes, may have been inherited. Mackenzie's father was naval officer Alexander Slidell Mackenzie, who, as commanding officer of the brig *Somers* in 1842, hanged three mutineers from the yardarm, one of them the son of Secretary of War John Spencer, in the only documented mutiny in U.S. Navy history. Confederate admiral Raphael Semmes would later, in the Mexican-American War, command the top-heavy *Somers* into to a watery grave off Vera Cruz.[29]

Before Sheridan could move against the Sioux, his superiors had other non–Indian-fighting plans for him, plans that would return him to one part of the country that, with Texas, he despised the most, Louisiana. There, as 1875 began, insurgent Southern Democrats and their Republican betters were engaged in internecine political warfare for control of the state legislature. President Grant, fearing a Democrat takeover, sent the one man he thought could manage that approaching disaster. Accordingly, it was, once again—to the searing regret of Louisiana residents—Sheridan time in the Deep South.

Grant essentially gave Sheridan—Sherman, to whom Little Phil reported, knew nothing of Sheridan's orders—carte blanche to manage the Louisiana political situation as he saw fit. Sheridan immediately intervened in the Louisiana Legislature, where Democrats had taken control. The army, under Sheridan's orders, marched into the legislature with bayonets fixed and ejected five Democrats who had won disputed elections. The rest of the Democrats stormed out, and the Republicans seized control of the House. Sheridan then proposed to suspend habeas corpus and to try civilians before military tribunals. Louisiana was in an uproar. Sheridan received threats on his life, and many citizens of the state urged that the people of Louisiana rise up and fight again. What Sheridan proposed smacked of the worst aspects of Radical Reconstruction, and whenever he entered the restaurant of the St. Charles Hotel, where he was living, he was greeted with a chorus of hisses and boos. Indeed, crowds shadowed him wherever he went.

Not only were the people of Louisiana incensed, but their outrage spread to Washington and, indeed, to the halls of Congress, whose members attacked Sheridan, Secretary of War Belknap and Grant. The war was ten years past, and the country was ready to move on. Sheridan did not get his military courts or the suspension of habeas corpus, and Washington engineered a compromise that gave Democrats control of the Louisiana House and Republicans control of the Senate. Sheridan left Louisiana for the last time to the joy of the many to whom he represented the worst of Northern oppression.[30]

Upon his return to Chicago, Sheridan's personal life took a major turn when he, at age forty-four, married the twenty-two-year-old daughter of Colonel Daniel H. Rucker, the assistant quartermaster of the army. The wedding took place on June 3. Irene was a tall, elegant society woman of grace and not an inconsiderable amount of charm and beauty. For the wedding, attended by President and Mrs. Grant and Generals Sherman, George Crook and John Pope, Sheridan wore his full dress uniform and, of all things, gold spurs.[31]

And now it was time to deal with the Sioux and their Cheyenne allies on the Northern Plains. Like their southern counterparts, the Sioux were starving on the reservations, as Washington failed time and again to honor its obligation to feed them. The Indians thus faced a classic Catch-22: either starve on the reservations or leave the reservations and fight the U.S. Army. Moreover, even if the Sioux left the reservations, their situation was made even direr by the disappearance of the buffalo at the bloody hands of the white man. Finally, the Sioux lived in a large area around the Black Hills, which they held sacred, and with the discovery of gold there, white gold miners streamed onto their sacred grounds. The army had been protecting—or trying to protect—the Sioux lands from encroachments by whites, but in a secret meeting during the autumn of 1875, military leaders agreed to pull the troops, and they concomitantly ordered the Sioux out of the Black Hills and onto reservations. The Sioux refused to comply, and the table was now set for the 1876–1877 Sioux Indian War, which, because of one battle, would be the most famous Indian war in U.S. history.

The Sioux were led by two chieftains, Sitting Bull and Crazy Horse, both able war chieftains, and a winter campaign orchestrated by Sheridan that began on January 31, 1876, failed miserably. Neither Sheridan nor his troops were prepared for the winter weather on the Northern Plains. They would have to wait until spring.

Ignoring warnings of a large concentration of Sioux and northern Cheyenne, Sheridan ordered General Alfred Terry to formulate a plan to attack the Sioux. Terry's plan was for Custer and the Seventh Cavalry—seven hundred men strong, with the colorful Custer in buckskins—to head west. They were to rendezvous with another column, with infantry, coming in from the west under General John A. Gibbon. General Terry would come down from the north. He told Custer not to approach the Little Bighorn until he had linked up with Gibbon's column from the west. A fourth column under General George Crook was to come up from the south, meet with the other three and smash the Sioux. The plan was for some three thousand men to attack in unison. At least that was the plan.

Crook's troops ran into a large force of Sioux at Rosebud River, were mauled badly and went home. This removed one thousand men from the equation. Compounding that error was Custer's boneheaded decision to split his regiment into three columns, one under Major Marcus Reno, one under Custer and the other under Captain Frederick Benteen. That split left Custer with about 250 men to face off with a mass of between ten thousand and fifteen thousand Sioux, Cheyenne, Arapahos and small contingents from other tribes. Custer did not know how many Indians he faced and did not know the lay of the land. Undaunted, on June 25, 1876, he led his men on a wild charge across the Little Bighorn River and into immortality.[32]

Sheridan, in Philadelphia with Sherman for the Centennial Exposition, did not receive word of the massacre until July 4. At first, Sheridan refused to believe the reports, but he soon realized that the worst had happened, and that Custer, twenty officers and 232 men had been lost to the Sioux. But, like Pickett's Charge, the Seventh Cavalry and the Battle of Little Bighorn would forever be immortal. Of the battle and Custer, Sheridan wrote, "Poor Custer, he was the embodiment of gallantry.... But I was always fearful that he would catch it if allowed a separate command.... He was too impetuous, without deliberation; he thought himself invincible and leading a charmed life. When I think of the many brave fellows who went down with him that day, it is sickening."[33] And it was.

Sheridan did what the army usually did after a catastrophe: he reorganized the command, removed Crook and Terry and replaced them with younger men—Colonels Nelson Miles and Ranald Mackenzie, one of Sheridan's favorites. Those two pursued and harassed the Sioux until Sitting Bull had enough and, with Crazy Horse, led the Sioux into Canada at the beginning of 1877. The great Sioux War was over. Sheridan visited the Little Bighorn in July 1877. His brother Mike took what was believed to be Custer's body to West Point, where, in 1861, he had finished last in his class. Those remains—Custer's or not—are buried there.[34]

During the remainder of the 1870s, several small Indian fights took place as the cavalry rounded up the remainder of the northern tribes and shepherded them onto reservations. Sitting Bull eventually returned with his band of Sioux. During this time, Chief Joseph of the Nez Perce led his tribe on the fabled march ahead of the pursuing cavalry. Once he left the Pacific department and moved into Sheridan's territory, Colonel Nelson Miles took up the chase and eventually cornered the Nez Perce in the Bear Paw Mountains of Montana, where Joseph uttered those famous words, "From where the sun now stands I will fight no more forever."[35]

The 1880s came, and Sheridan began to mellow in his attitude toward the Indians. Rather than maintaining the reservations, with their bloated bureaucracy and problems with the supply of food, Sheridan began to advocate that the government give the Indians land upon which to farm. "We took away their land and their means of support, broke up their mode of living, their habits of life, introduced disease and decay among them, and it was for this and against this they made war.... Could anyone expect less?"[36]

Then began a love affair that no one who knew Little Phil, the savage warrior of the Shenandoah and the plains, could have predicted. Going back to 1870, Sheridan had become involved with the Yellowstone region, and in 1871, 1873, 1875 and 1876, he sent expeditions into what became, in 1872, Yellowstone National Park. The 1871 expedition established Sheridan's "enduring connection" to the park, when it named a 10,000-foot-plus mountain for him.[37]

In spite of Yellowstone's status as a national park, tourists, hunters and the railroad all encroached on its lands, killed its game and defaced its landmarks. This activity led Sheridan to mount a counterattack against those encroachments, until finally, in 1883, Sheridan personally led a large expedition of notables into the park. On the trip were President Chester A. Arthur, Secretary of War Robert Todd Lincoln, Governor John Schuyler Crosby of Montana, Senator George G. Vest—he had led the fight to make Yellowstone a national park—New York judge Daniel G. Rollins and Anson Stager of Western Union. The group was attended by a seventy-five-man escort from the Fifth Cavalry. Once on the plains, five hundred Shoshone and Arapaho Indians "galloped into their midst on their ponies, garishly painted and ornately dressed in assorted styles of feathers and beadwork. Reining in a hundred yards away from the official party, they were saluted by a wave of the hat by the president, before continuing their routine."[38] Congress, at Sheridan's urging, denied permission for the railroad company to build a railroad into the park. In 1886, Sheridan—of all people—outraged at the continued slaughter of game by renegade hunters, sent a detachment of the Fifth Cavalry to take over operation of the park. Army supervision of Yellowstone lasted until 1918, when the National Park Service took over.

Another momentous event occurred in 1883, when General William Tecumseh Sherman, the commanding general of the army, announced his retirement. The president immediately named Sheridan to replace him, and in February 1884, Sheridan took command of the army, at least in theory. The secretary of war actually ran the army, issuing orders directly to the commanding general's subordinates. Congress did not confer the four-star rank that Sherman and Grant, his predecessors in that position, had. Still, it was a signal achievement for Sheridan, who moved his family—he and Irene now had four young children, twins Jane and Louise, daughter Mary and a son, Philip Jr.—to Washington. A group of his wealthy friends in Chicago, out of gratitude for his services to the city during the great fire, bought him a $44,000 house at Rhode Island Avenue and Seventeenth Street. That group included his friends Anson Stager, Philip Armour, Marshall Field and George Pullman.[39]

One of the sad aspects of Sheridan's life at this point was the final rupture of his relationship with his old friend, West Point roommate and attendee at his wedding, George Crook. The seeds of that break were planted during the Valley campaign when Sherman did not publicly recognize Crook for his role in that campaign. Crook felt, as do many historians, that he was the architect of victory at several of the battles, and then Sheridan blamed Crook for his defeat at Rosebud, which Sheridan rightfully thought had led to the Custer debacle, and his later failure to catch Geronimo, blame that led Crook to ask to be relieved. As an aside, Geronimo surrendered on September 4, 1886, the last tribal leader to give up. He lived at Fort Ord, California, until 1909, making his living selling his photograph and "souvenir hunting bows inscribed with his name."[40]

Sheridan served as ninth president of the National Rifle Association in 1885–1886, and he began his memoirs in 1886 and finished them in 1888. The years as commanding general were peaceful years for him. He and Irene entertained frequently, from foreign dignitaries to President Grover Cleveland. In addition, Sheridan represented the army at various ceremonies such as the dedications of the Washington Monument and the Statue of Liberty, and he frequently attended veterans' reunions, at which he enjoyed talking with his comrades of the old campaigns.

Irene Rucker's father, seventy-year-old Colonel Daniel Rucker, had served as assistant quartermaster of the army for many years, under General Montgomery Meigs, whose son had been killed by Confederate partisans in the Shenandoah Valley and whose death prompted Sheridan to issue an order to take into custody all males within a five-mile radius of the killing and to burn all houses within that same area. Sheridan later rescinded that order at the urging of his subordinates. At Sheridan's insistence, President Arthur forced the sixty-six-year-old Meigs into retirement and named the older Rucker as his replacement. Ten days later, Rucker, now a brigadier general, retired.

Sheridan's last battle was against the old Confederacy that he despised. In 1887, Secretary of War William Endicott ordered the return of captured Confederate battle flags to the states from which they had been captured. Endicott had not served in the Union Army and thus did not know how much anger that decision would provoke. Sheridan led the anti-flag-return forces, which included members of the Grand Army of the Republic, a political force of major significance, and various politicians hopped on board the anti-flag-return train. Feeling the heat, President Cleveland rescinded Endicott's order.

General and former President Grant, who was like a father to Sheridan, died July 23, 1885, and Sheridan was a pallbearer at his funeral in New York. Grant had won a race against time to finish his memoirs before succumbing to throat cancer. For Sheridan, who refused to visit Grant on his deathbed—he did not want to see the wasted Grant—it was a huge loss. Grant had been his mentor, had seen to his promotions, had appointed him head of the Army of the Potomac's cavalry, had rejoiced in his victories and had heaped lavish praise upon him. For Sheridan, it was a terrible loss.

The little Irishman's looks had changed:

> He wore upon the back of his round, bullet head an old-fashioned silk hat about two sizes too small; a short, light overcoat that had only two buttons and they were ready to fly off from the undue strain of Sheridan's round figure. The trousers were a gray plaid and fitted very snugly on the General's fat legs. His boots were thick-sided and un-blacked.

Sheridan was no longer Little Phil; he had become, instead, Fat Phil. Nevertheless, "he still bore himself with 'the quick, elastic gait, erect figure, and soldierly presence required as a cadet,' wrote his brother Michael.... People liked his amiable, low-key manner. 'Politeness is a cheap commodity that every one may possess,' he liked to say."[41] It was a far cry from the Sheridan who abrasively demanded from Robert E. Lee the return of the two notes that he had earlier written and was, therefore, excluded from the grand review. It was also a far cry from the Sheridan, who, when Lee surrendered, said, "Damn them. I wish that they had held out an hour longer and I would have whipped hell out of them."[42] And it was certainly not the Sheridan who was responsible for "The Burning" in the Shenandoah, the slaughter of the buffalo on the plains or the winter wars that decimated the Indians and drove them, starving, onto reservations, where they would continue to live on the razor-sharp edge of starvation. He had mellowed. Finally.

In November 1887, Sheridan complained to his army physician, Major Robert M. O'Reilly, that he did not feel well and had not felt well for several months. Dr. O'Reilly examined him and found that he was suffering from heart disease. No longer Little Phil, Sheridan now packed two hundred pounds on his five-foot-five frame. His face was flushed, and he was short of breath. Sheridan's lifestyle was not salubrious; he ate and drank to excess. That spring he spoke to the graduating class at West Point, telling the prospective graduates that West Point had fully prepared them for a career in the army, just as it had him. He urged them to do as he had: always do their very best, no matter how remote the post or seemingly insignificant the task. That, he said, was the key to his success.

On May 22, 1888, Sheridan suffered what had become the inevitable heart attack, and a few days later, more, albeit smaller, attacks. Congress, learning of his illness, quickly passed legislation promoting him to full general, the rank held previously by only Washington, Grant and Sherman.

Tormented by the debilitating summer heat and stultifying humidity of Washington, Sheridan and Irene bought a summer cottage in Nonquitt, Massachusetts, on the west shore of Buzzard's Bay, next to the home of Louisa May Alcott of *Little Women* fame. On June 30, 1888, the family departed Washington for Nonquitt. Sheridan finished his memoirs three days later. Like Grant, he had won his literary race against time.

On August 5, around 10:30 p.m., General of the Army Philip Henry Sheridan died in Nonquitt at age fifty-seven. His death left only General Sherman of the great Union triumvirate. Sherman would live only two and a half years after Sheridan.

They took Sheridan's body back to Washington, where there was an outpouring of grief and praise for the little general. His body lay in state in his parish church. President Cleveland, among other dignitaries, attended his funeral. He was buried on August 11, 1888, at Arlington Cemetery, not far from Robert E. Lee's house, from which the cemetery took its name.

Irene Sheridan never remarried. "I had," she said, "rather be Philip Sheridan's widow than any living man's wife."[43] Neither did any of his three daughters ever marry, just as none of Robert E. Lee's daughters ever married.[44] The overhanging greatness of their fathers was simply too much for any suitor to overcome.

Congress voted Irene a lifetime pension, and it was said that each morning his three daughters leaned out their window to shout good morning to the general, astride Rienzi in Sheridan Circle. Irene died in 1938, and of the daughters, Louise was the last to die, in 1969. Mike Sheridan, the general's brother, served his country in the Spanish-American War. He retired from the army as a brigadier general. Philip Jr., like his father, also graduated from West Point, in 1902. One of his classmates was the son of another Union hero, Arthur MacArthur: Douglas MacArthur would achieve five-star rank and military apotheosis in World War II. Philip Jr., like his father, died of heart trouble, in 1918. Sheridan's grandson, Philip III, graduated from

Harvard Law School, eschewing an army career. "There have been enough fighting men in our family," he said. Nevertheless, he joined and served in the Army Air Force in World War II.[45]

Like Nathan Bedford Forrest,[46] it is hard to overstate Sheridan's influence upon subsequent generations of military leaders and the warfare that they practiced. His use of cavalry, infantry and artillery combined into one mobile strike force would contribute to the deadly concept of mobile warfare in the twentieth century, and its ultimate, and horrific, child would be the German blitzkrieg of World War II. Moreover, like Sherman, Sheridan practiced the dark science of total warfare, and those same Germans would apply that horrible concept with stunning, mind-numbing efficacy in that same war.[47]

Yet, in startling contradiction to his warrior ethos, Sheridan also had his "soft" side. His love of, and work with, what would become Yellowstone National Park would create a lasting legacy for generations to come. And his change of heart with respect to the Indians represented a stunning shift from his earlier advocacy of total war, not only against the Indians but also against the buffalo, their primary food source. Indeed, after the beginning of his love affair with Yellowstone, he became an admirer of those great beasts and fought hard for their preservation. Both the warrior side and the conservationist sides of that complex little man would be part of his legacy.

Of him, at the 1908 unveiling of his statue on Sheridan Circle, President Theodore Roosevelt, whose mother was an ardent Southern sympathizer during the war, said:

> Not only was he a great general, but he showed his greatness with that touch of originality which we call genius. Indeed, this quality of brilliance has been in one sense a disadvantage to his reputation, for it has tended to overshadow his solid ability. We tend to think of him only as the dashing cavalry leader, whereas he was in reality not only that, but also a great commander.[48]

Those words, then, constitute Little Phil's epitaph.

CHAPTER FIVE

William Tecumseh Sherman

"Cump," "Uncle Billy"

Early Life

William Tecumseh "Cump" Sherman was born the sixth of eleven children to Charles and Mary Holt Sherman on February 8, 1820, in Lancaster, Ohio. The Shermans had immigrated to America from Essex County, England, and had been in this country since at least 1636. Robert Sherman, a signer of the Declaration of Independence, was a member of this family. The Sherman family lived in Connecticut until William Tecumseh's grandfather acquired land in Ohio and moved his family there. William Tecumseh's father, Charles, was a lawyer and then a justice of the Ohio Supreme Court. The boy, christened Tecumseh Sherman, got his name from the Shawnee chieftain, whom Charles admired for his courage and military acumen. Charles's sixth child would carry on that name and, one day, that tradition.[1]

Charles, however, participated in a financial scheme involving the collection of revenue for the federal government, and when it began accepting "only specie or Bank of the United States notes," Charles Sherman found himself with a pile of worthless paper, and, thus, "a large debt."[2] Charles attempted to pay off his debt but

William Tecumseh Sherman (1861–1865).

died unexpectedly in 1829, "virtually penniless."[3] Cump Sherman, nine years old, was taken in by neighbors, the family of Thomas Ewing, a successful Lancaster attorney and politician. It was in Thomas's house that young Cump would grow up. His foster mother was a devout Catholic, and she had the boy christened in her church. The priest, however, was not taken with Cump's given name and, because he was baptized on Saint William's day, added the name "William" so that the young Sherman became William Tecumseh Sherman.

Sherman would never call the Ewings "mother" and "father," but he would grow up as one of their children, and Thomas Ewing would ensure that the boy received the same education as his biological children. Nevertheless, "the financial difficulties resulting from his father's death and the breakup of his family were pivotal events for Sherman. Throughout his life he would worry about his financial situation, fearing that the same might happen to him. But young Sherman had been fortunate: his foster parent Thomas Ewing was one of the leading citizens of early Lancaster. He was known for his intelligence, professional success, and happy family life. Sherman grew to admire and respect his foster father."[4]

In 1836, Ewing secured an appointment for Sherman to the United States Military Academy at West Point. There is some debate with respect to whether Sherman wanted to attend West Point and to become an army officer or whether he would have preferred a career as an attorney. Nevertheless, he accepted the appointment and entered West Point in 1836, likely feeling an obligation to Thomas Ewing.[5] Cump was sixteen years old, tall and thin, an excellent athlete and an outstanding student.

His academic success would continue at West Point; however, he was an indifferent military cadet and did not keep his uniform—or its accoutrements—clean and shiny. Based only on his academic record, he would have finished fourth out of forty-three cadets in the class of 1840, but his military record knocked him down two notches to sixth in his class. He then embarked on a checkered military career—said to be "somewhat unexceptionable"—for the next thirteen years.[6]

Indeed, his career would afford him little opportunity for combat experience, other than a few desultory skirmishes with Seminole Indians in Florida, where he spent two years.[7] Then followed four years at Fort Moultrie in Charleston, South Carolina, where he made many friends in the community and became an admirer of Southerners and the South. Sherman missed the Mexican War,[8] when so many of his colleagues gained valuable experience for the conflagration to come. Instead of fighting in Mexico, he spent that time in Pennsylvania and California. There, in 1848, he saw the coming of the California gold rush at Sutter's Mill, about which he reported to President Polk.[9] Two years later he married his foster sister,

Ellen Ewing, now living in Washington with her father, who was secretary of the interior. Given Ellen's father's status, the wedding was a major society event attended by, among others, President Zachary Taylor. Then, in 1853, at the urging of his Ewing foster siblings and parents, he left the army and joined a St. Louis bank in its San Francisco office.[10] At this point in time, a recent graduate of the Academy, future Confederate general John Bell Hood, met Sherman and described him as "a nervous, red-headed former army officer ... with [a] piercing eye and a nervous, impulsive temperament."[11] Sherman would learn to control his impulsiveness, which would serve him well in the great conflict to come. Hood, unfortunately for the Confederacy, would not.[12]

The San Francisco bank collapsed,[13] and Sherman feared that he would follow his father into penury. The St. Louis bank then moved him to New York to manage that branch, but it, too, failed in the Panic of 1857.[14] Next came a stint in Kansas, where he worked as an attorney and commercial real estate agent. That venture, too, failed. Sherman wrote to Ellen, "I look upon myself as a dead cock in the pit."[15]

Future Union general Don Carlos Buell, who would fight with Sherman at Shiloh, told him of a position in Louisiana at a military school. Backed by two future Confederate generals, P.G.T. Beauregard and Braxton Bragg, Sherman secured the position and moved to Louisiana to serve as president of the Louisiana Military Seminary of Learning and Military Academy, the forerunner of Louisiana State University.[16] Ellen and the children remained behind in Lancaster and urged Sherman, who actually enjoyed his time in Louisiana, to come home to Lancaster. He was torn between the two, so that this was another dark period for the mercurial Sherman. He thus "entered the Civil War years unhappy with his life and unsure about his future."[17]

The Civil War hung large like a dark, miasmal cloud over the country, and then, as the country unraveled following Abraham Lincoln's election in 1860 to the presidency, war came on like a Louisiana hurricane. "When Sherman learned that South Carolina had seceded from the Union, he was brought to tears. He loved the South. Since entering West Point, his closest male friends had been Southerners. During the twenty-five years since leaving home, he had been under the social influence of the South. At West Point, Southern ideals were prevalent. His stay in Florida and South Carolina, his four years of working closely with Southern-born army officers in California, his six years representing Missouri bankers, and now his last year as superintendent of an academy in Louisiana had all left him with a favorable impression of the South.

"In reality, Sherman considered himself a Southerner. He was hoping to spend his life there and was in the process of building a house in

Louisiana. His old army comrades, he knew, were preparing to follow South Carolina's lead. But Sherman could not join them. It was not the slavery issue that stopped him; he considered slavery the appropriate status for Blacks. But he was passionately devoted to the Union and regarded secession a form of revolution and anarchy. Within three weeks, Sherman sadly resigned his position."[18] He reentered the army as a colonel in May 1861. For Cump Sherman the die was cast. While he loved the South, he loved the Union more.

Sherman took charge of a brigade of volunteers in General Irvin McDowell's army and, with McDowell in command, marched with the Union Army directly into the debacle at First Bull Run on July 21, 1861, He had already expressed his dismay with the raw recruits, who were prone to run and, as one-year volunteers, mostly just wanted to go home. Notwithstanding the proclivities of his men, however, Sherman held his men together, and for the most part, his brigade performed well and did "heroic work" that day.[19]

A promotion to brigadier general followed in late August, and Sherman received orders to Kentucky as second-in-command to his old West Point professor and the hero of Fort Sumter, Robert Anderson. Anderson was head of the Department of the Cumberland, but he soon became ill, and Sherman, to his great chagrin, assumed that command. "Sherman almost caved under the stress of his first major command. Convinced that his troops were outnumbered, he asked Lincoln for the impossible—two-hundred-thousand more men."[20] He also feuded with reporters, who hit back by writing stories that hinted—some would say "shouted"—that "he had gone insane."[21] "After Sherman came close to suicide, the army sent him home to pull himself together."[22] Those pesky-as-flies reporters would come back to bite Sherman time and again, but they would find that he could bite back.[23] One of the headlines—in the *Cincinnati Commercial*—howled, "General William T. Sherman Insane" and screamed that he was "stark mad." As a result of their attacks, he wrote to Ellen, "I am almost crazy."[24]

General Ulysses S. Grant, known as "Sam" at West Point, nevertheless selected Sherman to command a division in Grant's Army of Tennessee. What greeted the unstable general was the abattoir at Shiloh Church, near Pittsburg Landing, Tennessee. In two days of savage combat, Sherman's Fifth Division acquitted itself well, and Grant hailed Sherman as the linchpin of victory, which came on the second day after Grant's army had almost been driven into the Tennessee River on the first day. That night, Sherman's old friend Don Carlos Buell came up and brought fresh troops with which Grant launched a crushing counterattack on the second day of the battle that drove another old Sherman friend—P.G.T. Beauregard—back to Corinth, Mississippi.[25] Sherman had three horses shot out from under him and suffered a hand wound. Grant credited Sherman for the Union victory and promoted him to major general.[26] The promotion restored his self-confidence, and he would never again look back. "Shiloh, for Sherman, was the turning point in his life."[27]

The next major campaign was to capture the Confederate "Gibraltar of the Mississippi," Vicksburg. Grant and Sherman met in Oxford, Mississippi, in December of 1862 and laid out their plan for the campaign. The campaign was anything but smooth, but with Sherman feigning an attack on the city, Grant moved south to Grand Gulf, crossed the Mississippi and, with Sherman joining him, headed east toward Jackson. After whipping the Confederate garrison there, Grant, with Sherman in command of the Fifteenth Corps, turned west, beat John Pemberton's army at Champion Hill and then laid siege to Vicksburg. The Gibraltar fell on July 4, 1863, the day after Meade's signal victory at Gettysburg, and although Jefferson Davis—whose home was just south of Vicksburg—did not know it, the outcome of the war was now preordained. It would take, however, two bloody years for the South to realize that it was defeated.[28]

An interesting footnote to the Vicksburg campaign arose out of Sherman's perturbation with the press, whom he loathed as "the most contemptible race of men that exist."[29] An intrepid reporter, Thomas W. Knox from the *New York Herald*, hid aboard a ship in Sherman's flotilla that delivered Union troops into a debacle at Chickasaw Bayou, north of Vicksburg. Knox's presence on the ship contravened one of Sherman's orders prohibiting civilians aboard navy vessels. After the battle, Knox wrote "a scathing attack on Sherman's generalship." Sherman, of course, was no man to be savaged in the press, or anywhere else for that matter. He had the reporter "arrested and then court-martialed for disobeying the order and for being a spy, the only such event in American history. The board of officers found Knox not guilty of being a spy but guilty of disobeying Sherman's orders to stay off the ships and expelled him from the area." Sherman was not pleased with the sentence: he wanted the death penalty[30] or, at a minimum, time in prison.[31] The press, needless to say, was not pleased with Sherman. They again reported that he was insane.[32]

After Vicksburg, "Sherman sent for Ellen and two of their children, Minnie and Willie, to join him at his camp. While visiting with his father, Willie became ill with typhoid fever and died shortly afterward. Sherman took the loss of his son hard, mourning his death deeply."[33] Willie was Sherman's "Pride & Hope of Life," and he would grieve his death for the rest of his life.[34]

That autumn, Lincoln and Secretary of War Stanton gave Grant command of all Union forces in the West, and Sherman relieved Grant as commander of the Army of Tennessee. Toward the end of 1863, Sherman assisted Grant in breaking Braxton Bragg's siege of Chattanooga and then hurried east to assist Ambrose Burnside, who was under siege in Knoxville.

Grant's time in the West was about up, and in March 1864, he received a promotion to lieutenant general and assumed command of all Union armies involved in the war against the Confederacy. At that point, Sherman relieved Grant as overall commander of Union armies in the West.[35]

Lincoln and Grant formulated the final assault on the Confederacy. The Army of the Potomac, commanded by General George Gordon Meade, would attack Lee's Army of Northern Virginia in Virginia, and Sherman was to move from Chattanooga into Georgia simultaneously, seeking to destroy Confederate general Joseph Eggleston Johnston's army while inflicting savage property damage to the Confederacy's gut as he made his way east.[36] The two-front attack would prevent the Confederacy from moving troops back and forth as it had done with General James Longstreet's corps in the autumn of 1863 at Chickamauga.[37]

Ellen sent good news to Uncle Billy: she had given birth to a son, Charles Celestine. "I am glad that you are over the terrible labor," he wrote. "It is the last you will have to Endure." He believed that his new son would fill the vacancy left by Willie's death, which still haunted Sherman, and always would. "I fear we will never again be able to lavish on any one the love we bore for him.... I agree with you that we should retain Willie's name vacant for his memory, and that though dead to the world, he yet lives fresh in our memories."[38]

Sherman had one hundred thousand men, vastly outnumbering Johnston, but Johnston made a masterful retreat toward Atlanta, making Sherman's army pay in blood for every inch of Georgia soil that they crossed.[39] Nevertheless, Sherman pressed on, his army living off the land and flanking Johnston whenever he stopped to fight. Sherman eschewed frontal attacks on the strongly entrenched Johnston's Army of Tennessee with one exception: Kennesaw Mountain, where, contrary to his staff's advice, he sent his army head-on into Johnston's fortified position, costing Sherman "2500 of some of the North's best soldiers dead or wounded. Sherman was apparently unphased [sic]. He was becoming hardened to war, writing to Ellen two days later: 'I begin to regard the death and mangling of a couple of thousand men as a small affair, a kind of morning dash.'"[40]

Like the tank that would one day bear his name, Sherman's army moved inexorably toward Atlanta, flanking Johnston time and again. Johnston, no fool, understood the game, and when he dug in on a natural line of defense, he sent work crews on to prepare the next line of defense, knowing that Sherman, no fool either, would pin him down with part of his army and then send the rest around Johnston's flank, except at the aforesaid Kennesaw Mountain, where Sherman learned an expensive, and not unprecedented, lesson, just as Grant was learning in the Overland Campaign, just as Burnside had learned at Fredericksburg and just as Lee had learned at Malvern Hill and Gettysburg.

Jefferson Davis, in one of his many bonehead moves, decided that Johnston would not stand and fight Sherman, so he removed him, replacing the steady Johnston with the unsteady, unpredictable John Bell Hood, who, Davis believed, was just the tonic that the Army of Tennessee needed. That tonic, however, turned into bitter gall, and Hood wasted his army in a series of ill-advised attacks that Sherman, having studied his opponent, anticipated. The story is well-known: Sherman drove Hood back until finally, Atlanta fell, and the feckless Hood fled north into Tennessee, where he would meet his doom at the hands of John Schofield at Franklin—"Pickett's Charge of the West"—and George Thomas at Nashville, the final undoing of Hood's army.[41]

Sherman's victory at Atlanta receives—and received then—credit for Lincoln's reelection in November 1865.[42] But the high-strung Yankee was not done. Then followed a campaign that made his march east from Meridian look like child's play. It was a campaign that the South would cloak in infamy: "Sherman's March to the Sea," during which his army cut a brutal sixty-mile-wide swath through Georgia from Atlanta to Savannah. At Christmas, Sherman wrote to Lincoln, "I beg to present to you a Christmas gift, the city of Savannah, with 150 heavy guns, plenty of ammunition and 25,000 bales of cotton." Lincoln responded: "I was anxious if not fearful, but feeling that you were the better judge.... Now, the undertaking being a success, the honor is all yours.... It is indeed a great success."[43]

But there was one issue that dogged Sherman and that, to Lincoln, was an important aspect of the war: freeing and collecting the slaves to give them succor and support. Sherman did not see this as a part of his military mission, and indeed, because of his views of the slaves and "Negroes" in general, he ignored Lincoln's pleas to accommodate them.

Accordingly, "Sherman did not attempt to protect the freed slaves on his march." His proslavery and racist views were well-known. When Halleck cautioned him about what he said to others, particularly the press, on this issue, Sherman responded, "Military success, not protection of 'Sambo,' is my main priority." When others called for better treatment of African Americans, the answer was, "The Negro should be a free man, but not part of any equality with whites.... Indeed it appears to me that the right of suffrage in our country should be abridged rather than enlarged."[44]

The loss of son Willie in 1863 still stabbed at his heart like a Confederate sword. But there was more to come. In January 1865, while in Savannah, Sherman received word that his six-month-old son, Charles Celestine, had also died. He had, Sherman said, "gone to join Willie."[45]

Sherman now turned north toward the birthplace of the rebellion, South Carolina. He would, he said, "punish South Carolina as she deserves."[46] And punish her he did. Beginning his march north on February 1, 1865, his troops "burned and looted with renewed fury."[47] Said one soldier, "The whole army is burning with an insatiable desire to wreak upon South Carolina. I almost tremble at her fate but feel that she deserves all that seems in store for her...." At the end of the march, a soldier wrote, 'We burnt every house, barn and mill that we passed."[48] They did not, however, burn Columbia, although they received credit for that catastrophe. Confederate soldiers actually set the fire "touching cotton as they retreated [with] high winds that fanned the cotton fires, and liquor that Union soldiers and white and black southerners consumed in the city."[49]

Sherman and his army did not inflict the destruction that it had dealt to the Palmetto State on the Tarheel State. The rebellion had not begun there, and for some reason, the Union soldiers felt "more kindly" toward North Carolina than they had South Carolina. Sherman had faced little opposition when he marched through South Carolina, but old adversary Joseph Johnston awaited him in North Carolina. Sherman had orders to attack Johnston to keep him from moving north to support Lee, now being besieged in Petersburg, Virginia. Then Lee's lines collapsed, and the Army of Northern Virginia fled west, with Grant, Meade and Sheridan on its heels. The end was near, and for Lee and Grant and their two armies, it came on April 9 at the McLean house in Appomattox, Virginia.

Joseph Johnston and his remnants of the Army of Tennessee were still active in North Carolina, but Johnston contacted Sherman and asked for a meeting to discuss surrender. Sherman set out to meet Johnston on April 17 near Durham Station. En route, he received a telegram from Stanton that Lincoln was dead. Sherman decided to keep Lincoln's assassination secret to avoid further conflict initiated by his own troops seeking revenge for Lincoln's death.

He and Johnston met at a small farmhouse owned by James Bennett.[50] The two old adversaries had never met in person. Sherman first told Johnston of Lincoln's assassination, and Johnston said that it was not the South's doing, which Sherman accepted. They did not arrive at final surrender terms that day and met again on April 18. Johnston was accompanied by John Breckenridge, a Confederate major general and former vice president of the United States. Sherman produced a bottle of whiskey from his saddlebags, and the three men had a convivial drink. Then Sherman, without offering the other two another drink, poured himself another one and began to write the terms of surrender. Under those terms, Confederate soldiers would be granted a full pardon restoring all of their rights of citizenship.[51]

But there was more: Sherman agreed that the North would recognize the existing state governments when those governments took an oath of allegiance to the United States. Then, in places where there were two state governments, the U.S. Supreme Court would determine which one was valid. The document stated that federal courts were to be reestablished throughout the South, and the people of the Confederacy were to be granted "their political rights and franchises, as well as their rights of person and property as defined by the Constitution of the United States."[52] Sherman "allowed Johnston's soldiers … [to] keep their horses, mules, and ten days' rations for the journey home. Sherman, it turned out, believed in pitiless war and a merciful peace."[53]

The treaty was "so lenient that the nation's press and officials of the new Andrew Johnson administration, particularly Secretary of War Edwin Stanton … labeled Sherman a traitor."[54] Subsequently, Stanton forced Sherman to negotiate new surrender terms, and Sherman's "anger at Stanton and at his old friend Henry W. Halleck for accusations against his loyalty, caused him [later] to snub both men."[55] Indeed, "Stanton accused Sherman of insubordination, stupidity and treason."[56] Sherman was quite—rightfully and not unexpectedly—incensed.[57] As the grand march of his army through Washington approached, Sherman "ignored Halleck in Richmond and during the Grand Review of Union armies in Washington snubbed Stanton by noticeably refusing to shake his extended hand, but there the controversy ended."[58]

On May 30, 1865, Sherman bade farewell to his troops: "Our work is done and armed enemies no longer defy us…. You have done all that men could do." He urged them to be good citizens. Sherman now looked forward to peaceful days.[59] He had a "tumultuous reception" during the Grand Review in Washington, and the adulation followed him during a tour that he took with Ellen. In "New York, the crowds were so large that the police had difficulty controlling them. It was an impressive sight: a grateful nation expressing its thanks."[60] And Sherman determined one thing during his New York visit that would prove useful to him later: women of all ages were drawn to the Union lion.[61]

Postwar

1865–1869

Sherman was forty-five when the war ended, "his narrow, slant shouldered, nearly six-foot frame packed with vitality, destined to carry him easily into old age." As biographer Robert L. O'Connell writes, "Physically, professionally, and emotionally, Cump Sherman had found his sweet spot, and he was determined to stay in it." The part of his life that lay in front of him would be the happiest, but he would, nevertheless, be troubled by three nettlesome problems: money, Ellen's Catholicism and, later, army chain of command problems that would begin in 1869.

The first two problems—money and Catholicism—arose out of one fundamental problem: Cump and Ellen both had alpha personalities, and they clashed over the children, their Catholic faith and their parochial education, for which she fought—hard. Although Sherman had been baptized a Catholic, he had never practiced that faith, and he wanted his children educated in secular schools. In addition, Sherman was always concerned with the family finances and accused Ellen of overspending, although he was no miser himself. He worried about the family "hemorrhaging funds and Ellen as the bleeder in chief." Haunted by his penurious childhood, he was a constant worrier about money.[62]

Sherman complained when the city of St. Louis raised the taxes on his house and about the cost of sending his children to Catholic schools. His salary at this point was $1,070 a month, and he complained that he could "barely get along."[63] Notwithstanding Sherman's fears, money, however, followed Sherman and Ellen like the scent of roses. His old friends in Lancaster, Ohio, conducted a fund drive in Ohio and raised $100,000.[64] Another drive in St. Louis raised enough to buy him a $24,000 house in St. Louis and an extra $5,600 "for his bank account."[65] Subsequently, in 1869, when be relieved Grant as commanding general, a group bought him Grant's house in Washington for $65,000 and gave him $37,000 on top of that.[66] Although Sherman would never admit it, Ellen and Uncle Billy were flush.[67] His salary as general in chief of the army would be a very generous $19,000, later reduced to $15,000.[68]

Ellen continued to spend, and Sherman, notwithstanding his fear of penury and debt, was generous with his children and with any Union veteran who asked for help. Ellen gave generously to Catholic charities, especially the Little Sisters of the Poor and, indeed, gave away her entire inheritance, described by O'Connell as "a small fortune."

Moreover, Ellen did not like being the wife of an American hero. She thought that people—especially other women—were staring at her, and she railed about "odious comparisons" with other, younger women, who, she knew, admired and wanted her famous husband. "Of course," she said, "every good-looking young fashionable thinks it a pity so distinguished a man could not have her for his wife instead of the worn down old woman before." This was the beginning of a run of negativity that would overtake Ellen's life, leading her to reject the social life that her husband so enjoyed and instead focus on her religion "with its promise of a better life after death."[69]

Ellen put on weight with age and after giving birth to eight children. She carried 165 pounds on a five-foot frame. Sherman, lean and fit, blamed her weight on indolence that was, he believed, an outgrowth of being waited upon all of her life. Another area of conflict between the two was sex: of him, she wrote to her father, "I think he missed his calling when he took a civilized wife, as nature made him the spouse of a squaw." The problem with the marriage after the war essentially boiled down to this: in the years from their wedding to the end of the war, Cump and Ellen had spent as much time apart as together, and after the war, thrown together full-time, the marriage became a bubbling cauldron of tension between the two.[70]

Unlike his friend Grant, Sherman abhorred politics almost as much as he abhorred the press. So what was a forty-five-year-old general to do in the peace that followed the defining event in U.S. history? President Andrew Johnson and General of the Army Grant quickly answered that question. They divided the country into five military divisions, each consisting of several districts. Sherman got the second division, embracing an enormous territory running from the Mississippi River to the Rocky Mountains. Initially called the Division of the Mississippi, it soon became known as the Division of Missouri.[71]

Reconstruction followed in its various iterations, with each version harsher than the one before. Sherman still loved the South, and he urged a "soft peace" with minimum restrictions. While he acknowledged that slavery was dead, he did not accept Blacks as equals to whites, just as he had not accepted them as soldiers or even camp followers during his march through the South in 1865. Sherman spent the early Reconstruction years in St. Louis, so he did not have to be involved in it.[72] His family joined him there, and he spent precious time with them at the circus, at minstrel shows and at the theater.[73]

Of the South and Reconstruction he said, "We cannot keep the South out long, and it is a physical impossibility for us to guard the entire South by armies; nor can we change opinions by force…. Negro equality will lead to endless strife, and to remove and separate the races will be a big job." Sherman hoped that Johnson would, instead of listening to the Northern voices urging revenge, implement Lincoln's policies of restoration and reconciliation. He saw "Radical" Reconstruction as simply an effort to make the South "grovel" and an effort to "impose Negro suffrage," which Sherman opposed, and he watched with dismay as his friend Grant veered left into the Radical camp.[74] Sherman, surprisingly, thought that the same Southern whites who had brought on the war were in the best place to run the South after the war.[75]

Sherman's mission in St. Louis was to support the country's western expansion by "removing" the Native Americans. He understood that he "was to gain 'absolute and unqualified control of the Indians.'"[76] He and his "terrible swift sword," Little Phil Sheridan, did just that.[77] Actually, Sherman bore no particular animus toward the Indians.[78] He even acknowledged that the white man had done the Indians grievous wrong, but he believed that the two peoples could not coexist and that, therefore, the Indian must either be exterminated or moved to reservations. Sherman would later tell a congressional investigating committee that "the Indians, in the aggregate and in detail, have suffered great wrong at our hands," but "he rhetorically wondered how the continent could possibly be settled without doing some harm to the Indians who stand in the way.... There has to be violence somewhere."[79] Grant, his superior, supported Sherman fully.

Westward expansion in the years immediately following Appomattox rode on the backs of the men laying down the railroad tracks across the vast western wilderness. Sherman was enraptured with the railroad, and from 1866 to 1868 he quickly threw his considerable weight behind the unprecedented project until the eastward and westward tracks were joined in Promontory, Utah.[80] When the Indians objected to what they saw as an egregious expansion by the white man into their space, Sherman told them, "You cannot stop the locomotive anymore than you can stop the sun or the moon."[81] An engineer said of Sherman, "There is no one who has taken so active a part and who has accomplished so much for the benefit of the Government, in the building of the transcontinental railroads, as General Sherman."[82] Sherman helped the crews cross the Rockies at an elevation of eight thousand feet, and they named the crossing "Sherman."[83] This was where Sherman wanted to be instead of dealing with Reconstruction, which he considered more destructive than constructive. He slept in a blanket roll, boiled his own coffee over a campfire and spent hours in the open plains. Many of his former soldiers worked on the crews laying the tracks, and they joked with him about how their railroad work had changed: they had gone from *tearing up* tracks to *laying* them. He would sit at night around a campfire, sipping whiskey and telling war stories; then it would be up at dawn to do it all over again.[84]

In the summer of 1867, Sherman became a member of the eight-man—four military and four civilian—"Indian Peace Commission," which decided to place the Indians on two enormous reservations, one in the Northwest and one in the Southwest, both of them far away from the railroad. There, he hoped that with the support of the federal government, they could become self-sufficient. That support, however, would not be forthcoming, and problems with the western Indians would continue throughout Sherman's four years in charge of the Missouri Division.

While on the commission, Sherman decided to meet with some Sioux and Cheyenne leaders, but "Sherman wrote Ellen that the night before the conference, 'the Indians got on a big drunk and are not now in condition to have their talk.'"[85] Then in the spring of 1868 he traveled to southeastern New Mexico to meet with the Navajos. They had been placed on a reservation there but were starving. Of New Mexico, which he despised, Sherman said, "I want to see this country lay hold of Mexico again … and thrash her till she promises to take those damned territories [Arizona as well as New Mexico] back again." He said that "the New Mexicans [were] 'a mixed band of Mexican, Indian & Negro, inferior to any of those three races' if pure."[86] Sherman talked with the Navajos and was moved by their plight. He thus agreed to let them return to their ancestral homeland in northwestern New Mexico, where they have remained, largely successfully.[87]

The task of maintaining the Indian and facilitating western expansion of the country engendered internal conflict for Sherman. In addition, he had an army of only twenty-five thousand men obligated to enforce Reconstruction in the South and to police a territory of over a million square miles in the West. But then, in the autumn of 1868, after his successful visit with the Navajos, Sherman told his brother Senator John Sherman that all of the Indians who refused to go to their reservation were hostile and would have to be killed off. He resolved to attack them in the winter through his district commander, Phil Sheridan, and he told Ellen, "Probably in the end it will be better to kill them all off."[88] Sherman was, thus, terribly conflicted about the western Native Americans.[89]

Also during the fall of 1868, Grant assigned Sherman to escort Lewis D. Campbell, who was to be the minister to Mexico, to Mexico City. Mexico was under the control of Maximilian, Louis Napoleon's puppet, supported by about twenty thousand French troops, and Campbell's mission was to hook up with President Benito Juarez, who, they hoped, could soon depose Maximilian and run the French out of Mexico. Campbell, however, got drunk as soon as they boarded the ship and was drunk off and on for the remainder of the trip. When Sherman and Campbell arrived in Mexico City, Juarez was a thousand miles from Mexico City, and Cump, disgusted with Campbell and the trip as a whole, left the putative minister behind and returned to New Orleans, intending to be home in St. Louis for Christmas of 1868. Of Mexico, he wrote to his brother, "I would deplore anything that would make us assume Mexico in any shape—its territory, its government, or its people."[90]

1869–1876

Grant was elected president, and Sherman and Ellen moved to Washington in 1869, when he succeeded Grant as general-in-chief of the army, attaining four-star rank. In promoting Sherman, Grant passed over Halleck, Thomas and Meade, Sherman's seniors. Heartbroken, Meade moved to his hometown of Philadelphia. Thomas chose to move to San Francisco, and Sherman would always think that passing over Meade and Thomas hastened their early deaths. He complained about the "ungenerous failure of the Government to recognize their services at the cheap price of allowing two more lieutenant generals."[91]

The general-in-chief position was not a particularly happy job for him, although he would hold that position for fourteen years. The gravamen of Sherman's complaint as commanding general was that the secretary of war actually ran the army, and in Washington, politicians hung around and over his office like noxious clouds. He hated them, hated the press, hated the contumacious Indian agents in the West, and he even began to dislike Grant, who sided with his own political friends rather than his old wartime friend and military comrade.[92]

Sherman's salary as general-in-chief was $19,000 a year, but still, he worried about the cost of living in Washington with higher property taxes and the social obligations arising out of his new position, which he thought would be "financially intolerable."[93] He was still haunted by the financial ruin of his father and always would be, no matter his salary or the fact that he was living in Grant's "mansion," which had been given to him by Hamilton Fish—soon to be Grant's secretary of state—and a group of wealthy New Yorkers.[94]

On the home front, Cump and Ellen continued to experience problems with one another. The big issue with Sherman was his wife's increasingly numbing Catholicism and her concomitant refusal to accompany him to the myriad social events available to the couple in Washington. Ellen, in a letter to her father, said that "she was treated as the subordinate of the General, who has consented to tolerate my religion provided I do not presume to express my devotion to it.... I feel so totally estranged from Cump and we are so out of sympathy with one another, & with each other's friends, that life with them is a burden."[95]

But there was more to rankle Sherman: taking over for Grant as general-in-chief got Sherman involved in politics, and he had to deal with bureaucratic red tape, conflicts with and between personnel and all of the dysfunction of a hidebound bureaucracy. Moreover, Congress took umbrage at what they considered his excessive expenditures for travel and entertainment and, as previously noted, cut his salary from $19,000 to $15,000 a year. In addition, Grant did nothing to change the dysfunction of the army chain of command, even after Sherman asked him to grant the new general-in-chief direct authority over the entire army instead of having some of the bureau chiefs report directly to the secretary of war.

Grant refused, and their old friendship suffered as a result. Sherman would, therefore, never again consider Grant as the friend he had been during the war.

By the spring of 1871, Sherman was frustrated. He was also short of money and thus rented out part of the mansion—he called it the "elephant"—given to him by Fish and the New Yorkers. Cump decided to get out of Washington and to conduct an inspection tour of forts in the Southwest. First, however, he stopped in Baton Rouge to visit the scene of his prewar employment, the Louisiana Seminary of Learning and Military Academy, where he was greeted warmly. The next stop was New Orleans, where he made a speech in which he said that "Northern reports of Southern outrages against blacks were exaggerations." Once again, he hated that Northern troops were involved in Reconstruction and "thought that Southern problems could best be solved by Southerners." Needless to say, the speech received prominent play in Southern newspapers, and some Southerners expressed a hope that Sherman would run for president.[96]

From New Orleans he headed for the Southwest, where, with a small troop of "buffalo soldiers"—Black soldiers so called by the Indians, who thought them the color of buffaloes—he and some staff officers undertook an inspection of a line of forts running north from San Antonio some four hundred miles to Fort Sill in what is now Oklahoma. As the group approached the Red River—the northern boundary of Texas—a group of Kiowas and Comanches intently watched his contingent from a hill. Their leader told them that they would not attack because a bigger prize would soon follow. A few hours later, a wagon train arrived with ten wagons carrying supplies. The Indians attacked and killed seven of the teamsters. The rest of the men escaped because the Indians got distracted with looting the wagons.[97]

Fort Sill was commanded by Benjamin Grierson, the Union cavalry officer who had conducted one of the most famous raids of the war. A group of the Indians came in, and a chief—Santana—bragged that he had led the group who ambushed the wagon train. Sherman immediately had him arrested; other armed Indians appeared, and a standoff between the buffalo soldiers and the Indians ensued, with Sherman right in the middle of the two groups. Although the details remain murky, the situation was diffused, and Sherman had two other chiefs arrested. One of the chiefs was killed trying to escape, and the other two were tried in Jacksboro, Texas, and quickly found guilty and sentenced to hanging; however, a hue and cry arose in the national press, and authorities believed that if the two chiefs were hanged, the Kiowas would go to war. The governor of Texas commuted their sentences, and Sherman came home, his negative attitude toward the Indians firmly ossified.[98]

As a result of his problems with the secretary of war and other bureaucrats, Sherman spent as much time away from Washington as he could, touring Europe in 1871 and 1872.[99] He departed on November 11, 1871, and visited Gibraltar, Spain, southern France, Rome, Sicily, Malta and Egypt. Sherman also visited the Crimean War battlefields, Moscow, St. Petersburg and came back through Western Europe, England—he thought little of the British army—Scotland and Ireland. Altogether, he spent about a year on the trip, during which he, for the most part, avoided receptions and other formal events, although he still managed to meet the kings of Spain and Italy, Turkey's sultan, the Russian czar, the Austro-Hungarian emperor, two successive presidents of the French Republic and Queen Victoria and the future King Edward VII. He also had an audience with Pope Pius IX, to Ellen's delight, and met Helmuth von Moltke, the German field marshal and Europe's first man of strategy, who had just wiped the floor with France during the Franco-Prussian war.[100]

Upon his return, Sherman learned that some of his duties had, in his absence, been assigned to other military leaders. "Enraged, he said that was the last insult he would accept from Washington politicians. He would retire soon, he said, and he saw no benefit to putting up with congressional scolding and harassing for his last few months." He did not retire, however, and instead, true to his tradition, soldiered on.

Finally, sick of Washington and the great expense of living there, Sherman, in the fall of 1874, moved back to St. Louis with his family, glad to be rid of the capital and all of its attendant problems.[101] He sold the Washington house and, as he had rented the home in which they had lived when Sherman was in command of the Missouri Division, they returned to those familiar surroundings. Prior to leaving Washington, however, there was the matter of daughter Minnie's marriage to navy Lieutenant Thomas W. Finch. Cump and Ellen threw "one of the most splendid weddings ever seen in Washington."[102]

On Valentine's Day 1873, Sherman met Vinnie Ream, a sculptress. She was small—barely five feet tall—and filled with energy. Only twenty-six years old—Sherman was fifty-three—"she had long cascading curls and an utterly beguiling personality." Within days of their meeting, the two were lovers. The relationship was intense, until Sherman and his family moved back to St. Louis. After that he would see her when he was in Washington, but the relationship cooled, and in 1878 Vinnie announced that she was marrying a young army officer. She and Sherman remained friends, and contrary to his instructions to burn his correspondence, she did not, and his letters to her are a historically valuable insight into Sherman the man.[103]

During this period, there was constant talk of him running for president, an honor that he consistently declined. And then there was his old friend the press. Aware that Sherman hated Washington, they suggested that he resign his office. "By my office I am above party, and am not bound in honor or in fact to toady to anybody. Therefore I shall never resign, and shall never court any other office." He told his brother Senator John Sherman to convey that message to anyone interested in a political career for the general.[104]

Sherman fought fiercely to prevent his army from becoming an army of occupation in the South, which he described as "the distasteful demands of police duty in the occupied South, where 'black and tan' state governments, composed of the lowest elements, were maintained solely by the overawing bayonets of Northern soldiers who loathed their task."[105]

In March of 1875, D. Appleton published Sherman's memoirs, which were based on his prodigious memory, official battle reports and correspondence between him and other military leaders. As with most memoirs of Civil War generals, Sherman's were not uncontroversial, and with some eight hundred pages spread over two volumes, there were sufficient targets at which his detractors and enemies could fire away, which they did. The main complaint was that the memoirs lacked accuracy and that Sherman had relied too much on his own memory in compiling the material set forth in the books. Another complaint was that he had flattered himself, and yet another was that the devil was in the details and that Sherman had somehow missed the devil. Some criticized him for his opposition to the Fifteenth Amendment granting the vote to Blacks, and Southerners criticized him for the destruction of so much of the South, a point that he emphasized in his memoirs. They "were outraged by ... his description of the Confederacy as a criminal and senseless conspiracy." Of the South, he said, "We as the victors must stamp on all history that we were right, and they were wrong—that we beat them in battle as well as in argument."

Without doubt, the most savage of the attacks came from a newspaperman named Henry Van Ness Boynton, who had commanded an Iowa regiment during the war. As historian James Lee McDonough writes, "If Sherman considered himself a great general, and he did, which his memoirs clearly indicate, Boynton described him as little more than an egotistical blunderer."[106]

Nevertheless, the books were best sellers, and Sherman spent the rest of his days rebutting his critics in myriad magazine articles that he wrote.[107]

1876–1883

Eighteen seventy-six was an election year, and once again Republicans asked Sherman to seek the party's nomination. Once again, he

refused, and the nomination went to another Civil War veteran, Rutherford B. Hayes, who, to resolve a disputed election arising out of the chaos
extant in the South, agreed to pull the occupation troops out. After Grant's
tainted administration, Hayes restored honor to the federal government,
and Sherman's brother John became secretary of the treasury, charged
with cleaning up the financial mess left behind by his predecessor.

During this period Sherman served as president of the Society of the
Army of Tennessee and regularly attended various veterans' reunions, at
one of which he stated the famous military maxim, "Many look upon war
as all glory, but it is all hell." Today that statement has been shortened to
"War is hell."[108] In addition, in 1879, he toured the old battlefields and campaign sites in the South, where he was greeted with good humor. He said
that "people high and low received me with absolute cordiality and friendship." Another aspect of his conflict with President Grant and Congress
was their desire to cut the army's size. With only twenty-five thousand
men to "control" an enormous western area, cuts were anathema to a man
who had led an army of two hundred thousand men. He made the cuts
anyway, a process that served only to fuel his blazing hatred of the Washington, D.C., establishment.

Sherman homed in on his son Tom, or Tommy, for future greatness.
Cump told his son not to be a soldier or a priest but that he should become
either a doctor or a lawyer. He sent Tom to Yale, where he graduated in
1878. Then it was on to Washington University Law School in St. Louis.
Sherman was elated. But in a lightning strike, Tom wrote—a week after
graduation—that he was entering the priesthood. Sherman was devastated. And angry. He castigated his son, wrote angry letters and cut him
out of his will. But in 1880, the two reconciled, and Sherman shifted his
focus to his remaining son, Tecumseh, or "Cumpy." Cumpy followed in
Tom's footsteps, but, unlike Tom, he did become a lawyer in New York.
Tom, on the other hand, was "chronically depressed and ineffective as a
priest," and "he left the Jesuit order and spent the next two decades in a
solitary existence split between aimless travel and a little house in Santa
Barbara, before dying in a Catholic nursing home in 1933. Neither Tom—
unsurprisingly—nor Cumpy produced offspring."[109]

Sherman's love for West Point grew during his time as commanding
general, and he spoke at graduation each year.[110] He wanted to move the
West Point curriculum from engineering to more of a military education
and pushed the recalcitrant institution in that direction. In an effort to
improve the officer corps of the army, he instituted an advanced school for
infantry and cavalry officers at Fort Leavenworth, Kansas, "designed to
embody and impart the state of the art in active campaigning."[111]

West Point, however, became the scene of an incident that would draw national attention to the school. In the late 1870s, the first African American, Johnson C. Whitaker, entered West Point, and subsequently claimed to have been attacked one night by a group of white cadets. General John Schofield, the Academy superintendent, did not believe Whitaker, and neither did Sherman, both contending that Whitaker had concocted the story to avoid an exam for which he was unprepared and out of a revenge motive against white cadets who would have nothing to do with him.[112]

It was not that simple, however, as Sherman's old nemesis—the press—took the story and ran with it. Sherman said that the newspapers were "like a pack of hounds—one barks and the others join in without knowing the cause." President Rutherford B. Hayes, a Civil War brigadier general, intervened and replaced Schofield. He did so without going through Sherman. The matter eventually died down, and Whitaker remained at West Point.[113]

In 1878 Sherman moved back to Washington after he received assurances from the new secretary of war, Alphonso Taft of Ohio, that he would have command of the army and that all orders would flow through him.[114] His marriage was strained, and Ellen and the children spent the fall and Christmas in Baltimore. Sherman was alone for Christmas in Washington but finally rejoined his family for New Year's Day.[115]

During the winter of 1879, Sherman traveled through the Confederacy, retracing the route of some of his old campaigns. Accompanied by some of his staff and his daughter Lizzie, he was surprised by the warmth that the Southerners showed him. He visited Savannah, whose people he had fed in the desperate days of 1865, and then he headed west for New Orleans and Mardi Gras. In New Orleans he visited with his old adversary John Bell Hood, and then went up to Baton Rouge, where he spoke at the Louisiana Military Academy. From Baton Rouge he and his group traveled up the Mississippi River to Vicksburg and saw the old lines where he had fought so bitterly in the spring and summer of 1863.[116]

Sherman, not surprisingly, became an after-dinner speaker of the first magnitude and a highly desirable magazine writer. Through these mediums, and consistent with his memoirs, he "took on the task of presenting to the public what he believed was the true history of the war—that is, the moral superiority of the Union cause." He was quick to assign blame where he thought blame was due. This activity brought him into conflict with a variety of contemporaries, from Jefferson Davis to fellow Union generals.[117]

Sherman's relationship with Ellen remained difficult. He was gregarious and loved the theater, as well as dinner parties and dancing. Ellen, on the other hand, deep into Catholicism, had withdrawn from his social life, and in 1877 she even wrote a letter to a Mr. Rulofson, who had written a book against dancing, "in which she castigated 'the Evils of the Dance.'" Sherman had been a dancer since he was a teenager. Undoubtedly, he was not pleased with the letter or its attendant publicity. Undeterred by Ellen's reclusion, Sherman continued an active social life, usually accompanied by one of his daughters or other young women.[118]

Another woman entered his life about this time. Mary Audenried, the widow of Sherman's longtime aide John Audenried, who had accompanied him on his European trip in 1871 and 1872, was independently wealthy, and the two became lovers in 1880, after John's death. To outsiders, it looked as though the avuncular Sherman had merely taken Mary under his wing, but the relationship was a full-fledged affair, and Mary had the means to maintain it by meeting him anywhere, anytime. She was in her midthirties, and Uncle Billy was in his sixties. The affair lasted for most of the 1880s.[119]

In August 1880, Tom, who had been studying for the priesthood in England since 1878, returned to the United States. As noted, he reconciled with his father, who had threatened to cut him out of his will and had written angry letters to his family about Tom, but their relationship would never again be close, just politely proper. Tom visited his family in Washington and then left for Baltimore to continue his studies.

Elly married another naval officer that year: Lieutenant Alexander M. Thackeray, whom Sherman believed to be "a first-class officer."[120] Of the eight children born to Cump and Ellen, two of the boys—Charles Celestine and Willie—died; two—Tom and Philemon Tecumseh, known as "Cumpy"—were alive but would never marry; two of the girls—Elly and Minnie—would marry; and the other two—Rachel and Lizzie—would not.

In November 1881, Sherman visited Atlanta and spoke to a large crowd that included Confederate veterans. He emphasized that the country now stood united and that, as a united country, the future looked great. He, and his speech, were warmly received. But all of that goodwill was changing with the rise of the "Lost Cause" movement, which held that the South seceded because of state's rights rather than slavery, had fought valiantly until overcome by overwhelming manpower and resources, and that the Southern way of life was superior to that of the North. With the rise of the Lost Cause catechism, Sherman would, in the South, morph from a warmly received—on multiple occasions in the South—to the beast who burned and destroyed everywhere he went.

In June 1882, Congress passed a law requiring all army officers to retire at age sixty-four. Sherman would be sixty-four on February 8, 1884, but he decided to retire on November 1, 1883, when Congress promised him full pay and benefits and an army clerk to help him with his "enormous correspondence." With his relief by Philip Sheridan, Sherman, Ellen, Rachel and Lizzie moved back to St. Louis in 1884.[121]

1884–1891

In the presidential election year of 1884, both parties sought him as a candidate. He refused the Republican nomination in a telegraph containing this famous line: "I will not accept if nominated, and will not serve if elected."[122] Amazingly, after moving back to St. Louis, Sherman had Mary come to visit him and his family there. Mary moved into the Sherman home, and Ellen was outraged, as Sherman seemed to be throwing his affair into her face. She blew up, as did daughter Lizzie, when Mary made what Ellen perceived as an anti–Catholic statement. Mary departed for Washington soon after, but the affair continued.

With retirement, Sherman's life changed dramatically. He now had more time to devote to social events and the theater. He became courtly and loved and was loved by women of all ages. Like his Confederate counterpart Robert E. Lee,[123] he loved young women, and he loved to kiss—and did kiss—droves of them.[124]

His other major activity was attending, and speaking at, reunions of soldiers and, as noted, each year at West Point graduation. He was "wildly in demand" and, at one point, turned down a speaking engagement in Cincinnati because he was booked for the rest of the year. Indeed, he could have spoken every night of his life if he had chosen. He also spoke at funeral services for a number of Union generals and other officers until he finally tired of it. Strangely, for all of his conviviality, he hated shaking hands and thrust his hands into his pockets to avoid it. Most important to him was the Society of the Army of Tennessee, of which he served as president from 1869 until his death.[125]

Days, he spent in his basement office, which bore a sign over the door that said simply, "General Sherman's Office." He spent time there answering letters from his former comrades and occasionally smoking a cigar. He read his favorite books over and over: Walter Scott, Robert Burns and Charles Dickens. In the evenings Sherman attended the theater and opera and, of course, attended balls. As a speaker, he remained much in demand for reunions of his old comrades-in-arms. And although he feigned annoyance at being asked to speak as much as he was, in reality he enjoyed the attention.[126]

In 1885 he revised his memoirs, which were again published by D. Appleton and again became a best seller. Sherman added two chapters to cover his childhood and boyhood and the period of his life following the Civil War up to his retirement. The two-volume set was an "instant best seller" and netted Sherman $25,000.[127]

Then in 1886, he and Ellen moved to New York, and, after a stay in the Fifth Avenue Hotel, Sherman bought a four-story brownstone near Central

Park. Ellen wanted to be near her married daughters and Cumpy, who was at Yale. In addition, Cump was again angry about the city of St. Louis raising the taxes on his home and assessing him for paving the street. The household in New York consisted of himself, Ellen, Rachel and Lizzie.[128]

Of all of the deaths of his fellow Union generals, one in particular touched him deeply: that of Philip Henry Sheridan, who was ten years Sherman's junior. They buried Sheridan in Arlington Cemetery across the Potomac from Washington, and after the crowd left, Sherman stood alone at the grave and wept.

Ellen had become a recluse, and her health, which had not been good in years, declined rapidly in 1888. After two heart attacks, she died on November 28 of that year. "Wait for me, Ellen," Sherman cried as he raced up the stairs to her deathbed, "no one ever loved you as I loved you." She did not wait, however, and was gone when he got to her. Following a service at the New York brownstone, they took her back to St. Louis to Calvary Cemetery, where Willie and Charles Celestine were buried and where Sherman intended to be buried.[129] On Willie's tombstone was written: "Our Little Sergeant; From the First Battalion, 13th U.S. Infantry. In his breast was no guile."[130]

After a period of depression following Ellen's death,[131] Sherman returned to the New York social whirl, sometimes escorted by one or both of his daughters and often accompanied by Mary Draper, "the socially prominent widow of pro–Sherman historian John W. Draper," on his arm. There is no evidence, however, that she was ever more than a friend to, and dinner date for, him.[132]

In June 1889 he spoke at West Point graduation and then accompanied Lizzie to the Catskills. In July he made another trip out west, which caused him to miss Tom's ordination as a Jesuit priest. Then there were veterans' meetings in Cincinnati and Boston. It was an exhausting regimen.

Sherman's financial fears—always present—were especially driven by a $14,000 mortgage on the New York brownstone. He made plans to pay it off over the next several years. The social whirl continued unabated, and he went to four or so dinner parties a week. He had noticeably declined as 1891 arrived, but he refused to give up his social life.

On February 4, 1891, Sherman went to a dinner party and awakened the next morning with a severe cold. Nevertheless, he attended a wedding the next day but was too sick to attend a dinner party at the Union Club, one of his favorite venues. The cold, combined with his asthma, morphed into pneumonia, and the end came rushing at him like one of John Bell Hood's wildly unsuccessful charges, except that this charge would be successful. He died on February 14, 1891, but not before his daughters had a Catholic priest administer extreme unction to him while he lay unconscious. Cump, who thought Catholicism "irrational," would not have approved.[133]

He was to be interred in St. Louis, but first, New York had to tell him goodbye. And they did. His body lay in state at his home, and Tom conducted his funeral there. Then, while thousands watched from rooftops and beside the streets, thirty thousand men—former soldiers—escorted his body to a waiting ferry that took him across the Hudson to New Jersey and then on to Pennsylvania, where his body was placed on a train headed west. Along the way people lined the tracks, also to say goodbye to the old warrior. In St. Louis, they buried Cump in Calvary Cemetery with his wife and his son Willie, whom Sherman grieved right up to the end. His epitaph, which he chose himself, is "Faithful and Honorable.[134] He had been true to his word, in both war and peace."[135]

Was he a military genius? Although this question is susceptible of many different answers and opinions, the answer has to be yes on two accounts: one, he developed and implemented a new form of warfare designed to terrorize and break the spirit and will of an opponent, and two, his tactical acumen in flanking Joe Johnston in Georgia without an undue loss of life was brilliant. Indeed, "he possessed an extraordinary mind and was quick to grasp major military problems. The Civil War was the defining moment of his life. He helped preserve the Union and was proud of it. He remained a soldier and patriot always."[136]

So what, besides his genius, is the old warrior's legacy? Like so many other Civil War generals on both sides of the conflict, it remains to this day a source of controversy. Given his war of destruction waged against civilians on his two "marches"—Jackson to Meridian and Atlanta to Savannah and then up to Columbia, South Carolina—there could be no other outcome. It is interesting that in the South, in the immediate aftermath of the war, Sherman was accepted well for the generous terms that he accorded Joseph E. Johnston at the surrender of the Army of Tennessee at Durham, North Carolina, on April 17, 1864. In the immediate aftermath of Johnston's surrender, the Northern press, as it had in December of 1861, contended once again that Sherman was insane.

Then, during Reconstruction, Sherman's "friendly attitude toward the South" softened his "brutish image" and burnished his tarnished reputation in the South. "He supported white Southerners, his old friends, whom he considered the best hopes for restoring order in the postwar region. He opposed enfranchisement of Blacks, agreeing with conservative whites that it was foolish and dangerous to do so. He took such strong pro–Southern positions that, in 1871, after a speech in New Orleans, there was a presidential boomlet for him in several Southern newspapers and among some Southern politicians."[137]

There was, however, no one Southern position with respect to Sherman in the early years after the war. Some saw his brutal campaign of destruction as just a part of war, while others hated him for it. "When Sherman toured the region in 1879, most Southerners greeted him warmly. Atlanta and other locales he visited on this triumphal tour displayed little animosity. In New Orleans he was the honored guest of Rex during Mardi Gras, and General John Bell Hood also enthusiastically appeared with him in public. Since this tour occurred four years after the 1875 publication of his memoirs, it seems evident that these two volumes did not convince white Southerners to consider him a pariah."[138]

It was later, during the rise of the "Lost Cause" catechism, that Sherman became the beast—the "brute"—who had waged a war of destruction against a defenseless civilian population. Jefferson Davis, not surprisingly, attacked him in a vicious polemic, calling him a liar. Then, in 1888 Sherman—upset by anti-Black behavior in the South—published an article urging fair treatment of Blacks. Between the attacks of Davis and others, the publication of that magazine article and the Lost Cause coda that venerated Robert E. Lee and damned Union generals and the North in general, Sherman's reputation in the South sank like a stone. And as the two sides reconciled, rather than focusing on the philosophical differences—especially over slavery—that led to the secession of eleven Southern states, the North and South instead focused on the heroism of the common soldier. Lee, during this surge of interest in the war around the turn of the twentieth century, became the exemplar of all that was good and the brute Sherman of all that was bad.

Subsequently, less judgment-loaded treatments of Sherman began to appear, extolling his "military greatness" and insisting that "the bloodbath of World War I might have been avoided had Sherman's Civil War lessons been followed." A number of biographies followed, treating Sherman as everything from a general comparable to the Nazi generals of World War II to a model for the U.S. effort in Vietnam. "Michael Fellman, in his … [biography] insists that the key to understanding Sherman's personal and public life is suppressed rage. His portrayal depicts an unattractive individual who acted out his anger against the South in his marches and against his wife through a lifetime of marital discord."[139]

Thus Sherman's legacy, like so many other Civil War commanders, is, to say the least, controversial. But as John F. Marszalek argues persuasively, "there now exists … a much more positive view of the man and his warfare. Sherman was a fallible human being whose quirks and weaknesses were traceable to the earliest days of his childhood. He rose above them all to become one of the major figures of the Civil War and of all American military history. He was an American pioneer in the use of destruction for the psychological purpose of convincing the other side to end the war. His psychological warfare was so effective, in fact, that it has affected the American mind from the 1860s to the present day."

CHAPTER SIX

Ulysses S. Grant

"Uncle Sam," "Unconditional Surrender," "Sam"

Boyhood

"My family is American, and has been for generations, direct and collateral."[1] Thus wrote Ulysses S. Grant in the opening of his memoirs. Grant was descended from pilgrims—Matthew and Priscilla Grant—who migrated to Massachusetts in 1630 aboard the *Mary and John*, one of thirteen ships that sailed for America within about six months of each other that year. There is some dispute about the number of generations of Grants who lived and died in what was to become the United States. Grant claimed to be part of the eighth generation, while some historians contend that he was a member of the seventh generation. One fact about his ancestors does stand out: a grandfather, Noah, had a drinking problem, "a fact worth flagging because of the hereditary component in alcoholism."[2]

Grant's father, Jesse, was an Ohio tanner and a strident abolitionist who once worked for Owen Brown, the father of abolitionist John Brown, someday hence to be of Harpers Ferry fame. Grant's mother, a quiet, reserved woman,

Ulysses S. Grant (1860–1865).

83

was Hannah S., and Grant was the first of five children born to that couple. Grant's birth name was Hiram Ulysses Grant, but that would change later.

As a boy, he learned to ride at age five and attended schools in Georgetown, Ohio. The boy had a special, quiet way with horses, which he trained for money. That acumen with, and love of, horses would stay with him for life. When Ulysses—known to his family as "Lyss" or "Lyssus"[3]—was seventeen, his father decided unilaterally that Grant would attend West Point. That was not Grant's choice, but regardless, Jesse used his connections to wrangle an appointment for his son out of a congressman, Thomas Hamer. Hamer completed Grant's application, but he did not know Grant's real name, so put his name down as Ulysses S. Grant, using Hannah's maiden name. Grant, passive and reticent, did not resist the change.[4]

At the time that he entered the Academy at age seventeen, he "weighed 117 pounds and was five feet, one inch tall," barely over the West Point minimum of five feet. "His hair was sandy brown; his fair skin was freckled. His hands and feet were small, and then, as later, his body was not tightly muscled but smoothly turned. He would grow to be five feet, eight inches tall while at West Point."[5]

Grant was a small country boy in rough-hewn country clothes when he entered West Point in the summer of 1839 as Ulysses S. Grant, but he was soon to become simply "Sam" Grant. Future Confederate general James Longstreet described him as "fragile" with a "delicate frame," but he had "a noble, generous heart, a loveable character and a sense of honor." Another cadet, William Tecumseh Sherman, said of Grant, "A more unpromising boy never entered the Military Academy."[6] But Grant persevered and finished solidly in the middle of his class—twenty-one out of thirty-nine—although when measured against the cadets who actually entered with him, his rank was twenty-one out of seventy-three. He would also graduate as the finest horseman at the Academy, perhaps in its history.

West Point, with its largely patrician class of cadets, transformed Grant from a country bumpkin into a semi-sophisticate. There, he had indulged his love of literature—mainly Sir Walter Scott novels—and had developed considerable skill as a painter. Still quiet and shy, Grant proved to himself and his family that he could measure up to the standards of one of the nation's finest educational institutions.[7] Upon graduation, Grant wrote to a friend that the happiest day of his life was when he left West Point.[8]

Grant's plan was to put in one year in the army and then resign to pursue a civilian career at which he could make more money than as a lowly army lieutenant, and upon graduation he received orders to

Jefferson Barracks in St. Louis, the largest military base in the United States, through which would pass an all-star cast of future Civil War generals on both sides of that conflict. Grant soon met and wooed Julia Dent, sister of a West Point classmate. She was "stumpy," with "more neck than chin." Moreover, she was cross-eyed, but notwithstanding those physical drawbacks, she was charming and warmhearted, and offered Grant the unconditional love he had never had. They became engaged in May 1844.[9]

Julia lived on a plantation called "White Haven" north of St. Louis. Her father, Colonel Frederick Dent—the title was honorary—was a slaveholder and an avowed Southern sympathizer. He opposed the marriage but grudgingly, in the face of his wife's support for Grant, eventually accepted the union. He required, however, the couple to wait a year to marry. The war tocsin began to sound, however, on the southern border with Mexico, and Grant's regiment moved south to Louisiana. Grant's immediate superior was Richard Ewell, soon to achieve fame in the Confederate Army. Grant respected and admired Ewell.[10]

War with Mexico came, a war that Grant thought was unjust. He saw it as a war to affirm statehood already granted to Texas and to allow slavery there. In command of the army was General Zachary Taylor, affectionately known to his men as "Old Rough and Ready," of whom Grant would later say, "There was no man living, who I admired and respected more highly than Taylor."[11]

Grant became quartermaster of his regiment, and that experience would serve him well during the Civil War when he would put that background to use in supporting entire armies. He participated in multiple battles and once, at Monterrey, when ammunition ran low in house-to-house fighting, raced on the side of his horse to get ammunition in a wild and spectacular demonstration of the horsemanship that had made him a legend at West Point.[12]

During the war he met future generals Robert E. Lee, Joseph E. Johnston, Jubal A. Early, P.G.T. Beauregard, George Gordon Meade, John Pemberton, Winfield Scott Hancock, Joseph Hooker and Braxton Bragg. He also renewed his acquaintance with Thomas Jonathon "Tom" Jackson—who had entered West Point Grant's senior year—and James Longstreet and George B. McClellan.[13] Winfield Scott now commanded the American army, and Grant accompanied him as he repeatedly defeated the numerically superior Mexican forces and eventually captured Mexico City. The "unjust war" resulted in the Mexican cession of part of Texas, New Mexico, most of Arizona, Nevada, Utah, part of Colorado and all of California.[14]

Grant married Julia at White Haven on August 22, 1848, with James Longstreet, Julia's cousin and Grant's friend, as best man. He and Julia served a tour in Detroit, where Julia became pregnant with their first son,

Frederick Dent Grant. It was in Detroit that Grant began drinking, but he stopped and even joined the Sons of Temperance. That membership, however, would be only temporary. Grant then left with his regiment for San Francisco, leaving a pregnant Julia behind. After a brutal crossing of the Isthmus of Panama, his regiment reached San Francisco and then moved on to Oregon. In the meantime, Julia had given birth to their second son, Ulysses S. Grant, Jr., known as "Buck."

It rained and snowed almost constantly in Oregon, and Grant, without the stabilizing influence of Julia, sank into melancholia and depression and, once again, began drinking. The following year, 1853, he received orders to Fort Humboldt in Northern California, which he found even more depressing than Oregon. Mail was sporadic, so he heard little from Julia and gradually sank into the deep well of booze-fueled depression. Eventually, his drinking caught up with him, and his commanding officer gave Grant an ultimatum: either resign or be court-martialed. Grant resigned in April 1854.[15]

He returned to St. Louis by way of New York, where, broke, he got drunk, got in a fight and ended up in jail. Future adversary Simon Bolivar Buckner bailed him out and loaned him money for a hotel room. He borrowed money from his father, Jesse, for the trip home.[16] It was the beginning of the most difficult period of his life.

Penurious, Grant took up farming on sixty acres adjacent to White Haven that Julia owned and built a house by hand—they named it "Hardscrabble"—in which he and his family would live for the next three years. This was a period during which he failed at everything he tried. Grant reached the nadir of his struggles during this period—and perhaps of his entire life—when, in December 1857, he pawned his gold pocket watch for twenty-two dollars to buy Christmas presents for his family.[17] Julia, however, never gave up on Grant, even telling her family that she had a dream in which Grant was elected president. They laughed. Grant was now selling firewood on a street corner in St. Louis, wearing his old, faded army overcoat.

After a failed attempt at farming White Haven—Julia's mother had died, and her father had moved to St. Louis—Grant tried to take up real estate in St. Louis with a cousin of Julia's. This too was a disaster: Grant was too softhearted to collect the rents owed the firm, and he was incapable of keeping the firm's books. The cousin fired him.

Finally, Jesse extricated Grant from the Missouri muck and sent him to Galena, Illinois, where the father owned a leather-goods store that his sons Simpson—who was dying of consumption—and Orvil ran. He was there two years, two happy years in which he did not drink, attended church regularly and joined, in 1860, the Republican Party.

Then war came, and Grant helped organize a company of Galena volunteers, but he refused command and instead sought, based upon his West Point and regular army experience, a higher command. He knew that his time had come, and he intended to make the best of it.

Galena Congressman Elihu B. Washburne had watched Grant organize the company there, and he intervened with Illinois Governor Richard Yates, who offered Grant a colonelcy and command of the Twenty-First Illinois infantry regiment. Grant promptly took that outfit from chaos to competency, and by July 1861, it was deemed ready for combat.[18] He then led that unit into southern Missouri to take on a Confederate force, but the Confederates fled, and the Union press, starved for victory, hailed Grant as a bold leader. He next took Paducah, Kentucky, without a fight, and with help from Washburne, Grant received a promotion to brigadier general and command of the Department of Southeast Missouri, with a princely salary of $4,000 a year. He was on his way.[19]

Next up was a battle at Belmont, Missouri, where Grant's men smashed the Confederate lines, but, rather than following up their success, fell to looting the Confederate camp, while the Confederates, reinforced, regrouped and then counterattacked. Grant's men made it back to their boats and escaped, but once again, Grant received hero's accolades. Once again, however, the ugly charge of drinking arose, with salacious details of Grant's misbehavior while drunk. It was the genesis of the repeated wartime tales of Grant's drinking, which usually followed a battle.[20]

Grant and Henry Halleck then hatched a plan for Grant to begin clearing the Mississippi, and Grant did so by taking Forts Henry and Donelson, where, when his old friend Buckner asked the terms of surrender, Grant replied tersely, "No terms except unconditional and immediate surrender. I propose to move immediately upon your works." In reply, Buckner said that he would "surrender in accordance with your ungenerous and unchivalrous terms." Grant would later say that if he had enjoyed command of the entire region, he could have marched to and taken Chattanooga, thus dramatically shortening the war.[21]

The twin victories brought a promotion to major general of volunteers to Grant and command of the District of West Tennessee—"limits not defined." That promotion and designation led to creation ultimately of one of the great fighting forces of the Civil War, the Army of Tennessee, which in time would take Vicksburg, Atlanta, Columbia and South Carolina, and end up receiving Joseph Johnston's surrender in North Carolina.

Once again, the miasma of the drinking allegations arose and hung over Grant like a cloud. Aware of the rumors, Halleck relieved him of command, but once again, Congressman Washburne intervened, this time with Abraham Lincoln. Grant was restored to command and, with

six divisions instead of three, moved up the Tennessee River to Pittsburg
Landing in Tennessee, setting the stage for one of the great battles of the
Civil War—and the costliest, in terms of casualties, up to that point. The
battle took place at Pittsburg Landing, Tennessee, but it would be forever
after known simply as Shiloh.

Confederate forces under General Albert Sidney Johnston attacked
Grant's unprepared force on April 6, 1862, and routed it, almost driving
his army into the Tennessee River. However, Johnston was killed, P.G.T.
Beauregard took command and the attack, at the critical moment, fizzled.
Reinforced by troops of Don Carlos Buell, Grant unleashed a savage counterattack the next day and drove the Confederates down to Corinth. In the
aftermath of the battle, Grant received criticism for the first-day debacle
and for failing to catch and destroy the Confederates before they reached
Corinth. Halleck thus relieved him again and took personal command. He
moved at a glacial pace toward Corinth, and the Confederates fled. Grant
was restored to command and initiated the Vicksburg campaign.[22]

The point of the Vicksburg campaign was to sever the Confederacy
and stop the flow of supplies from the Confederacy west of the Mississippi to the eastern Confederacy. But first, Grant fomented a controversy
that would dog him for the rest of his life: he promulgated a ban of Jews
from the Department of West Tennessee, believing that they were buying
and selling contraband Confederate cotton. The howls of protest eventually reached President Lincoln, who forced Grant to rescind the order.[23]

The Vicksburg campaigns—there were five—were exercises in frus-
tration for Grant and his protégé Sherman, until finally, on the fourth
attempt, Grant succeeded in crossing the Mississippi—David Dixon Porter's fleet ferried his army across—at Bruinsburg, Mississippi. Grant led
his army east to Jackson, looped back west and defeated the Confederates
under John Pemberton at Raymond, Big Black River and Champion Hill.
Grant then laid siege to the city, which surrendered on July 4, 1863. With
the fall of New Orleans and Natchez to Admiral Farragut, the Confederacy was cut in two.[24] It was "one of the most brilliant strategic campaigns
in American military history."[25] As Lincoln exclaimed, "The father of
waters again goes unvexed to the sea."[26] For his success, Grant received
a much-coveted promotion to major general in the regular army[27] and
the adoration of a grateful nation and president. He took command of
the Military District of the Mississippi, which included all territory
between the Appalachians and the Mississippi River, except for the Gulf
region.[28]

Then, in the autumn of 1863, Confederate general Braxton Bragg,
aided by James Longstreet's corps from the Army of Northern Virginia, attacked the Army of Tennessee under William S. Rosecrans at

Chickamauga Creek and drove him back into Chattanooga. Grant relieved Rosecrans and took command. Subsequently, in a series of battles at Orchard Knob, Lookout Mountain and Missionary Ridge, Grant broke out of Nashville and drove Bragg into north Georgia. Grant also sent Hooker to eastern Tennessee, where he secured that region for the Union.

Lincoln promoted Grant to lieutenant general—he would be the first to hold that rank since George Washington—and brought him east to take command of all Union armies. Grant laid out a strategic plan for bringing the Confederacy to its knees: the Union would attack simultaneously on all fronts and prevent the Confederacy from moving troops back and forth, as they had done with Longstreet's corps at Chickamauga. Grant made his headquarters next to George Meade's with the Army of the Potomac at the beginning of 1864, and he told Meade that he was to go where Lee went, without fail. The Grant who appeared in northern Virginia was unadorned by the regalia of uniform or rank. He wore a plain blue uniform without sash, sword or trappings of any type, other than three stars on his shoulder straps. Grant had a full beard, kept his left hand thrust into the pocket of his pants, chewed on an unlighted cigar and had a "square-cut face whose lines and contours indicate extreme endurance and determination."[29] He was quiet, shy, soft-spoken and determined.

On May 4, 1864, Grant launched what would be known as the "Overland Campaign," which would consist of three major battles and a number of skirmishes as the two armies moved east, Grant trying to flank Lee and get at Richmond, and Lee moving sideways to prevent the flanking movement. At the Wilderness, the two armies struggled in the nightmarish undergrowth of part of the Chancellorsville battlefield, where the bones of skeletons poked ghoulishly from the ground. The undergrowth and the terrain neutered Grant's numerical advantage, which was almost two to one. At the end of the Wilderness battle, nothing had changed, except Grant had lost eighteen thousand men and Lee twelve thousand. Grant could afford those losses; Lee could not.

Grant moved east toward Spotsylvania Courthouse, but Lee beat him there. Thus ensued one of the longest and bloodiest battles of the war, a battle that would give the world two names that would live in bloody infamy: the Mule Shoe and the Bloody Angle. In those places, Grant would batter Lee, trying to break him, but he would not, and he paid a terrible price for his attacks: 17,666 men lost against Lee's 7,500. It was a "long, fierce and useless battle" that lasted from May 8 to May 19.[30]

The aftermath of Spotsylvania brought Grant the imbroglio between Sheridan and Meade, both of whom presented their highly charged cases to Grant, who listened quietly, a study in contract with his two enraged subordinates, before "suggesting" that Meade turn Sheridan loose as an independent command. Sheridan, cut loose, caught up with Confederate nemesis J.E.B. Stuart at Yellow Tavern, where Stuart died. Sheridan reached the gates of Richmond and then returned to the Army of the Potomac.

Summer came, and Lincoln and Stanton, concerned with the mounting losses and the lack of progress on taking Richmond, asked Grant of his intentions. In one of the famous lines of the Civil War, he replied, "I propose to fight it out on this line if it takes all summer."[31] He would do that, and it would take all summer, and more.

Grant again moved east, but Lee cut him off at Cold Harbor. It was Burnside at Fredericksburg all over again, only this time it was Grant at Cold Harbor, whose ground in the aftermath of the battle would run red and cold with Union blood. Here, Grant ordered a frontal assault on entrenched Confederate positions, a decision that he would regret for the remainder of his life. The losses were staggering. In one charge alone, Grant lost seven thousand men in about thirty minutes to Lee's fifteen hundred. After Cold Harbor Grant had lost roughly fifty thousand men in the Overland Campaign, 41 percent of his army, but Lee had lost thirty-two thousand men, over 50 percent of his army. It was a war of attrition, and Lee could not afford the attrition.[32]

In the North, a cloud of furor arose like the humidity that came out of the swamps of northern Virginia. The hoary "butcher" sobriquet reappeared, and the Northern press questioned the efficacy of Grant's war of attrition. Walt Whitman wrote, "I steadily believe that Grant is going to succeed ... but oh what a price to pay." Lieutenant Oliver Wendall Holmes wrote "how immense the butcher's bill has been."[33] But Grant, undeterred, drove on.

Then came one of the great tactical moves of the war. Grant rested his army eight days and then moved suddenly around Lee's right to the James River, which his enormous army crossed on a 2,100-foot-long pontoon bridge hastily—and ingeniously—constructed by his engineers. It was a marvel of engineering that matched Grant's maneuver.[34] He moved on Petersburg, but Lee got there in time to repulse yet another frontal attack. Then the two sides entrenched, and siege warfare along the lines of Vicksburg—a harbinger of another great conflict to come fifty years later—came.

The siege was punctuated by various skirmishes and battles, the most famous of which was "the Crater," which Grant called "the saddest affair I have ever witnessed in this war." Meade wanted to court-martial its author, Burnside, but Grant intervened and allowed Burnside to retire. The siege dragged on into 1865. Union and Confederate lines were often only one hundred yards apart. The men met in no-man's land and swapped tobacco, coffee and newspapers. "Ordinary soldiers had already established patches of peace.... Rebs and Yanks washed clothes together in the streams, and the kidding that went along with the laundering led first to good-natured horseplay and then to organized foot races and wrestling matches.... But then they had to go back to killing one another."[35]

Grant moved his line westward, trying to outflank Lee. Finally, Sheridan won at Five Forks, and the next day a direct assault ruptured Lee's lines. Lee evacuated Petersburg. Grant's forces caught up with Lee at Sayler's Creek and whipped him thoroughly, and Sheridan cut him off at Appomattox. Grant then sent the first of several notes in which he shifted the responsibility for "any further effusion of blood" to Lee by asking for Lee's surrender. Then ensued a further exchange of memos that led Lee to surrender the Army of Northern Virginia to Grant in Wilmer McLean's living room at Appomattox.

Lee wore a fresh dress uniform with sash and a gold sword. His only aide was Lieutenant Colonel Charles Marshall, grandson of Chief Justice Marshall. Grant, on the other hand, wore a private's "blouse" with the three stars of a lieutenant general, the only insignia on his mud-splattered uniform. Lee, who had known nothing but success in his life until this moment, now faced off with Grant, who had prior to the war known little but failure. It was Grant, however, who was self-conscious, not because of his or Lee's success or failure, but because Grant feared that the impeccably dressed Lee would be offended by Grant's dress. Grant would later write of these moments when the war came to a virtual end, "What General Lee's feelings were I do not know. As he was a man of much dignity, with an impassable face, it was impossible to say whether he felt glad that the end had finally come, or felt sad over the result, and was too manly to show it."[36]

Although not in the surrender document, Grant verbally agreed to allow Confederates who claimed ownership of horses and mules to keep their mounts, to be used, he said, to break ground on their "little farms," as Grant described them, in the spring. After the surrender, Lee told Grant that his men—and their Union prisoners—were badly in need of food, and Grant authorized the transfer of twenty-five thousand rations to the beleaguered Army of Northern Virginia. Grant would later write:

> I was accompanied by my staff and other officers, some of whom seemed to have a great desire to go inside the Confederate lines. They finally asked permission of Lee to do so for the purpose of seeing some of their old army friends, and the permission was granted. They went over, had a very pleasant time with their old friends, and brought some of them back when they returned. When Lee and I separated he went back to his lines and I returned to the house of Mr. McLean. Here the officers of both armies came in great

numbers, and seemed to enjoy the meeting as much as though they had been friends separated for a long time while fighting battles under the same flag. For the time being it looked very much as if all thought of the war had escaped their minds.[37]

On April 14, in Washington, Mary Lincoln invited the Grants to accompany her and the president to the theater in Washington the next night. Julia Grant did not like Mary Lincoln because of a bad experience she had with her at City Point, Virginia, during the war, so Grant declined. John Wilkes Booth assassinated Lincoln that night at Ford's Theater. Grant was on the conspirators' list to be killed. He, by the grace of God and Mary Lincoln's rudeness to Julia, had avoided the assassin's bullet.[38]

The "Grand Review" followed in Washington on May 23 and 24. Meade's Army of the Potomac marched the first day—it took eight hours for them to pass—and Sherman's Army of Tennessee marched on the second. In all, two hundred thousand soldiers marched down Pennsylvania Avenue. The two armies were a study in contrasts: Meade's army was well-equipped with uniforms; Sherman's men wore frazzled and worn uniforms, and they marched with less precision than Meade's men, but they carried "themselves with swagger." Grant, however, reported that the marching of Sherman's army "could not be excelled."[39] The war was over. It was time for Grant to move on to the next phase of his life.

May–December 1865

After the Grand Review, Grant wrote his report of the war, pointing out that when he assumed command of all of the Union armies, those armies did not act in concert, which allowed the Confederacy to move troops from one theater to another as the threat arose there and even allowed the Confederate commanders to send soldiers home in the spring to put in their crops. Grant, therefore, made his subordinate generals—Sherman, Canby, Wilson and Stoneman—move in concert with the Army of the Potomac, which made the outcome of the war against the rebellious Confederacy a certainty.[40]

Then Grant undertook reduction of the million-man army to a size necessary only to maintain order in the South, which he placed at eighty thousand men.[41] He retained his wartime staff: John Rawlins as chief of staff; Cyrus Comstock, Orville Babcock, Horace Porter and Frederick Dent—Julia's brother—as aides; Adam Badeau and Ely Parker as military secretaries; and Theodore Bowers and Robert Lincoln as assistant adjutant generals. He also began the acceptance of myriad gifts from various courtiers, which was "standard recompense for war heroes." A group of New Yorkers bought a home for him in Georgetown, paying $34,000 for the house, investing for him $55,000 in government bonds and handing over $16,000 in cash.[42] He also accepted ownership of a home in Philadelphia, from which he intended to commute to Washington on a weekly basis, but he did not like being gone from his family all week, and Julia and daughter Nellie in particular objected,[43] so they moved to the Georgetown house, from which Grant walked to work as general-in-chief of the army, puffing on a cigar and window-shopping as he walked. His unreconstructed rebel father-in-law, Frederick Dent, moved in with Grant and his family, and Grant had to listen as the old man railed constantly about Yankees. Andrew Johnson appointed Grant's own father, the ever-ambitious Jesse Grant, postmaster in Covington, Kentucky.[44] Nepotism and money flowed.

Then followed a victory tour of various Northern cities: New York, Boston, Chicago, St. Louis, with a stop in between at West Point. There, he called upon the Northern apotheosis General Winfield Scott, who had been born before the Revolution, and Scott gave him a copy of his memoirs, inscribed "From the Oldest to the Greatest General of the Army of the United States."[45]

But trouble for Grant arose out of the ashes of the Confederate defeat. The ever-vindictive Andrew Johnson wanted blood from the leaders of the rebellion, so the United States, through abolitionist federal judge John C. Underwood in Norfolk, Virginia, convened a grand jury, which returned indictments of Lee, James Longstreet, Joseph Johnston and others. Grant was "flabbergasted," and Lee was "stunned," both believing that the terms of Lee's surrender precluded legal action against him, as did Sherman's terms to Johnston.[46]

Grant told Johnson that Lee never would have surrendered the still-lethal Army of Northern Virginia at Appomattox had Grant not offered terms that included amnesty for all officers and men then fighting for the Confederacy. The same conditions applied to Johnston's surrender to Sherman. Grant argued forcefully that there would have been "'endless guerrilla warfare' without this leniency" and that the sainted Lincoln had approved the terms of surrender. On June 13, Lee wrote to Grant and asked if the terms to which the two generals agreed at Appomattox precluded prosecution, and Grant replied that those terms did. Grant then played his trump card: he would resign if the North pursued prosecution of Confederate officers. Johnson, fearing what would have been enormous blowback against him personally, relented, and "at Johnson's behest, Attorney General James Speed ordered the U.S. attorney in Norfolk to abandon Lee's prosecution. On the same day, Grant informed Lee that no further actions would be taken to place him behind bars."[47]

Then, it was on to Galena, where Grant had arrived as a failure five years before. There, he intended to maintain his legal residence, and there the citizens gave him yet another house. When asked whether he had any political ambitions, Grant replied that "I am not a candidate for any office, but I would like to be mayor long enough to fix the sidewalks, especially the one reaching to my house."[48] From there it was on to St. Louis, where he had sold firewood on winter-enveloped street corners and tried to work in real estate, the latter a "dismal failure."[49]

As the end of 1865 approached, Andrew Johnson, anticipating the return of Congress, dispatched Grant on a sixteen-day tour of the South, from which he was to compile a report of conditions there. At Cape Fear, North Carolina, a reporter observed Grant in inconspicuous civilian clothes, purchasing an apple. It was an act characteristic of this hubris-free man.

At the conclusion of his tour Grant reported to the president, Gideon Welles and Congress that "The people are more loyal and better disposed than [I] expected to find them."[50] He urged that army troops remain in the South, but without "colored soldiers."[51] That report would subsequently arise from the ashes of his past to haunt him.

The new year—1866—arrived, and with it came new challenges and opportunities for Grant. It would be the first of three transition years, as Grant made his way along a pathway that would lead him out of the army and into the political world that he had always detested.

In March 1866, Grant's fifteen-year-old son, Fred, made application to West Point, and in no surprise, was admitted.[52] That same month, the embryonic struggle between President Andrew Johnson and Congress began to take shape when Johnson vetoed the Civil Rights Act, and the Radical Republican–dominated Congress overrode his veto. It was the first in a series of legislative battles that would find their denouement in Johnson's 1867 impeachment. "This is a country for white men," Johnson said, "and, by God, as long as I am President, it shall be a government for white men."[53]

On April 6, the Grants hosted a "gala reception" at their I Street home, "the final event of the Washington social season." President Johnson attended the "grand affair" and stood with Grant in the receiving line, to the chagrin of Radical Republicans such as Edwin Stanton and Charles Sumner, who were already on a collision path with the president. Also in attendance, surprisingly, was Alexander Stephens, former vice president of the Confederacy.[54]

The South was far from settled in the aftermath of its bitter defeat and in the face of increasing pressure from Washington to grant suffrage and equal rights to Blacks. That anger boiled over in race-fueled riots in New Orleans and Memphis, as well as trouble in north Mississippi.[55] These events engendered a change in Grant's views of the postwar paradigm: he moved from a proponent of reconciliation to an advocate of Black enfranchisement and equal rights, which were codified in the Fourteenth Amendment, passed by Congress in June 1866, and subsequently ratified by the states.[56] Grant's change in position and philosophy was tectonic for both Grant and the nation, especially the South. It threw him in with the Radical Republicans and their revenge-loaded Congressional—as opposed to the mild Presidential—Reconstruction. Nevertheless, Johnson, who opposed the Fourteenth Amendment, supported legislation that Congress passed on July 25, 1866, creating the rank of full general and giving Grant a fourth star and a salary of $20,000 a year.[57]

One of Grant's tasks was to demobilize the one-million-strong Union Army. By the end of 1865, roughly eight hundred thousand had been released. Grant's objective was to have an army of only twenty-six thousand men to occupy the South and the western forts. That army, he soon found out, would be stretched too thin.[58] Its responsibilities expanded exponentially when Congress passed the First Reconstruction Act, which divided ten of the eleven Southern states that had seceded—Tennessee had already been readmitted to the United States—into five military districts, each headed by one of Grant's generals: John Schofield, Daniel Sykes, George Thomas, Edward Ord and Philip Sheridan.[59] The generals were to ensure that the states convened constitutional conventions "to invest former slaves with full citizenship rights" and to ratify the Fourteenth Amendment to the U.S. Constitution before being readmitted to the Union. Grant was to oversee the generals and, as their supervisor, became responsible for overseeing Congressional Reconstruction and, thus, a political agent of Congress. Grant had thus moved left along the Washington political continuum.[60]

Still, although moving away from Andrew Johnson, Grant, ever the dutiful soldier, recognized that Johnson was his commander in chief, and although he balked at doing so, accompanied, along with Admiral David Farragut, Johnson on a three-week, two-thousand-mile speaking tour in August 1866.[61] It was a purely political ploy, designed to bolster Democratic representation in Congress with November's midterm elections looming, and Grant hated every minute of it.[62] When he spoke, Johnson was vulgar and coarse, and when the crowds baited him, he became even more so. Some observers thought he was drunk, and Grant, who was mere "window dressing" on the tour and, away from Julia, miserably unhappy, began drinking again.[63] It was one of Grant's binges, and at one point his aides had to move him from a passenger car on a train into the luggage car, out of sight. Sober, he left the tour to the vitriolic Johnson, who called Radical Republicans "traitors," and Grant returned home to Julia. Johnson's campaigning, and Grant's and Farragut's "window dressing" notwithstanding, the Republicans carried the House of Representatives 173–47 and the Senate 57–9.

Congress continued with Radical Reconstruction and passed a second and a third Reconstruction Act, both of which fell on Grant to enforce. But Johnson, knowing Grant now sided with Congress, had other ideas for the general and proposed sending him to Mexico on a diplomatic mission to get him out of town. Grant refused, contending that while he must take orders from Johnson on military matters, the trip to Mexico was a political matter that he was not obliged to perform. In a cabinet meeting, Johnson "exploded in rage" when Grant refused the mission and slammed his hand into the table. Grant rose and said, "I am an officer of the army, and bound to obey your military orders. But this is a civil office, a purely diplomatic duty that you offer me, and I cannot be compelled to undertake [it]." The room was gravid with stunned silence. Grant then left the room, and Johnson, excoriated in front of his cabinet and embarrassed, sent Sherman instead.[64] Grant, exhausted, rented a house on the beach in Long Branch, New Jersey, for the summer of 1867. Long Branch would provide him with a badly needed rest, time and again.[65]

At this point in his life, people who knew him characterized Grant as an introvert who hated public speaking and abhorred conflict, an interesting personality trait for a man who had just won the Civil War by hammering his opponent to death. Moreover, it was said that he was "sickened by violence, especially toward women, and was extremely protective of animals." Grant was still plagued by the headaches that had haunted him throughout the war. He was considered sensitive and empathetic.[66]

The general-in-chief, always the putative farmer, retained his interest in the Dent properties around St. Louis, and in 1867, he bought the old Dent place, White Haven, as well as several adjoining properties belonging to Julia's sister Emily Dent Casey and her brother John Dent, those two properties consisting of 280 acres. It was a dramatic turn of fortune. Julia's father, Frederick, now eighty-one and invalided by a stroke, lived with the Grants in Washington, and Grant, the feckless captain of Hardscrabble, now owned the Dent home and land.[67]

Back in Washington, Edwin Stanton had become a lightning rod in the Johnson administration, and Johnson wanted him gone. Congress had passed the Tenure in Office Act, which expanded the Senate's "advise and consent" role for appointees to include that function for dismissed cabinet members. The act, however, was applicable only to cabinet members appointed by the current administration. Lincoln had appointed Stanton; thus, the act, in Johnson's opinion—and logically—did not apply. Johnson then suspended Stanton, and Grant became interim—and reluctant—secretary of war. He worked, therefore, at his military office in the morning and in the office of the secretary of war in the afternoon.[68] After another tumultuous cabinet meeting scene with Johnson, Grant resigned from the interim position.[69]

In December 1867, the House of Representatives began work on articles of impeachment, and on January 25, 1868, the House voted to impeach Andrew Johnson. There were eleven articles of impeachment, nine relating to Johnson's suspension and subsequent firing of Stanton, and two arising out of his general conduct. One article accused him of "intemperate, inflammatory and scandalous harangues against legislators." His trial began in the Senate on March 5, 1868, and Johnson, on May 16, was acquitted by a single vote. Grant supported impeachment of the man he called an "infernal liar."[70] Johnson thus began the last months of his presidency. The presidential election loomed in November, but first the Republican Party had to nominate a candidate.

A rising tide of support for the nomination of Grant as the Republican candidate for president resulted in his unanimous nomination on May 21, 1868. He received 650 out of 650 votes, and when Edwin Stanton rushed into Grant's office to tell him that he had been nominated, Grant looked up at him, implacable as ever. There was "no shade of exultation or adoration on his face, not a flush on his cheek, nor a flash in his eye." It was a pure poker face, the same one he had projected during the most savage fighting of the war.

Grant dreaded a life in politics, but once again, his sense of duty to his country and his party commanded that he enter the political arena. Democrats were quick to brand him an imbecile and a dolt. He was "a commonplace man," the *New York World* said. "He has no military talent [and] is hated by the army. He is generally drunk."[71] His opponents would hurl myriad accusations at him: he was "the butcher," the father of a daughter by an Indian woman in Vancouver, Washington, the author of the infamous general order relating to Jews, a Black Republican and a "nigger lover."[72] The Democrats' campaign platform could be summarized in one sentence harking back to Andrew Johnson: "This is a white man's country; let white men rule it."[73]

The Republican vice presidential candidate was Schuler "Smiler" Colfax, the speaker of the house. The Democrats' nominees to oppose Grant and Colfax were Horatio Seymour, the governor of New York, for president, and for vice president, General Francis Preston Blair. Grant told Julia that he did not want to be president but that he felt duty-bound to run. He would, however, later say that "I wasn't sorry to be a candidate ... but I was very sorry to leave command of the army." In so doing he was leaving a salary of $20,000 a year for one of $25,000 a year, but the army job carried with it a generous pension. The presidency, amazingly, offered no pension.[74]

Grant's campaign style was consistent with his personality: he did not campaign, at all. Instead, he, Sherman, Sheridan and Grant's sons, Fred and Buck, took a tour of the West, visiting various military installations all the way across the plains and into the Rockies. After the western tour, Grant returned to Galena, where he remained through November, 1868. Surrogates did the heavy political lifting, and Grant won the Electoral College 214–80.[75] The reluctant warrior and the reluctant candidate now would be the reluctant president of the United States.

Inauguration Day, March 4, 1869, was cold and rainy. "A sleety mist cloaked the capitol … for the inauguration."[76] Grant had not invited Andrew Johnson, and Johnson holed up at the White House doing last-minute work. Grant rode alone to the Capitol for the swearing-in ceremony, but at the last minute he stopped at the White House and sent one of his attendants to invite Johnson to accompany him, but Johnson refused, stating that he was "too busy." He would be the third president, after John Adams and John Quincy Adams, not to attend his successor's inauguration. He would not be the last either.

At age forty-six, Grant became the youngest president in the history of the republic. Outfitted in "a finely tailored black suit," Grant took the oath of office from Supreme Court Chief Justice Salmon Chase. Grant, the reluctant public speaker, then delivered his inaugural address, which was only twelve hundred words long. He read the speech, in which he spoke in favor of the Fifteenth Amendment, which would, if ratified, give Blacks the right to vote. He advocated paying all federal expenditures in gold, and in an unexpected twist, said, "The proper treatment of the original occupants of this land—the Indians—is one deserving of careful study. I will favor any course toward them which tends to their civilization and ultimate citizenship."[77] The speech was well-received by the press.[78]

After the ceremony, Grant paid a brief visit to the White House and then moved on to his I-Street residence. Fred Dent, his brother-in-law, was in charge of all inauguration activities, and that night, the Grants attended the inaugural ball at the Treasury building. It was now time for Grant to construct his cabinet.[79]

In an effort to avoid hectoring by supplicants for cabinet positions and in keeping with his tight-lipped custom as a military leader, Grant did not release the names of his cabinet picks to anyone, even Julia. This was a mistake, not because of Julia but because he did not include congressional leaders in the process. This meant that he sent the names of all of his nominees to the Hill at one time, and the Congress was as blindsided as the public.

The nomination process in the Senate was not salutary. Elihu Washburne, the congressman from Galena and Grant's old friend and sponsor, received Grant's nomination for secretary of state. The Senate granted

Washburne approval, but in a deal made earlier, he shortly resigned and accepted the ambassadorship to France. Grant then made his best appointment: Hamilton Fish, the patrician former New York governor, congressman and senator, to be secretary of state. Fish would serve for both of Grant's terms.

Other appointments that bear discussion include that of Alexander Stewart as secretary of the treasury. Stewart gave Grant $65,000 for the I Street house, and the next day Grant announced the appointment. An old statute, however, prohibited an appointment to that position of anyone who had financial dealings with the Treasury Department. Stewart, a wealthy New York merchant, had customs dealings with Treasury and was thus forced to resign after a week in office. George Boutwell, former governor of Massachusetts, replaced Stewart. He would play a major role in a scandal yet to unfold.

As secretary of war, Grant appointed his old aide John Rawlins. Grant's "conscience," Rawlins was the man who had kept, and could keep, Grant off the bottle. Rawlins was also Grant's filter against bad advice and was one of the few men who could deal effectively with William Tecumseh Sherman. Rawlins was an important appointment, although his tenure in office was to be all too brief. Finally, as commissioner of the Bureau of Indian Affairs, he appointed his old army secretary Ely S. Parker, a Seneca Indian who had been with Grant at Appomattox.[80] In keeping with the custom of the time—one that would be resurrected in modern times on a much grander scale—he appointed family members to minor positions. He also appointed old friend and Civil War foe James Longstreet to a position as surveyor of customs for the port of New Orleans.[81]

Grant's style in dealing with his cabinet was the same as his style in dealing with his subordinate army commanders: he let the cabinet heads run their departments. Thus, uninvolved in the minutia of governing, Grant was able to establish a daily routine with time for himself, one aspect of which seems incredible now. He rose at seven, read the Washington newspapers, had breakfast at eight thirty with his family, two members of whom were gone. Fred was at West Point, and Ulysses Jr., known as "Buck," was at Phillips Exeter Academy preparing for Harvard. His children Nellie and Jesse lived at the White House with their parents. After breakfast, Grant went for a walk around Washington, greeting other pedestrians as he walked. He worked from ten until three, when he and his son Jesse and, upon occasion, his daughter Nellie would go for a ride. "If boys were playing ball in the park, he would often stop to watch, smoking a cigar."[82] He would call on old friends, especially from the army, and they were always welcome to call upon him, both visits unannounced.[83] Dinner was at five, followed by coffee and a cigar, and he and Julia would retire sometime between ten and eleven.[84]

Julia began remodeling the White House almost immediately, and she hired a professional chef. For dinner, she had the table set for twelve to make places available for those whom the Grants would invite during the day. Twice a week, one afternoon and one evening, the Grants received guests—Julia handling the afternoon visits, and both the president and Julia a Wednesday evening affair.[85]

The White House had several occupants in addition to Grant's nuclear family. First, old Colonel Dent, outspoken and reactionary, was there. Next, Julia's brother Frederick came to live with the Grants. He would serve as Grant's appointments secretary. And finally, two of Grant's wartime secretaries—Horace Porter and Orville Babcock—lived in the White House. Although nominally assigned to the War Department, their duties were to act, once again, as Grant's secretaries.[86]

Grant, over Julia's highly vocal objection, contracted to sell the I Street house for $40,000 over ten years. Subsequently, Grant reneged on the contract, and the erstwhile secretary of the treasury, Alexander Stewart, now back in New York, formed a committee to raise money, which they did. The committee then bought the house from Grant at an inflated price and, true to the traditions of that time, gave the house to the new general-in-chief of the army, Sherman, who would spend his time there complaining about the high upkeep of the house.[87]

One of the first issues that Grant confronted as president was one that had startled the public when he mentioned it in his inaugural address: his Indian policy. The problems arising out of the white man's interaction with the western Indians were myriad. White men were destroying the great buffalo herds, the Indians' primary food source. Those Indians who moved onto reservations were cheated and starved by corrupt Indian agents. When they left the reservations seeking food, they were attacked mercilessly by the army, now led by Philip Sheridan, who, as he always did, conducted scorched-earth campaigns winter and summer.

With Native American Ely S. Parker as commissioner of Indian affairs, Grant moved to reform the country's policy toward the Indians. First, Grant and Parker believed in assimilation. Thus, rather than viewing the tribes as sovereign nations, they proposed that the individual Indians be "Christianized" and made citizens. Next, the tribes must be confined on reservations, which seemed in conflict with the treatment of Indians as "individuals." The administration would replace the corrupt agents with honest ones. Finally, they would use education to prepare the individual Indians for citizenship.[88]

The administration's policy ran head-on into the belief of a large segment of American society, including Sherman, that the only course for the savage Indian was extermination. Sherman's—and Sheridan's—army generally fell into the latter camp. Thus, there would be during Grant's eight years over two hundred battles with Indians, and Grant's policy would often be punctuated by massacres at places like Sand Creek—the Cheyenne—and of other tribes like the Piegans, who were slaughtered in January 1870. These merciless attacks engendered outrage in the East, but the tension between Grant's policy and that of the settlers and the army remained high. The problems that haunted Grant's administration—assimilation and citizenship—remain to this day, and this country's record of dealing with its Native Americans remains a shameful chapter in its history.[89]

The summer of 1869 came, and Congress went home. By July, Grant, having had enough of the energy-and-stamina-sapping Washington heat and humidity, headed north to Long Branch, where, once again, some of his supporters bought him a house, this one a three-story, twenty-eight-room "cottage." It would become his summer White House. There he would spend a few hours each day on the veranda conducting business, but only after breakfast and a ride around the area.[90]

While there, Grant in New York City visited his recently married sister, Virginia, known as "Jennie." The thirty-seven-year-old Jennie, teetering on the edge of permanent spinsterhood, had moved to New York in June, 1869 and had immediately become the toast of the city and a highly desired guest on the dinner party circuit. Jennie then married a New York businessman named Abel Rathbone Corbin. Twenty-five years older than she, Corbin—and thus, Jennie—would soon become important players in an incident that would arise in the not-too-distant future.[91]

There were three main players in this drama: Corbin, Jay Gould and James Fisk. Fisk and Gould were New York operatives of the first magnitude, while Corbin, although wealthy, was only moderately successful as a speculator. Gould had made his fortune smuggling contraband Southern cotton through Union lines. Fisk had taken on, and bested, Cornelius Vanderbilt for control of the Erie Railroad. Corbin, Grant's brother-in-law, was in fast company.

The scheme, hatched by Gould and Fisk, was to corner the market for gold and drive the price up, then sell and get out with a sizable profit. Corbin, because of his proximity to Grant, was an obvious third player. The key element in the scheme involved Grant's government and specifically the Department of the Treasury, which could bust the scheme by selling government gold. So the question for the three manipulators became, "Would the government sell its gold?"[92]

They first put the question to Grant on a steamer that was taking him to Boston for a conference. He declined—wisely—to answer. A second meeting ensued, this time between Corbin and Gould on one hand

and Grant on the other. According to Gould, in this meeting Grant said that "the government would do nothing during the fall months of the year [1869] to put down the price of gold or make money tight."[93] Many historians question Gould's veracity on this subject. Grant saw the issue in a larger light than most: to him it was about the price of grain and other "foodstuffs," which were being produced in the American Midwest and West in surplus quantities, and the farmers needed to export the surplus. To do this, they needed a weak dollar to make the commodities more affordable to foreign purchasers, and the dollar moved inverse to the price of gold. Thus, the high price of gold produced a cheap dollar, which, in comparison with foreign currencies, made the price of commodities lower for foreign purchasers, a significant advantage for farmers. Although Gould was an unreliable source as to what Grant said, George Boutwell, Grant's secretary of the treasury, said that he received a letter from Grant basically saying that the government should sell no gold in order to maintain a cheap dollar and thus facilitate exports of the surplus crops.

The battle between the gold bulls and the bears raged, and the bulls were prevailing. The price of gold climbed. And climbed. And climbed. Finally, Boutwell went to Grant and told him what was happening. He recommended that the government intervene and stop the madness by selling gold and thus avoiding a financial panic like that of 1853. On Friday, September 24, Grant and Boutwell agreed to sell from $3 million to $5 million in government gold. The gold market collapsed when news of the sale reached the market in New York, and many speculators were wiped out. Corbin was damaged to the extent that he and Jennie were forced to give up the fast Manhattan lifestyle and move to Jersey City, New Jersey.[94]

One member of Grant's administration was implicated: Daniel Butterfield, a Treasury employee who purportedly passed information on the government's plans to Gould. Grant and his administration were completely exonerated, although this finding by the congressional committee that investigated the matter did not extend to Grant's in-laws.[95]

But there was more to it than just Grant's in-laws: Julia Grant's alleged participation in the scheme. Later, after the scandal, there was evidence that Grant's brother-in-law Corbin was managing a gold account for Julia Grant and that she made some $27,000 on the price rise, $25,000 of which one of the co-conspirators purportedly shipped to her in a box. This aspect of the Black Friday scandal remains murky, as the congressional committee declined to call both Julia Grant and Jennie Grant Corbin to testify.[96]

Grant addressed three major foreign policy issues during the first two years of his administration: Great Britain, Cuba and Santa Domingo (now the Dominican Republic). The genesis of the issues with Great Britain arose out of the wartime deprivations of five Confederate raiders that had been built in Great Britain: the *Alabama*—the primary offender—the *Shenandoah*, *Florida*, *Georgia* and *Rappahannock*. But there was more; fishing rights off of New England, the boundary with British Columbia and the U.S. citizenship of naturalized former subjects of Great Britain, the Fenian raiders along the eastern border with Canada and the claims of the United States for annexation of Canada.

Britain did not so much contest the principle that compensation was due to the United States for the deprivations of the Confederate raiders as it did the calculation of those damages. Senator Charles Sumner, whom Grant disliked intensely and who disliked Grant equally, posited that the United States had suffered damages of $2.5 billion. Sumner's figure included both direct damages—the loss of ships and cargo—and indirect damages: a hodgepodge of items originating in Charles Sumner's fertile imagination. Grant's secretary of state, the aristocratic Hamilton Fish, calculated direct damages at $48 million.

Under Fish's tutelage, Grant gradually came to believe that good relations with Great Britain were vital to the United States' future and thus that settlement of all of these claims and counterclaims would benefit both nations. The two sides then agreed to a joint commission to settle the issues, and the commission settled all of the issues, including reparations of $15.5 million for the losses caused by the Confederate raiders. The settlement was codified in the Treaty of Washington, a watershed treaty that over time would lead to Great Britain becoming the United States' closest ally.[97]

The second foreign relations issue concerned Cuba, where Cuba's colonial overlord, Spain, was involved in a military conflict with Cuban insurgents who wanted independence. Extant in the United States was a move to intervene and to annex Cuba as a state. There were any number of problems arising out of putative annexation, not the least of which was that slavery was still legal in Cuba, and there were a half-million slaves there. Grant's cabinet was split on the issue. In the end, Grant decided against intervention and instead offered to mediate between the two sides. Spain rejected Grant's offer, and in the end, the United States neither intervened nor mediated.[98]

The third issue was that of Santa Domingo, and it was more complicated and, for Grant, more troublesome than the other two put together. The drama began when government officials there wrote to Hamilton Fish and proposed that the United States annex Santa Domingo. Grant dispatched Orville Babcock to explore the proposal, and Babcock returned with a recommendation for annexation, which Grant embraced. Once again, however, a foreign policy issue brought Grant into contact—and conflict—with Charles Sumner, who loathed Grant as a reeking-of-tobacco bumpkin. Grant thought Sumner effeminate and overbearing but recognized that Sumner's support was essential. Grant also thought that Santa Domingo could function as a refuge for Southern Blacks.

The critical event in the annexation process occurred on January 2, 1870, when Grant, hat in hand, walked across Lafayette Square to the home of Charles Sumner and paid him a call. It was an unprecedented event, but annexation of Santa Domingo was so important that Grant believed calling on Sumner would carry the day. At the door, the butler, unimpressed by the presence of the president of the United States, began to dismiss Grant by telling him that Sumner was at dinner, but Sumner heard Grant's voice, intervened and invited him into the dining room, where Sumner was dining with two journalists. There, Grant engaged Sumner in a discussion of annexation and eventually departed with what he thought was an agreement that Sumner would support him.

He was mistaken. Sumner led the Senate Foreign Relations Committee to oppose annexation. Grant rushed to Capitol Hill and directly lobbied senators for support. The measure required a two-thirds majority to pass, and the votes were simply not there. Annexation failed, and although there would be one more attempt to resurrect the issue, the annexation dog was not going to hunt.[99]

There was one other development during this period that profoundly impacted Grant: the death of Secretary of War John A. Rawlins of consumption. Grant's conscience and filter, Rawlins was the only cabinet member who could argue with Grant, and his loss was enormous to the president on both a personal and a professional level. Rawlins had been his friend—his *only* friend—filling a hole in Grant's life that had existed since boyhood. He had been with Grant throughout the war. He had seen Grant grow from general to president, knew him—his strengths and his weaknesses—as did no other man. Grant would now face the next six years of his presidency without the one man he considered indispensable.[100]

The new year—1871—rolled around, and with it came more challenges to Grant's administration arising out of Reconstruction in the South. Six Confederate veterans had formed in 1866 a fraternal organization called the Ku Klux Klan, in Pulaski, Tennessee. Gradually, however, the Klan morphed into something far more sinister: an organization whose sole purpose was to "keep blacks in their place" using violence and intimidation. A Black's "place" meant no voting, a prohibition against holding office and serving on juries, and economic serfdom. It also meant that the Thirteenth, Fourteenth and Fifteenth Amendments would be without force and effect in the South.[101]

Grant did not want to use the army to force compliance with those amendments,[102] but it increasingly appeared obvious that he would have to do so. Congress responded to the widespread violence by passing three acts. Known as the "Enforcement Acts," they gave Grant specific powers to enforce the three amendments to the Constitution. The first gave the federal government the power to supervise elections, and the second made it a federal crime to interfere with anyone's voting rights. The third of the three acts targeted the Klan and made it a federal crime to prevent voting, serving on juries and holding office.[103] Grant had to take his entire cabinet to Capitol Hill to lobby for the Klan act, which seemed doomed for failure until presidential lobbying pulled his political chestnuts from the fire. On April 20, 1861, Congress passed the Klan Act.[104]

The Klan Act needed a predicate upon which to base *federal* jurisdiction, as the crimes it targeted had always been under the jurisdiction of the state where the crimes took place, and the states were not even considering prosecution. Thus, Grant personally came up with two bases: the violence, he set forth, was interfering with the federal postal system, as well as the collection of revenues. That was sufficient to provide Congress with all it needed to invoke federal jurisdiction.[105]

The three acts, among other powers granted to the executive branch, allowed the use of the armed forces and the suspension of habeas corpus. Grant fired Hoar, his attorney general, and appointed Amos T. Akerman (pronounced with a long "a," like "Amos"). Akerman was an unusual case. A Georgian, he had served as a Confederate general during the war; however, he had somehow become a liberal Republican activist and was just the man to unleash on the former Confederate states that refused to comply with the three amendments to the Constitution. Grant also had Congress create the Department of Justice as a cabinet-level organization and staffed it with attorneys who would help the state U.S. attorneys to enforce the three acts.[106]

The army went after those who used violence against Blacks, and Akerman was a bulldog. He obtained about three thousand indictments and six hundred convictions during the remainder of 1872. He allowed, however, many of those indicted to plead guilty and escape jail sentences, so that, in the end, only sixty-five went to prison.[107] The legal offensive put the Klan on its heels, but Grant eventually tired of Akerman's rants about the Klan—the only subject about which he could talk, Grant thought—so he fired him. With Ackerman's removal, much of the federal government's enforcement action in the South ended.[108]

In 1872, Grant continued his routine: up early, read the papers, breakfast with Julia and then work from ten to three every day except Tuesday, when he conducted the weekly cabinet meeting in the afternoon. He had gained thirty-five pounds from White House cooking, and he now took carriage rides in the late afternoon instead of the horse rides he had once enjoyed. Colonel Frederick Dent, Julia's brother, continued as his appointments secretary, and Secretaries Orville Babcock and Horace Porter still lived at the White House.[109] Grant was heavily involved in the lives of his children and was happiest when he was around them. Under Julia's stewardship, the White House became the "center of a lively, youthful hospitality."[110]

There was another devilish issue that confronted Grant and that would not go away: the question of what to do with the western Indians. Grant was convinced that the Indian Bureau, with its corrupt agents, was the root cause of the problem that caused continued clashes between settlers, and, therefore, the U.S. Army, and the western Indians. Grant created an Indian Commission comprised of philanthropists and others sympathetic with the Indians to examine the question. The commission put the blame for the condition of the Indians on the white man, who, it asserted, was the underlying cause of violence between the two parties. It condemned previous government policies as "broken treaties and unfulfilled promises." Further, the members stated that "the history of the … white man's connection with the Indian is a sickening record of murder, outrage, robbery, and wrongs committed by the former as a rule."

Somewhat amazingly, three different delegations of Indians visited Grant in Washington. The Sioux chief Red Cloud brought a delegation of braves. Grant tried to sell him on a move to Oklahoma where the Sioux could be trained to farm and raise cattle and sheep. The government would construct schools for Indian children, teach them to speak English and to read and write it. Red Cloud took it under advisement. Two more delegations also visited the White House, and the head of the third delegation, Chief Spotted Tail, wished Grant success in the presidential election of 1872.[111]

In January 1872, the Republican Party selected Philadelphia as its convention city. The party was ascendant. They argued that Grant had fulfilled all of his election promises: all seceded states had rejoined the Union, the government had taken measures to protect voting rights in the South, Grant had reduced the national debt, he had overseen reform of the post office and the civil service, and Grant's administration had largely restored international relations.[112] The press and the public were happy with his performance as president. Of him, Postmaster General John Creswell said, "Grant is so good and pure that all he needs for his perfect vindication is simply that the people know him and his works. The more I see of him the more devotedly do I love and admire him."[113]

There was, however, more trouble on the horizon. A group of dissident liberal Republicans met in Cincinnati a month before the Republican convention and nominated Horace Greeley, the firebrand editor of the *New York Tribune*, as its candidate for president.[114] Of Greeley it was said that "he was a genius without common sense." Greeley had once written of Blacks: "They are an easy worthless race ... taking no thought for the morrow."[115] Amazingly, the Democrats fell in behind the liberal Republicans and also nominated Greeley. For the only time in history one of the two major parties nominated the candidate of a third party.[116]

Grant and the Republicans jettisoned Schuyler "Smiler" Colfax in favor of Radical Republican Henry Wilson.[117] As before, Grant did not campaign, using, also as before, surrogates to do it for him.[118] The liberal Republicans attacked him on several fronts. They argued that Grant was too passive, but incongruously, argued that he was a tyrant who had used armed force too liberally and moved powers granted to the states to Washington. They also tried to resurrect the drinking specter, but that dog had long ago quit barking. Their platform: reduce tariffs to reduce the power of corporations and lobbyists, civil service reform to remove corruption from politics, withdraw federal troops from the South and, finally, remove the coarse Grant from the White House and replace him with someone more refined.[119]

Grant's minions, on the other hand, took Greeley's hundreds of editorials and crammed them down his throat. Then, two months before the election, the Geneva arbitration panel ordered Great Britain to pay the United States $15.5 million for Civil War reparations.[120] That, of course, did not hurt Grant's reelection campaign. The result of all of this was predictable by election time: Grant took 56.5 percent of the popular vote to only 43.5 percent for Greeley. It would be the largest popular vote majority until the twentieth century and the largest since Andrew Jackson had defeated John Quincy Adams in 1828. Grant captured thirty-one of thirty-seven states and won 286–66 in the Electoral College. In addition, Republicans captured two-thirds of the Senate and the House of Representatives.[121] The Republican triumph was aided by "the fairest and freest" election in the South until 1968.[122] The table was now set: Grant and the Republicans could do whatever they chose during the next two years, as long as what they chose to do was constitutional. The only questions were whether and how they—and Grant—would take advantage of their overwhelming political position.

The Second Term

1873–1877

The new administration began with a legacy that extended back to the Andrew Johnson administration—the Credit Mobilier scandal—which, unfortunately for Grant, did not come to light until his second term in office. That scandal—one of several that would dog Grant—involved inflated fees to the federal government to build the Union Pacific Railroad. Insiders raked in staggering "sums of money—in one case 348 percent" by charging exorbitant amounts to the government. The *New York Sun* called it "the most damaging exhibition of official and private villainy and corruption," and alleged that the shadowy corporation "had received $72 million in contracts to construct the Union Pacific Railroad—valued at $53 million." The revelation unleashed the congressional dogs of war in December 1872, and congressional hearings began in January 1873. Then the names began to drop: Vice President "Smiler" Colfax; Senator George Boutwell, the former secretary of the treasury; John Logan, a famous Civil War general; and Massachusetts senator Henry Wilson, the vice president-elect. "Many of these politicians were close to Grant. Some said too close."[123]

Then came more congressional chicanery: "The lame duck session of … Congress had voted the president a 100 percent pay raise—from $25,000 to $50,000—increased salaries for Supreme Court justices, and approved hefty increases for themselves." Grant's increase was not unreasonable given that he had to pay the expenses of running the White House out of his salary, and salaries for congressmen had been flat for twenty years. Surely, the congressmen thought, the public would understand, and if the raises had been all there was to the legislation, perhaps the public would have understood. But there was more: Congress had made the increases retroactive to the beginning of the term that was ending. "The press dubbed the vote, 'the Salary Grab Act.'" When the new Congress met, it did stick with the pay raise for the president and the Supreme Court justices, but it abrogated its own pay raises. These two affairs did nothing to engender good feeling and confidence of the public with respect to either Congress or Grant's second administration, even though the miasma of corruption did not—except for Henry Wilson—reach its tentacles into Grant's cabinet.[124]

Grant, with most of his original cabinet gone, relied heavily upon Hamilton Fish, his ever-steady secretary of state. As historian William S. McFeely points out, "there was hardly anyone else in the cabinet worth talking to, and Grant felt deserted." Columbus Delano, a "dimwit," was secretary of the interior. George Robeson, a lightweight of the first magnitude, was secretary of the navy, and "the new Attorney General, George H. Williams, was neither learned nor concerned with much of anything but his career and his exceedingly costly wife." Orville was tainted with scandal, and John Rawlins's—perhaps Grant's most trusted and influential advisor ever—successor, William Belknap, "was a bluff, hypocritical, unimaginative man." But worse, in a habit that would repeat itself a hundred years later, Grant spent too much of his time dealing with minor appointments, which he sought to balance by state. It was an endless, energy-sapping task, and it allowed the forest to escape his watch while he tended to the trees.[125]

Another matter piqued Grant's interest: architecture. He became involved in the design of federal buildings, and with his architect, a young Englishman named Alfred Bult Mullett, designed many, only two of which remain today. One, the majestic Executive Office Building next to the White House, exemplified what would become known "General Grant style … a term of common usage among architectural historians." That style was based upon the Second Empire style of architecture in France.[126]

In a harbinger of other deaths yet to come, Jesse Grant died in January 1873, at age seventy-nine. George Meade had died two days after Grant's reelection, and "Colonel" Frederick Dent, Julia's father, would die on December 15 at the age of eighty-six.[127] In addition, Vice President Henry Wilson suffered a stroke in May 1873, and while he would live another two and a half years, the stroke would incapacitate him for the remainder of his life. That year—1873—would see another loss, the loss of Northern political will. The zeal of the Northern public for Reconstruction began playing out at the inception of Grant's second term. That change was to dramatically affect Grant's ability to project the power necessary to protect civil rights for freed slaves, and it would engender a tectonic shift in the next Congress.[128]

Two other events took place in 1873, one that would greatly affect Grant personally and the other that would significantly affect both his administration and the nation as a whole. The first involved Grant's teenage daughter Ellen, or Nellie, as she was called. Nellie had, at age sixteen, sailed with the Adolph Bories to Europe, where, in London, she was presented to Queen Victoria. On the return voyage, she met an Englishman named Algernon Sartoris, a member of the "minor gentry," a "cad and a bounder."[129] He was, as was his father, a philanderer, and he was ten years older than Nellie. They would be married the next year.[130]

The second event would prove to be catastrophic for Grant and the country, which was enjoying a postwar economic boom and had not suffered a depression since 1837. That, however, was about to change, and it began, as many economic crises do, on Wall Street, from where it would quickly bleed over onto Main Street. It actually began when a Philadelphia investment banker named Jay Cooke borrowed heavily to finance construction of the Northern Pacific Railroad, the idea being that he would then monetize that debt with bonds that he would sell, the proceeds from which he would use to pay back the banks. There was one major problem:

he could not sell the bonds and thus defaulted on the bank debts, which caused the banks to fail, consuming the deposits of thousands of small depositors. Construction on the railroad stopped, hundreds lost their jobs and the financial consequences of the failed banks and the lost jobs and bank accounts snowballed into a bona fide recession that threatened to be even more. There was no Federal Reserve then. The money supply was controlled by the Treasury Department, which was in effect controlled by Grant, as the gold speculators had learned to their sorrow in 1870. Two sides began lobbying Washington, and thus Grant, to do something. The little people—the displaced factory workers, the farmers and western ranchers urged the federal government to pump more greenbacks into the economy. The problem, however, was that Grant was a gold standard true believer. His firm position was that United States currency should be redeemable in gold. Thus the money supply was a function of the amount of gold held by the federal government, and if that supply did not increase over time, the country was faced with a static money supply. So the two camps—the "tight" or "hard" money disciples—mostly bankers and large investors—and the "inflation" warriors, or "loose" money supply soldiers, lined up against one another, with Grant in the middle.

This time, unlike the gold crisis of 1870, there was no George Boutwell to assist Grant with the money supply. Instead, there was Grant's most trusted adviser, the hard money Hamilton Fish, who opposed any move to inject money into the economy, and there was Boutwell's—now treasury secretary—assistant, the feckless William Richardson, unimaginative and unresponsive, saying yes to his boss. The loose money people urged Grant at a minimum to print enough money to keep up with the country's population and wealth growth. He refused, toeing the hard money line, but he did authorize Richardson to reissue $26 million in greenbacks that had been retired. It was the proverbial deck chair thrown off the sinking ocean liner.

The economic collapse worsened. Millions lost their jobs. With no income and no social safety net, they became homeless and hungry. The panic of 1873 "was the first crisis of the Industrial Age," and it would balloon into a depression that would last for the rest of the decade. Moreover, because the world's economies were already interdependent to a significant degree, and in the aftermath of the Franco-Prussian War in Europe, the depression of the 1870s would spread to other regions as well.[131] That depression was a harbinger of what was to come in the 1890s and the 1930s. It would test the mettle of the Grant administration, and that administration would be found wanting in the cold clear light of hindsight and history.

Finally, in 1873 Grant proffered four candidates for two Supreme Court seats—one of them chief justice—all of whom the Senate rejected.

One was tainted by the Credit Mobilier scandal—he had also used public funds for private expenses—and another had written a letter to Jefferson Davis after Fort Sumter recommending a friend for a position in the Confederate government. The press savaged both. Grant at one point in 1873 was zero for four in the confirmation of candidates for the Supreme Court, and his party controlled the Senate.[132]

The new year, 1874, brought, on May 21, the culmination of Nellie's engagement to Algernon Sartoris: they were married that day, only the fourth wedding ever in the White House. It was a "small" wedding, limited to around two hundred family members and close friends. Grant stared at the floor and wept. Nellie and Algernon would have four children. Three of the children survived. Grant family tradition holds that Algernon was a "drinker," and that the marriage was unhappy. The Grants were right: the marriage would end in divorce five years after Grant's death.[133]

The recession roared into a full-blown depression in 1874, and Congress, responding to the shortage of money, passed what was to become known as the "Inflation Bill." The Inflation Bill would increase the amount of currency in the economy by $100 million, and Grant's cabinet, and a majority of Congress, favored the legislation. Grant, however, still a "hard money" man, vacillated until finally, he vetoed the bill, and Congress was unable to muster the two-thirds majority needed to override his veto. Farmers—and their congressmen—in the South, Midwest and West were outraged. Someone had to pay, and that debt would not be long in reaching foreclosure. Moreover, Grant's veto ossified the Republican Party's fiscal conservatism and political position as the staunch defender of hard money, a position that obtains to this day.[134]

The final blow came in November, when the Democrats took control of the House and regained ten seats in the Senate, although not control.[135] It was a crushing blow to Grant and to the Republican Party. Grant, notwithstanding that political catastrophe, was urged to run for a third term, and he apparently considered it, as the move was favored by Julia Grant, who enjoyed being first lady. Grant, however, decided to follow the George Washington model and decline, much to his wife's high dudgeon. And then the year on the Styx ended, finally.[136] Or did it? Would the faint miasma of corruption that had dogged the first two years of his second term disappear, or would the stench grow even more noxious?

Thus finally arrived 1875, and with it came more controversy. First up was the so-called "Whiskey Scandal," which involved federal tax agents— bribed by distillers and distributors—who underreported the amount of whiskey subject to taxation. One center of such activity was Grant's old—and unhappy—hometown, St. Louis. The scandal began to unfold when Grant's didactic secretary of the treasury, Benjamin James Bristow, undertook an investigation into the St. Louis operation. Determined to rid Grant's administration of the corruption that ran through it like whiskey ran through a sieve, Bristow plunged into the St. Louis scheme like it was a lake, and he came up with several fish, one of them a big fish: General John McDonald, the collector of internal revenue over seven states, whose headquarters was in St. Louis.

Grant "purportedly" agreed with Bristow with respect to McDonald's prosecution, but when the investigation moved up the whiskey ladder, it reached Grant's private secretary, Orville Babcock, and everything changed. Grant would not hear of Babcock's guilt, and the president finally agreed to a military court of inquiry, but he appointed the three generals who were to sit on that court, and they quickly acquitted McDonald. Then, a St. Louis grand jury indicted him, and Grant wanted to attend the trial and testify, but Bristow and Fish talked him out of it. The president thus gave a deposition in which he proclaimed Babcock's innocence. The trial jury found Babcock not guilty, but Grant, under pressure from Bristow and Hamilton Fish, fired him. There was a rumor extant in Washington that Grant's son Fred was on the receiving end of some of the ill-gotten gains, but that bog was never explored. Another rumor had it that Grant was having an affair. The correspondent remained a mystery. Finally the tumult and shouting died. It had not been Grant's finest hour.[137]

Next up was Secretary of War William Worth Belknap, whom Grant had appointed in 1869 when his closest adviser, John Rawlins, died. Belknap's first wife, Carrie, had gotten involved in a kickback scheme involving the Indian Agency at Fort Sill, Oklahoma. She had obtained the license to run the agency, and the agent who ran it skimmed revenue off the top and paid it to her. Carrie died and Belknap turned around and married her sister, Amanda, known as "Puss." Puss was a beautiful woman, but she was also an expensive woman for Belknap to maintain on his salary of $8,000 a year. The Belknaps entertained lavishly—Grant attended a New Year's Day party in their home—and the "voluptuous" Mrs. Belknap wore fine clothes and adorned herself with expensive jewelry. Many, including her friends and fans in the press, wondered how Belknap managed all of this.

The Indian agency paid her $6,000 a year and her co-conspirator, a New Yorker named Caleb P. Marsh, received the same amount. Congress, now controlled by Democrats, launched an investigation, which, at first, seemed to indicate that Belknap himself was untainted. But upon deeper inspection, the oversight committee determined that the money had been sent to Belknap in accordance with his instructions. The dogs of war were nipping at his metaphorical heels when, on March 2, 1876, Belknap rushed to the White House early in the day and tendered his resignation personally to Grant. In doing so he beat the Damoclesian sword that overhung him like doom by a few hours, and as an ex-secretary of war, the issue now was whether the House could impeach him. It thought so and thus undertook impeachment proceedings, which passed the House and moved over to the Senate. The Senate acquitted, not on grounds that Belknap was innocent but rather that it lacked jurisdiction because Belknap was no longer in office. Belknap became holder of the dubious honor of being the only former cabinet member to be impeached.[138]

But that was not all that arose out of the Indian Reservation Agency corruption. It was rumored that Grant's son, Orville, was also involved in this kickback scheme, as was Julia Grant's brother John C. Dent. Those dark, narrow alleyways were never explored.[139]

And there would be more. Next up was Grant's Secretary of the Interior, Columbus Delano. Delano's problems arose out of surveying contracts let by the surveyor general, Silas Reed, to parties that would then form partnerships with Delano's son, John Delano, to perform surveying work. The problem was that John Delano would then receive payments pursuant to his partnership agreements but would perform no surveying. Moreover, another person was implicated in the scheme: Orvil Grant, Grant's brother and former boss in the Galena, Illinois, leather goods store. It was a nasty entanglement, and Grant's aggressive attorney general, Benjamin H. Bristow, dumped it into Grant's lap. The president did nothing, but eventually public opinion, as expressed through the press, forced Grant to accept Delano's resignation on August 7, 1875.[140]

Next up was Grant's Secretary of the Navy, George M. Robeson, who had taken Adolph Borie's place. Roberson, whose net worth was about $20,000 when he took office, entered into an arrangement with a Philadelphia grain merchant firm, A.G. Cattell and Son, to supply foodstuffs to the navy. "The firm flourished, and so did Roberson." A congressional investigation ensued, and the congressional committee forced Robeson to hand over his bank records, which showed a balance of $320,000, achieved when Roberson's salary was only $8,000 a year. Moreover, there was evidence that the firm had purchased a house for Roberson in Long Branch, New Jersey, where Grant summered.[141]

The congressmen next reviewed Cattell's records, but those were in such disarray that they could find no evidence of payments to Roberson. Amazingly, the congressional committee concluded that the evidence was largely "circumstantial" and, although the committee considered impeachment, they were preoccupied with the Belknap impeachment in the Senate, and let it go, instead condemning Roberson's "gross misconduct."[142]

The next up was Grant's brother-in-law James F. Casey, who was Emmy's husband and collector of customs in New Orleans. Bristow investigated Casey for fraud as part of the "customhouse ring." Casey told Grant that Bristow's prosecutions were motivated by Bristow's own political ambitions. The investigation went nowhere.[143] Then came George Williams, Grant's attorney general, whose wife had accepted a $30,000 payment from a New York brokerage firm that Williams refused to prosecute. Williams, exposed, resigned.[144]

Then came Grant's Minister to Great Britain, Robert Schenck, who was accused of using his position "to promote investments in which he had a personal stake." He, too, fell like a bowling pin and resigned under pressure from Congress's long investigative arm.[145] With the stink of these scandals was born the mantra that Grant's was a corrupt administration. There is no question that it was riddled with corruption, some of it reaching into Grant's own family. And Grant? He was hesitant to pursue much of it, although Bristow, his secretary of the treasury, did, as did the Democratic Party-controlled Congress. In spite of all of it, however, none of it reached Grant, though rumors placed it near him. Through it all, however, the president remained imperturbable. And remarkably, in the spring of 1876 there was again talk of a third term. That, too, went nowhere.

On May 10, 1876, the centennial celebration opened in Philadelphia. It would run for two and a half years, and millions would see this exhibition of America's industrial innovation and might. Earlier, Grant had ordered Sherman to send the Seventh Cavalry into Indian country to force the Sioux back onto their reservation. Sherman, although he harbored serious reservations about the competence and state of mind of the Seventh's commander, George Armstrong Custer, sent him in. The result, while not quite predictable, certainly, in hindsight, was not surprising. Custer split his force and, vastly underestimating the number of Sioux facing him, attacked and was wiped out. Grant received that news on July 8 while in Philadelphia.[146]

So in 1876, Grant's administration ground to an ignominious end. The Republican Convention that summer on the seventh ballot nominated for president Rutherford B. Hayes, governor of Ohio and a "minor general" who had been wounded at South Mountain and was a "tight money man" in keeping with the highest traditions of the Republican Party. His opponent would be the Democrat Samuel J. Tilden, governor of New York, and Tilden would win the popular vote but come up one vote short in the Electoral College. There was no vice president to count the votes, so Grant and Congress created a commission to do it. In the South, electoral pandemonium reigned. Louisiana, Florida and South Carolina had disputed returns and proffered two sets of electoral votes. Not surprisingly, the Republican-majority committee accepted *all* of the Republican ballots from the three contested states in return for a promise by Hayes to restore self-rule in the South. With that promise, Hayes won by one electoral vote, and Reconstruction died a sudden death.[147]

The inauguration was March 4, 1877. Julia Grant, who had loved her time in the White House—and resented her husband's refusal to run for a third term—told Hayes's wife, "Mrs. Hayes, I hope you will be as happy here as I have been the last eight years." Grant, on the other hand, told an associate that "he was never happier than the day he left the White House. 'I felt like a boy getting out of school,'" he said.[148]

Grant's next undertaking was major trip: he and Julia would undertake a journey to much of the then "civilized" world. They departed Philadelphia on May 17, 1877, on board the passenger and freight liner *Indiana*, bound for Liverpool. Grant, it was said, remembered the freedom of the military campaign, the joy of life in a tent and on horseback. While he couldn't reproduce his wartime existence, he could recapture some of those experiences.[149] He was fifty-seven years old and still in the prime of his life. Grant had invested—one of the few good investments of that life—in the Comstock silver mines, and he had made $25,000, enough to finance his trip.[150] A publisher asked him to write his memoirs, but he declined. That book, if it came at all, would come later.

The Grants were accompanied by their younger son, Jesse; a maid; and a thirty-seven-year-old reporter named John Russell Young, who worked for the *New York Herald*. The *Herald*, which had sponsored Henry M. Stanley's trip to find Dr. David Livingston in the heart of Africa with great financial success, wanted almost day-by-day coverage of Grant's trip. Young was just the man to give their readership that coverage, and his work would subsequently result in a two-volume set titled *Around the World with General Grant*.[151]

There is some dispute among historians with respect to who actually accompanied the three Grants. One source posits that Grant's "manservant" made the trip; however, historian-biographer Ron Chernow notes that Grant had his "black manservant," Bill Barnes, put ashore before departure. H.W. Brands identifies only the three Grants and Young, while Jean Edward Smith includes both the maid and the manservant. William S. McFeely refers only to the three Grants and Young. Joan Waugh includes son Fred "for a year." That year was actually during the second half of the grand tour when the party sailed to the Far East.[152]

An "immense gathering cheered the former president's arrival" in Liverpool, and Grant gave a "small speech of appreciation" to the crowd, not his favorite function. They made their way to London, where they were guests of Queen Victoria at Windsor Castle—actually thirty miles from London—and where Grant met literary lions Matthew Arnold, Anthony Trollope and Robert Browning, as well as Prime

Minister Benjamin Disraeli. The Prince of Wales came to Grant's theater box and introduced himself, and subsequently he hosted Grant at Epsom for a horse race, which Grant, the old and superb equestrian, thought was "a cruel sport."

There was confusion among Victoria's entourage about how to treat and address Grant. He was no longer president, and there was no protocol or precedent for a visiting ex-president. After discussion among her aides and the American ambassador to Great Britain, the British reluctantly agreed to address the ex-president as President Grant, although to the hordes who followed his progression from Liverpool and into London, he was "General Grant." A British newspaper wrote of Grant: he is "open-browed, firm-faced, blunt, bluff and honest, and unassuming, everybody at once settled in his own mind that the General would do."[153]

The overnight visit at Windsor was "a terrifying triumph." Upon their arrival there, the Queen kept the Grants waiting while she rode a horse. Victoria's aides had assigned son Jesse to dine with the "household," but he refused, and finally, the Queen's assistants relented, and he was allowed to join his parents at the Queen's table. Victoria found Julia "civil & complimentary in her funny American way." She pronounced (Jesse) "a very ill-mannered young Yankee." That night at "supper" was the only time that the Grants would see the Queen.[154]

The Grants visited with daughter Nellie, who was trying hard to convince herself and her parents that she was happy at her home in Southampton. Her husband Algernon was "dissolute," which precluded invitations to the young couple to grand parties in London. Nellie's "stubborn pride" demanded that she show her parents that she had done the right thing in marrying Algernon Sartoris.[155]

The Grant's travels continued, with trips to Belgium, where they met King Leopold, to Germany—the first of two visits—Switzerland and Italy, where Grant met Pope Leo XIII and King Umberto. They then traveled to Scotland, back to England, Paris, Southern Italy and Malta, Alexandria and Cairo, Egypt. There they saw the pyramids, then they went on to the Holy Land, Constantinople, Athens, traveled back to Italy, Paris, the Netherlands and Germany, where Grant called upon Otto von Bismarck, the "Iron Chancellor." Next up were Denmark, Norway, Sweden, Finland, Russia, where he met Czar Alexander, Poland, Austria, then back to Paris, from which it was reported that he had seen the cancan dancers. From Paris the Grants and their entourage traveled to Spain and Portugal. Having seen most of Europe, Egypt and part of Asia Minor, they were, however, not done traveling.

In Berlin, Grant, accompanied by his journalist friend who would record the visit, John Russell Young, walked nonchalantly from his hotel to Bismarck's palace, smoking a cigar the whole way. Upon arrival, he tossed the cigar, approached the grand entrance and knocked on the door like a tradesman. The military guards realized that the man was Grant and saluted, while the door attendants stood there, amazed that a former president of the United States and the hero of the American Civil War stood before them in a plain black suit with no medals.[156]

Bismarck was surprised by Grant's looks, which the chancellor thought youthful and which he attributed to a "military life." The two men discussed the Civil War, which Bismarck thought was the result of Lincoln's desire to preserve the Union. Grant agreed that preservation of the Union was the original impetus for the North's entry into the war, but subsequently, the abolition of slavery became the North's objective. Bismarck thought that a larger standing army might have prevented the war, but Grant thought that it would have made no difference because so many of the "old" army's officers were Southerners, and with their departure, the old army dissolved.[157]

The two men discussed Philip Sheridan, who had visited with Bismarck during the Franco-Prussian War. Bismarck thought Sheridan "a man of great ability." Grant said, "I regard Sheridan as not only one of the great soldiers of the world.... [I believe] no better general ever lived than Sheridan."[158] Bismarck invited Grant to a military review, a function that Grant eschewed but this time accepted, saying, "The truth is I am more of a farmer than a soldier. I take no interest in military affairs and although I ... have been in two wars ... I never went into the army without regret and never retired without pleasure."[159] Grant thought Prussia "militaristic," with flags flying and uniformed men evident everywhere he went.[160]

Bismarck treated Julia with all of the respect that she had always craved but never had received. "Humiliations—being laughed at for her uncontrollable eye, being regarded as married to a failure, being cut down by Mary Lincoln—all were made up for at Prince Bismarck's palace. She was at last the princess of childhood fantasies at White Haven. Julia could not get too many princely attentions."[161]

In Constantinople, Grant called upon the sultan, who gave him two Arabian stallions, which Grant shipped back to the United States. Those two stallions "became the foundation sires for the Arabian breed in North America." Grant noted with disgust that in Turkey "women are degraded even beneath a slave. The donkey is their superior in privileges."[162]

With $65,000 that his son Buck had made for him, Grant decided to extend the trip to the Far East. His entourage now consisted of Julia; his son Fred—Ulysses had returned home; his former Secretary of the Navy, Adolph E. Borie; Borie's nephew, the physician John M. Keating of Philadelphia; and Young. Together, they would travel through Suez to India, then through Southeast Asia, Hong Kong and Singapore to China and, finally, to Japan. Although he thought the Taj Mahal was beautiful, he was once again struck by the treatment of women in India, where they were devalued more than animals. The viceroy, Lord Lytton, would later recount that Grant "got drunk as a fiddle," fondled at least four different women and tried "to ravish" one of them. The viceroy then claimed that it took six sailors to subdue the drunken ex-president and deposit him at "the public saloon," where he attacked the "unresisting body of his legitimate spouse, and copiously vomited during the operation. If you have seen Mrs. Grant you will not think this incredible."[163]

Grant found Hong Kong "stunning" and in Canton was "carried by porters through a crowd of 200,000 and feted with a sumptuous banquet." Grant said of the Chinese, "My impression is that the day is not very far distant when they will make the most rapid strides towards modern civilization and become dangerous rivals to all powers interested in the trade of the East."[164] He thought that the nation was still "mired in the past" but said that "China will rapidly become a powerful and rich nation. Her territory is vast and full of resources. The population is industrious and frugal, intelligent and quick to learn. They must, however, have the protection of a better and more honest government to succeed."[165]

Prince Kung, the Chinese emperor's son, asked Grant to mediate a dispute that China had with Japan over the Ryukyu Islands, and when he went to Japan, he spoke to the Meiji emperor about the dispute, urging him to settle it peacefully. The emperor listened, and a short time after Grant left, Japan annexed the islands. Nevertheless, Grant thought the Japanese people "the most kindly and most cleanly in the world." Japan, of all the countries that he had visited, was his favorite.[166]

One of the many interesting conversations that Grant had with Young concerned Grant's memories of the war and the personalities he had encountered during those tumultuous years. He was generally positive when discussing McClellan, whom he thought was a victim of the Union's—and the Union Army's—unpreparedness to fight. He also discussed Southerners and thought that the South would have profited from "streams of immigration" from the Northeast and mid-Atlantic states. He felt sorry for poor Southerners, whom he had hoped the war would free from a slave-like bondage under the old planter class, but he believed that had not happened.[167]

Another conversation with Young—published in the *New York Herald*—concerned Grant's view of Confederate generals. He rated Albert Sidney Johnson, who was killed at Shiloh, highly and thought that if he had lived, "might have risen in fame." He also thought highly of Stonewall Jackson, who had been with him for a year at West Point. Nonetheless, he thought that much of what Jackson had accomplished early in the war—implicitly against lesser Union generals—would have been difficult to achieve against the likes of Sherman, Sheridan, Thomas and Meade. "No doubt so able and patient a man as Jackson, who worked so hard at anything he attempted, would have adapted himself to new conditions and risen with them." Grant was not that high on Lee, whom he acknowledged as only "a fair commander." He thought Joseph E. Johnston was a better Confederate general.[168]

The Grants sailed on the *City of Tokio* on September 3, 1879, for San Francisco, where they arrived on September 20 to a tumultuous reception. From San Francisco they visited Portland and Fort Vancouver, where they saw the house in which Grant had lived some twenty-five years before and the field in which he had once planted potatoes to make a little money on the side. They visited in Virginia City, Nevada, and explored a silver mine; then it was on to Chicago for a reunion of the Army of Tennessee. Philip Sheridan, outfitted in a plumed hat, led a parade of some eighty thousand veterans, and that night Grant attended a six-hour dinner at which sixteen speakers droned on and on about the war and their guest of honor. The last speaker was Mark Twain, who had once served "in an irregular Confederate unit organized in his hometown of Hannibal, Missouri."[169] Next, the Grants visited Galena and, finally, returned to Philadelphia, where they arrived on December 16, 1879, roughly thirty-one months after their departure.[170]

Grant's return raised the question: What now? As an ex-president he had no pension and no ready source of income. His travels abroad—trumpeted by Young to the American public—had rendered him a man of the world and a bona fide American hero, if he had not been so before. There was then a groundswell of support for him to seek a third term as president, as 1880 would be an election year. Hayes was not running, and as one wag, Robert G. Ingersoll, said, "Hayes couldn't be reelected if no one ran against him."[171]

The Republican convention would be held in Chicago on June 2, 1880, and Grant was an early favorite to capture the nomination. He had, however, returned home with months to pass before the convention, and that time was sufficient to take the bloom off Grant's rose. His popularity crested well before the convention, and by the time of the convention it had taken a decided downturn. His reviews in the press were mixed. The *St. Louis Post-Dispatch* declared, "The nation needs a man of iron to replace a man of straw."

Others, however, howled that he had been "driven mad by ambition," while still another tarred him as a "'puppet' of machine politicians."[172] As biographer William S. McFeely says, "There was no substance to clothe his campaign. It had developed no idea or issue. There was no reason at all why he should be elected president again. Grant had become nothing but a symbol—a mighty one perhaps, but with no more currency than an old battle flag."[173]

A driving force—perhaps *the* driving force—behind Grant's campaign was Julia Grant, who wanted another tour of duty in the White House. She urged Grant to go to the convention and to run as a "world statesman." He refused to visit the convention and never articulated a platform as a world statesman or as anything else. In the end his vote tally was stuck at 306—with 379 required to win the nomination—and Garfield won the nomination as a compromise candidate on the thirty-sixth ballot. Julia was sick. Grant was finished politically. He claimed to be "relieved."[174]

Garfield and his running mate, Chester A. Arthur, would be opposed by one of the heroes of Gettysburg, General Winfield Scott Hancock, of whom Grant said, "He was a very good corps commander. He was ambitious, and had courage and a fine presence; but he is vain, selfish, weak, and easily flattered," and "he could never endure to have anyone else receive any credit."[175] Grant "took to the stump" in support of Garfield, who won the Electoral College 214–155.

The Grants had no desire to live in Galena and preferred New York City, which they could not afford. Once again two groups of Grant's wealthy friends stepped up and created two trusts of $250,000 and $100,000, respectively. They also bought him a house at 3 East Sixty-Sixth Street, just off Fifth Avenue. Although personally finished politically, Grant could not resist dabbling in politics. Thus, just two months after the election, Grant wrote, "Garfield has shown that he is not possessed of the backbone of an angleworm."[176]

His first business venture after returning to the United States following his trip was as head of a Mexican railroad that would run from Mexico City to Guatemala, the Pacific Ocean and the Gulf of Mexico. Grant was president and established his headquarters at 2 Wall Street in New York City. The company paid him a salary, but the railroad eventually failed.[177]

Now came one of the lowest of Grant's many low points. His son Buck—Ulysses Jr.—was a partner with a Wall Street prodigy named Ferdinand Ward in an investment banking and brokerage business, and the firm was making money "hand over fist." Grant wanted to make money—a lot of money—and Grant and Ward seemed to be the way to do it, so Grant invested his entire liquid capital of $100,000 in the firm and became a silent partner. Ward was the managing partner, and Buck was as silent as his father. He, too, had invested $100,000, and Ward, who was also to invest $100,000, promised the two Grants a handsome return of $2,000 a month.[178]

Ward's father-in-law was James Fish, who was chief operating officer of the Marine Bank, which made loans to Grant and Ward for the firm's own investments, the collateral for which were securities held by the firm. In addition, James Fish was a partner in Grant and Ward, a conflict of interest of extraordinary proportions—even for that time—that would not inhere to the benefit of the Marine Bank.[179]

The returns were incredibly high—too high in fact. Wall Street began to talk when Grant and Ward paid its investors 40 percent dividends.[180] By the spring of 1884, Ulysses Grant was worth, on paper, in the neighborhood of a million dollars, and on paper, the firm was worth $15 million. But smoke curled up from the paper, because beneath it there was trouble. Ward was using the funds borrowed from Marine Bank—Fish had given Grant and Ward an open line of credit—to pay those 40 percent dividends. The line of credit was secured by securities. Ward, however, had used the same securities as collateral for multiple loans, which, obviously, was illegal.[181]

Horace Porter, Grant's old aide and now an executive with the Pullman Company and Wall Street savvy, smelled the rat extant in the scheme and went to Grant's house to tell him that there was no way that the firm was making the profits necessary to pay those kinds of dividends. However, when he arrived there Ferdinand Ward had beaten him to the punch and was extolling the firm and its profits. Grant, Porter observed, was excited, too excited for Porter to tell him that there was trouble in paradise, so Porter left, and Grant wallowed in, and swallowed whole, Ward's presentation.[182]

On May 4, 1884, Ward showed up unannounced at Grant's house. He told Grant that the firm had in the vicinity of $650,000 on deposit with Marine Bank, and the City of New York had withdrawn much of its money from the bank, which had created a cash flow problem. Ward said that if Marine Bank failed, Grant and Ward would lose its money and go under. He said that he already had raised $250,000 and needed another $150,000 from Grant, who did not have it. He then talked Grant into borrowing the money, which Grant eventually did from his friend William Vanderbilt. Grant turned the money over to Ward, who promised that Grant would get his money back within twenty-four hours.[183]

Two days later, Marine Bank failed and with it went Grant and Ward. Ward suddenly disappeared, as did Grant's $150,000. James Fish locked himself in his office. He and Ward had orchestrated a classic pyramid scheme, paying early investors high dividends with funds invested by later investors and from the Marine Bank loans under its line of credit. A later audit revealed that Ward kept two sets of books. The first set showed the firm's net worth at $15 million. Those books constituted fiction worthy of Charles Dickens.[184]

Ward was indicted, tried and convicted of fraud. He received a sentence of ten years of hard labor at Sing Sing. Fish was also convicted and got seven years in federal prison.[185] Grant, about whose culpability many wondered—the *New York Sun*'s headline: "Is Grant Guilty?"—was deemed by the majority of people to be a victim, as was Buck. Both had left the details of the firm's operations to Ward, and both had suffered egregiously for their lack of attention. Grant was left with a total $211 in capital. He had lost $250,000 with Grant and Ward. The first $100,000 had come from a fund set up by rich friends, and the $150,000 was the loan from William Vanderbilt. In addition, his $250,000 trust fund lost everything when it invested its entire corpus in the Wabash Railroad, which, true to Grant's record of investing, failed. Spending money was all that he had. Grant again teetered on the razor's edge of bankruptcy.[186]

Once again, however, friends stepped up to help. They gave the Grants $2,500. In addition, Julia sold two small houses that she owned, and Grant, looking for a way to make some money, agreed to write four articles for *Century Magazine* on the Civil War campaigns of Vicksburg, Shiloh, the Wilderness and Appomattox at $500 each, later increased to $1,000 each.[187]

William Vanderbilt wanted to forgive the $150,000 loan, but Grant demurred. He and Julia gathered all of their valuable personal property and gave it to Vanderbilt, along with the title to their house. Vanderbilt very reluctantly took the personal property and title to the house but told the Grants that he would hold the valuables in trust and at his death would turn them over to a museum. He would also allow the Grants to live in what was now his house for the rest of their lives.[188]

The *New York Times* wrote: "For the love of money the greatest military reputation of our time has been dimmed and degraded by its possessor. The people look on with shame." Grant said, "I could bear all the pecuniary loss if that was all, but that I could be so long deceived by a man who I had such opportunity to know is humiliating."[189]

The Death of Ulysses

The Grants went to their cottage in Long Branch for the summer of 1884. In June, while eating a peach, Grant experienced an excruciating pain in his throat. He thought something had stung him. When the pain persisted, and Grant had trouble swallowing, Julia insisted that he see a doctor. He did. The physician found a pea-sized growth in the soft palate at the base of his tongue. He recommended a specialist, but Grant's specialist—John H. Douglas—was in Europe until October, so Grant waited to see Douglas, which he did on October 10, 1884. The four months' delay was

Grant shortly before his death (April 1885).

critical, as it allowed the tumor to grow from pea-sized to plum-sized, and by October, the tumor was imbedded deeply in Grant's soft palate, which made it inoperable. If he had sought treatment earlier, a surgeon could likely have removed the growth, but it was too late for that now.[190]

Roswell Smith, president of *Century Magazine*, negotiated with Grant for his memoir, offering him 10 percent royalties. Smith, by October 1884, thought that he had a deal, albeit a *verbal* deal, with Grant. Then came Grant's friend Samuel L. Clemens, who, with his son-in-law, had formed a publishing company, Charles L. Webster and Company. Their company had recently published Clemens's book, *The Adventures of Huckleberry Finn*, destined to be an American classic. Clemens went to work on Grant, asserting that *Century*'s offer was far too low and that he could do better, *a lot better*. Indeed, Clemens offered a 20 percent royalty, or 70 percent of the book's net profits, with an advance of $50,000 on the spot. Grant worried about his "deal" with *Century*, but in the end, he opted for the advance and 70 percent of the net profits.[191] Clemens told Grant that they would sell the book by taking advance orders, and Grant went to work on his memoirs in his Wall Street office. By January, however, he was confined to his house at 3 East Sixty-Sixth Street.[192] In February 1885, the illness went public when the *New York World* published a letter from Grant to a friend in which Grant described the illness.[193] Grant now entered a race against cancer to complete his memoirs.

His writing process took form. He would write and then have what he had written reviewed by his "staff": his son Fred and Fred's wife, Ida; Adam Badeau; Horace Porter; Buck; Harrison Tyrell, his valet; and Nathan Dawson, his stenographer.[194] In March 1885, his family thought that he was gone, but he rallied in April and plowed ahead with his writing.

Trouble arose with Adam Badeau, who had convinced himself that he was indispensable to Grant and therefore demanded a portion of Grant's advance and the percentage of the net profits Grant would receive. The *New York World* published an article—likely written by Badeau—claiming that Badeau was the author of the book and that Grant could not write. Grant wrote a rebuttal and fired Badeau.[195]

On March 4, 1885, Congress restored Grant's rank and awarded him an annual pension of $13,500.[196] Three days earlier, the *New York Times* ran a headline "Grant Is Dying." Reporters began a death watch outside his house. Grant had lost forty pounds and was taking cocaine during the day and morphine at night to arrest his growing pain. The cocaine quit working, and his physicians switched him to laudanum and morphine.[197] He wrote to a friend: "If you could imagine what molten lead would be going down your throat that is what I feel when swallowing."[198] The drugs slowed the pain but also affected his writing. Still, he worked through the pain and stuck to his work like he had stuck to "this line" in the summer of 1864.

Nellie came from England in mid–June 1885. By now, speech had become difficult, so he communicated by notes. John W. Drexel gave him the use of a house in Mt. Macgregor, New York, about twelve miles north of Saratoga Springs. Grant traveled there in William Vanderbilt's private railroad car with Julia, Fred and Ida, Nellie, Dr. Douglas, Grant's nurse and his valet. His race against death continued, and his end came into sight. He worked on.

Visitors began arriving to tell him goodbye. His old friend Simon Bolivar Buckner, now a successful newspaper publisher and politician, came. John C. Fremont, Sherman and Sheridan visited him, as did

Fitzhugh Lee and Albert Sidney Johnston's son. Longstreet and Winfield Scott Hancock came, the latter to "make peace with the general."[199]

Grant wrote a five-hundred-word preface on July 1 and finished his memoirs on July 16, 1885. There were two volumes, together comprising eleven hundred pages. He now weighed less than one hundred pounds. He died a week later, having run, and won, the race against time and cancer.

Julia considered several places for his burial but in the end decided that New York had been their home and that she would bury him there. The general's funeral was one for the ages. First, it is estimated that 1.5 million people viewed his casket as it passed by rail from Mt. Macgregor to New York City. Then, Winfield Scott Hancock led some thirty-seven thousand veterans who followed the casket to Riverside Park, where Grant was interred, there to await construction of a mausoleum. The procession was seven miles long. Pallbearers included Sheridan, Sherman and Confederate generals Joseph Johnston and Simon Bolivar Buckner. Grant's tomb was completed and dedicated in 1897. In 1902, Julia, who did not attend her husband's funeral, joined him there.

Samuel Clemens sold three hundred thousand sets of Grant's *Memoirs*, which produced some $450,000 income for Julia. She wrote her own memoirs, which were not, however, published until 1975.[200] In 1893, she met Varina Davis, Jefferson Davis's widow, in New York City. They lived twenty blocks apart and became fast friends. In 1895, however, Julia sold her New York house and moved to Washington, D.C., where she was soon joined by Nellie, who had been living on Lakeshore Drive, north of Chicago. Nellie died in 1922.

Grant's son Fred became minister to Austria-Hungary under Presidents Benjamin Harrison and Grover Cleveland. Subsequently he worked as commissioner of police with Theodore Roosevelt in New York City. Fred died in 1912.[201]

Buck moved to San Diego, where Jesse lived. He was successful in real estate and built the state-of-the-art U.S. Grant Hotel, a "wonderfully successful memorial to his father." Buck died in 1929. Jesse searched the West and Mexico for wealth, participating in various schemes to make his fortune. He eventually settled in San Diego, became a Democrat and was the last to die in 1934, almost two years into the presidency of that quintessential Democrat, Franklin Roosevelt.[202]

James Longstreet said that Grant was "my lifetime friend, kindest when I was most fiercely assaulted. He was a great general, but the best thing about him was his heart."[203] Longstreet also said that Grant "was the truest as well as the bravest man that ever lived."[204] Philip Sheridan said that Grant "was the greatest soldier in our history."

When one considers the Grant story—his rise from selling wood in a

tattered coat on a St. Louis street corner to president of the United States—
it is an incredible story, almost unbelievable. His legacy, however, has been
marred by the corruption that haunted his administration, as well as by
the meteoric rise of the "Lost Cause" catechism, the concomitant deifica-
tion of Robert E. Lee[205] and the subsequent diminution of Grant's reputation as a military man in comparison with Lee. Thus, the conventional
wisdom became that Lee was a genius, while Grant was a "butcher" who
overcame the sainted Lee with overwhelming military might.

A hard look at the record reveals, however, that Grant was a strategic genius who knew that defeating the Confederacy would require three
armies to fight on three different fronts. He orchestrated this complex strategic plan over an enormous geographic area, and with his strategic genius
came victory. Grant's legacy is, therefore, one of a humble, quiet man who,
along with Abraham Lincoln, saved the Union from dissolution. For an
American, there is no greater praise.

CHAPTER SEVEN

Fourteen Others

Ambrose Everett Burnside

"Burn"

Andrew Everett Burnside was born May 27, 1824, in Liberty, Indiana, the fourth of nine children.[1] Educated in a one-room school, he was apprenticed to a tailor in the neighboring town of Centreville when he was fifteen. When his mother died, he moved back to Liberty and opened his own tailor shop but quickly decided that he preferred the army over garments and applied for an appointment to West Point. Through his father's influence and with the support of two former governors and a United States senator, he received an appointment there in 1843. Burnside entered West Point that summer at age eighteen.[2]

In his first two years at West Point, Burnside faltered, but the summer after his second year, while on summer leave, he worked on a farm, and the monotony and drudgery of that oeuvre convinced him that he preferred the military life to the farming life, so he buckled down his last two years. As the result of his increased effort, he finished eighteenth out of thirty-eight cadets.[3] Burnside received his commission as a second lieutenant in the Third U.S. Artillery,[4] and with the

Ambrose Burnside (1863).

127

Mexican War in progress, shipped out for Vera Cruz, but the war ended before he could see any action. He then received orders to Fort Adams in Newport, Rhode Island. Subsequently, he was posted to Las Vegas, New Mexico, where in a skirmish with Apaches he received an arrow in his neck, but it was not a serious wound.[5]

What he also came away with was a brilliant idea. Burnside recognized that cavalry troopers were at a disadvantage in fighting the Indians, as they could use only their sabers in a mounted fight. It was impossible for them to load a muzzle-loading rifle, and, for some reason, revolvers were not generally used by the cavalry. Burnside thus devised a plan for a new weapon: a breech-loading carbine to replace the muzzle-loading rifles, and he took a leave from active service in the winter of 1850 and 1851.[6]

While home he became engaged to Charlotte Moon, but at the altar, when the preacher asked her if she took him to be her husband, she said, "No siree, Bob," and walked out, leaving poor Burnside standing at the altar. Subsequently, she became engaged to an Ohio lawyer, and when they reached that point in the ceremony and before she could answer, the man pulled a pistol and said that there was either going to "be a wedding tonight or a funeral tomorrow."[7] She dropped the "no siree, Bob" line and took him to be her lawfully wedded husband. Subsequently Burnside married twenty-three-year-old Charlotte Richmond, whom he had met at his first duty station at Fort Adams in Newport, Rhode Island, a location that would play a large role in his post–Civil War career. In addition to marrying Charlotte Richmond, he received a promotion to first lieutenant.[8]

Burnside resigned from the army in 1852 and started the Bristol Rifle Company, to manufacture breech-loading rifles. Borrowing heavily to underwrite the increased production that a cavalry contract would require, Burnside thought that he had won a contract to supply that weapon to the U.S. Cavalry, but in what was thought to be the solicitation of a bribe by the Secretary of War, John B. Floyd, Burnside refused to pay and lost the contract.[9] He then was forced to take bankruptcy. He pledged everything he had, including the patent on his rifle, to his creditors, left his wife to move in with her parents and headed west. His friend George B. McClellan hired him to work at the Illinois Central Railroad in Chicago. By 1861, Burnside was the line's treasurer and worked at an office in New York. And after living with the McClellans in Chicago and conserving his money, Burnside paid off his creditors.[10]

Then came the war, and the governor of Rhode Island granted Burnside command of a regiment and a commission as a colonel.[11] From Washington, Burnside took his raw troops toward First Manassas. Along the way they lightheartedly picked berries. "That evening, what was left of the brigade staggered into Washington.[12] Burnside's brigade disbanded, and he was released from the militia."[13] It was an ignominious beginning to a military career that would have more than its share of ups and downs, mostly the latter.

On July 21, 1861, George McClellan took command of the Army of the Potomac and immediately gave Burnside command of a brigade and a promotion to brigadier general. Burnside then hatched a plan to mount attacks along the North Carolina coast, and with McClellan's approval, assembled a motley mélange of vessels to transport what was now a division of fifteen thousand men. He attacked and captured Roanoke Island, Elizabeth City and New Bern, which led to a promotion to major general on March 18, 1862.[14]

If a general can take only three strikes before he is out, then Burnside, at his next battle at Antietam in Maryland, took the first of his strikes. McClellan ordered him to cross what would become known as "Burnside's Bridge" on September 17, 1862, and although his troops could have waded across Antietam Creek, Burnside persisted in trying to cross the bridge— all day—in the face of several hundred Confederate sharpshooters. "To motivate the men, Burnside offered a ration of whiskey if they were able to secure the position on the opposite bank."[15] His dilatory performance, and Joseph Hooker's defeat on the Union right flank, allowed Lee to move troops along his interior lines into position to repulse the Union Army's piecemeal attacks.

Finally, late in the day, Burnside's four divisions crossed on the bridge and began their attack on Lee's right, now in peril because of the overwhelming superiority of Burnside's numbers. Then, at the last minute, came A.P. Hill's division, up from Harper's Ferry, on the run and slammed into Burnside's left flank. Burnside called off the attack and retreated back across Antietam Creek. The Battle of Antietam was over.[16]

Burnside's second strike was not long in coming. Literally *forced* by Lincoln to take command of the Army of the Potomac, Burnside reorganized—what else do generals do in the aftermath of a defeat?—and moved on to Fredericksburg. There, in December 1862, he planned to attack across the Rappahannock River and catch Lee unprepared for a decisive victory. The first problem was that it took ten days to get pontoons ready for his army to cross, which gave Lee time to mass his army along Marye's Heights, an escarpment tailor-made for defense. The second problem was that his troops—Burnside had 117,000 men opposing Lee's 72,000—after taking fire all day from Confederate sharpshooters in the town, finally drove the Confederate troops out and spent the night looting, drinking, singing and fighting—each other. Burnside's subordinates told him that an attack up Marye's Heights would be a slaughter, but he persisted, and he sent his men into the Fredericksburg abattoir, where in a day they suffered twelve thousand to thirteen thousand casualties. Following the catastrophe at Fredericksburg on December 13, 1862, Burnside hatched another plan to get at Lee. In January 1863, he undertook what would sadly be termed the "Mud March" toward the Rappahannock River in which his army became bogged down to its knees, and axles, and its mules up to their undersides. Burnside again used whiskey to incentivize his men. A brigade, however, got drunk, and once again fights broke out. The "Mud March" boondoggle precipitated a revolt among Burnside's generals, and Lincoln removed him from command.[17]

With three strikes against him, Burnside was not done. He rendered able service to Grant in eastern Tennessee, squaring off successfully with James Longstreet's army around Knoxville.[18] The denouement of Burnside's Civil War career came on July 30, 1864, when he took his fourth strike at the infamous "Battle of the Crater," in which he hatched a plan to send Pennsylvania miners beneath the Confederate lines to set off a large charge of explosives, open a gap in their lines and pour through it with federal troops, including a division of African Americans. Grant and Burnside's immediate superior, George Meade, opposed the plan, as did Grant, but in the end, much to their subsequent chagrin, went along with it.

The story is well-known. The explosives indeed created a gap in the Confederate lines. The problem was that the Confederates quickly closed the gap, and the explosion created a large "crater" in front of their lines, into which two divisions of Union soldiers rushed, only to be shot like ducks in a barrel. A number were captured and marched through Petersburg and Richmond. It was a disaster of the first magnitude—Burnside lost four thousand men—after which Burnside left and went home to Rhode Island, where he was when a court of inquiry firmly affixed blame to him. It was his fourth strike, and he was done. Burnside resigned from the army on April 15, 1865.[19]

Postwar

Drawing on his West Point engineering background and his prominence as a Civil War general, Burnside moved rapidly to enter the business world. Stockholders in the Illinois Central Railroad elected him a director, and that same year, 1865, he became president of the Cincinnati and Martinsville Railroad. In addition, the Rhode Island Republican Party selected him as a candidate for governor in April 1866, and he ran and won; however, he said that the position required little time, so he remained active in the business world, serving as president of both the Cincinnati Railroad and the Locomotive Works in Providence. In addition, he became president of the Indianapolis and Vincennes Railroad, and a director of the Narragansett Steamship Company. In the spring of 1868 he was named president of the Vincennes and Cairo Railroad.

Burnside went to London to solicit bonds for the Vincennes Railroad and was there when the Franco-Prussian War broke out. From London he went to Paris as a guest of the King of Prussia, and met Otto von Bismarck, the Kaiser's chancellor, in the Prussian lines outside Paris where they had laid siege to the city. Crossing the lines, Burnside entered Paris, where Grant's old friend Elihu Washburne was the U.S. minister. With French leaders, Burnside discussed a truce; however, the French proffered a nonstarter: the retention by France of the provinces of Alsace and Lorraine. The Prussians were not buying that. They had already annexed those provinces, so the siege dragged on.

Burnside encountered his fellow Union general Philip Sheridan while visiting with Bismarck, and after the failed negotiation in Paris, Sheridan accompanied Burnside back to London, and then Burnside returned home. In 1873 he attended a reunion of the Ninth Army Corps in New Haven, Connecticut. The next year, he was nominated to be a candidate for the United States Senate, and he won. That summer, he attended another reunion in Knoxville, where he had successfully led Union forces against James Longstreet's corps in the fall and winter of 1863–1864. Burnside remained active in Civil War veterans organizations and chaired the committee to erect a Civil War Memorial in Providence. A group of his old comrades from the Ninth Corps met with him in New York and formed the "Society of the Burnside Expedition and the Ninth Army Corps."

He and his wife acquired a farm near Bristol, which he named "Edghill Farm," the name taken from his father's first name and his great-grandfather's last. On March 5, 1875, he took his seat as a United States senator and was appointed to the Committees of Military Affairs, Commerce and Education, and Labor. On May 29, 1875, he visited Antietam, and in August of that year, President Grant visited him at Edghill Farm for two days. On the second day, Burnside hosted an informal clambake in Grant's honor.

Death entered Edghill when Burnside's wife died on March 9, 1876. Still, while mourning her loss, Burnside returned to Washington, where he became a member of the "High Court of Impeachment" hearing the impeachment case of former Union general William Belknap, who had most recently been Grant's secretary of war. Burnside became chairman of the Committee of Education and Labor and moved up to second on the Military Affairs Committee. He "kept house" in Washington, where, in spite of his sorrow at the loss of his wife, Burnside entertained friends and maintained "colored servants."

Democrats, who had already taken control of the House, seized control of the Senate, as well, and Burnside lost his chairmanship of the Committee on Military Affairs. The third session of the forty-sixth Congress began December 6, 1880, and the next year, President James Garfield—a former U.S. general—was assassinated, which caused Burnside to wonder how a man could survive the Civil War and then die at the hands of an assassin.

On September 13, 1881, Burnside died of a heart attack at Edghill Farm with only his servant, Robert Holloway, and his physician, a Dr. Barnes, present. Three days later, after a funeral service at the First Congregational Church in Providence, he was buried at Swan Point Cemetery. Members of the Grand Army of the Republic escorted his casket from the church to Swan Point Cemetery.[20]

Because of the four strikes against him—Burnside's Bridge, Fredericksburg, the Mud March and the Crater—his military record is tarnished, at best. His lasting legacy, therefore, was to give the English language the word "sideburn," based upon the magnificent muttonchops that he wore throughout his life. Thus, during the war, subordinates took his name, reversed it and produced the term "sideburn," which is still with us today.

George Armstrong Custer

"Autie," "Fanny," "Curly"

George Armstrong Custer (May 1865).

George Armstrong Custer was born in Ohio on December 5, 1839, and through the good auspices of a girlfriend's father who wanted him gone, received an appointment to West Point, which he entered in 1857. Prior to West Point he had taught school in Ohio, and at West Point he finished last in his class and faced expulsion each year because of excessive demerits. Indeed, he was under detention at the time of his graduation. It was thus an ignominious beginning to what would be, at times, a spectacular army career that would also end in spectacular fashion. Upon graduation, Custer received orders to the Second U.S. Cavalry.[21]

Unlike many of his senior officers, Custer had missed the Mexican War primer to the Civil War and the Indian Wars out west. He thus entered the Civil War without any combat experience. After joining the Army of the Potomac immediately after graduation from West Point, Custer quickly garnered that experience at First Bull Run, where he rode into battle for the first of many times. Subsequently he served in staff positions before a sudden promotion from first lieutenant to brigadier general on June 28, 1863. That meteoric rise made him the youngest—at twenty-three—general in the Union Army. His command was the Michigan Cavalry Brigade, the "Wolverines," which would, under Custer's leadership, distinguish itself at Gettysburg, where Custer led wild charges against the Confederate troopers of Major General J.E.B. Stuart and subsequently led the charge of a regiment against two Confederate brigades that saved the Union right flank.

Custer fought on through the post–Gettysburg summer and the autumn of 1863, and his reputation as an outstanding cavalryman grew. His preference was for saber charges, but he also developed "mounted infantry," who would ride into battle, dismount and then fight as infantry, similar to what Confederate general Nathan Bedford Forrest was doing in the Deep South.[22] Like Forrest, Custer led most every charge himself, and his Michigan cavalrymen loved him for it. "As one Wolverine wrote: 'For all that this Brigade has accomplished all praise is due to General Custer. So brave a man I never saw, and [he is] as competent as brave. Under him a man is ashamed to be cowardly. Under him our men can achieve wonders.'"[23]

Major General Philip H. Sheridan took command of the Army of the Potomac's cavalry, and Custer continued to polish his image as a dashing cavalry leader. He fought alongside Sheridan at Yellow Tavern, and his charge there resulted in the death of J.E.B. Stuart, a staggering loss for the Confederacy. Custer then followed Sheridan into the Shenandoah Valley and fought well throughout that devastatingly effective campaign. For his actions in the Shenandoah, Sheridan promoted Custer to major general and gave him command of the Third Cavalry Division. Then, with the destruction of Jubal A. Early's army, Custer returned as a major general with Sheridan to Grant's Army of the Potomac and fought well at Petersburg, where, at Five Forks, he turned the Confederate right flank in the battle that portended the end for Lee's Army of Northern Virginia. Custer's division was instrumental in the crushing defeat of a portion of Lee's army at Sayler's Creek, and he led his division around Lee's retreating army and cut him off at Appomattox Courthouse.[24] It was here that one of famous episodes of what was to be the last Virginia campaign occurred.

Custer, under cover of a white flag, crossed the Confederate lines and, led by an old West Point friend, Major William H. Gibbes, rode up to the Army of Northern Virginia headquarters, where Confederate lieutenant general James Longstreet sat, leaning against a tree. "In the name of General Sheridan I demand the unconditional surrender of this army," Custer exclaimed excitedly. Longstreet replied: "I am not the commander of this army, and if I were, would not surrender it to General Sheridan." Custer repeated his demand and was "visibly irritated." Longstreet shot back this time that the Army of Northern Virginia "was not whipped and that if Custer was not satisfied, he could attack." Longstreet then ordered Custer to get out of the camp and cross back through the Confederate lines. Custer, worried for his safety, asked for a guide, and the same West Point friend, Gibbes, led him through the line, chastened and somewhat embarrassed. A Confederate officer who was present for the colloquy would later write, "If I ever saw a man with his tail between his legs, it was Custer."[25]

After the surrender at the McLean house, Sheridan bought the table—reportedly for twenty dollars—upon which Grant had written the terms of surrender and gave it to Custer for his wife, Libbie. For the young major general, the war was over, and with it would go his brevet major general's rank. He became a lieutenant colonel in the newly formed Seventh Cavalry—a regiment at Fort Riley, Kansas, as opposed to the division he had commanded as a major general. The Seventh was a cavalry unit that would forever live in the collective memory of most Americans, for all the wrong reasons. It was an amalgam of disparate elements at both the command and the enlisted levels. One of its captains was Frederick W. Benteen, who hated Custer and was said to possess "a backbone of steel … and a soul of vinegar." Benteen thought that Custer was "a boisterous braggart." As a Custer hater, he would be prominent in Custer's life—and in the end of that life—fomenting difficulties for his commander all along the way.[26] Tom Custer, Autie's brother, was a lieutenant in the regiment, as were Captains Miles Keough and Robert M. West, who would serve with Custer until the end. There were others, but one lieutenant—Thomas B. Weir—would give rise to one of Custer's less admirable deeds.

His postwar career as an Indian fighter was marred by at least two incidents along the way. First was his court-martial for desertion when he left his command without permission on the Kansas plains and traveled far to the east to Fort Riley, where his wife, Libbie, was and was rumored to be having an affair with the handsome bachelor Weir. The source of the report was an alleged anonymous letter from Benteen. The trip and the abandonment of Custer's command caused Lieutenant General U.S. Grant, then general-in-chief of the army, to order a general court-martial for Custer at Fort Leavenworth. A second charge arose out of Custer's conduct in overmarching his men and the third arose out of his alleged neglect of duty by abandoning a group of his men who had been attacked by Indians and by not recovering and burying the bodies of two troopers who had been killed in a firefight with the Indians. Finally, "Captain Robert West of the Seventh filed a charge that accused Custer of ordering that deserters 'be shot down' without trial and of denying the wounded men medical treatment," a charge that arose out of Custer's orders not to treat three deserters who had been wounded in a fight with Custer's troopers.[27] What was not charged, but could have been, were the punishment of shaving troopers' heads for minor infractions and threatening to have them flogged, a punishment long since relegated to the dustbin of punitive actions authorized for use by army commanders.

The court-martial took place at Fort Leavenworth and lasted almost a month. The court found Custer guilty of the three charges and suspended him without pay for a year. Custer was, of course, dismayed and criticized the court publicly, which did nothing to endear him with his superior officers, especially Grant. He and Libbie returned to Michigan, where he would serve his suspension.[28]

Subsequently, Sheridan took command of the Department of the Missouri, which encompassed most of the country between the Mississippi and the Rocky Mountains, and, as the Indian Wars heated up, requested Grant to return Custer to duty, which Grant did, reluctantly, although not pardoning him.[29] Custer immediately returned to command and quickly attacked a Cheyenne village along the Washita River, destroying it and many of its inhabitants, including women and children.[30] And while the attack engendered praise in the West, in the East it was highly controversial. Custer then, at Sheridan's direction, employed the Shenandoah Valley winter warfare tactics on the Plains Indians in 1867–1868. Back at Leavenworth, a rumor circulated that Custer had taken an Indian princess as his mistress and fathered a son named Yellow Swallow or Yellow Tail by her. The controversial charge is the subject of much speculation among historians, but the consensus view now is that Autie's brother Tom Custer was Yellow Tail's father.[31]

At this point in his life, a female friend described "him as a man of about 165 pounds, with 'no spare flesh, well-knit— strong muscles lean & lithe.'" She thought that he appeared in photographs to be "much older looking" during the Civil War than when she knew him in the 1870s. "His eyes were a piercing blue; keen, thoughtful, observant & very quick in glancing at any object & sizing it up." His hair was "a real gold in color," and his fair complexion had been "bronzed by outdoors life." When he spoke, his voice was "pleasant in tone but quick and energetic with sometimes a slight hesitation as if words rolled out rapidly but not fast enough for the thought which preceded them. A nervous forceful manner in speaking." She also said, "all his motions were rapid—he ate rapidly & etc."[32]

The Indian Wars continued as the Grant administration sought some resolution to the Indian "problem," which, as noted earlier, was engendered by the greed of the white man in encroaching upon Indian Territory, and the stated policy of the federal government to move the Indians onto reservations and, in Grant's words, "Christianize" them. Custer was the point man in most of these western wars and the battles that comprised them. "Indeed, it was his expedition to the Black Hills that precipitated the great Sioux [and Cheyenne] outbreak of 1876."[33]

Now at Fort Hayes, Kansas, Custer sought in 1869 command of the entire Seventh Cavalry, and when he did not get it, he applied to be the commandant at West Point, a position that he also did not get. In the meantime, a small city arose outside Fort Hayes. Known as Hayes City, it was a hotbed of prostitution, gambling, drunkenness, crime and especially violence. Custer cracked down and incarcerated miscreant troopers in a hole twenty feet in diameter and twenty feet deep, covered with a roof of logs. It was at this time that he threatened head shaving and flogging.

Eighteen seventy-six came, and with it an order out of Washington for the Sioux to sell and abandon their sacred homeland in the Black Hills following the discovery of gold there. The Sioux, no slouches at warfare, refused. Then Sheridan ordered General Alfred Terry to undertake a campaign to remove the Sioux. A newspaper correspondent wrote, with little prescience, upon seeing Custer: "Here, there, flitting to and fro, in his quick eager way, taking in everything connected with his command, as well as generally, with the keen incisive manner for which he is so well known. The General [sic] is full of perfect readiness for a fray with the hostile red devils, and woe to the body of scalp-lifters that comes within reach of himself and his brave companions in arms."[34]

Almost as much has been written about June 25, 1876, as has been written about another disaster—the sinking of the *Titanic*—for like that tragedy, at Little Bighorn there were numerous accounts written by survivors, some of them eyewitnesses, and others based upon interviews with a number of Cheyenne and Sioux. The campaign began when Terry contrived the plan for the Northern Plains campaign, splitting his army into four groups: Custer's, who led 647 men of the Seventh Cavalry, with civilians, scouts and guides included in that number; a large unit with infantry commanded by General John A. Gibbon; another led by Terry himself; and the fourth, which would come up from the south, led by General George Crook.

So who were Custer's men? The troopers "wore dark blue flannel blouses and sky-blue kersey pants with the seats and upper legs reinforced with white canvas." They wore hats of gray or brown and were an average of five feet seven in height and 140 pounds in weight. They carried 1873 Springfield carbines and 1872 .45 Colt revolvers in holsters. Approximately one-fifth had no experience in fighting the Indians.[35]

Custer had explicit orders not to proceed toward the Little Bighorn River until he hooked up with Gibbon. On June 25, Custer's scouts, however, found what they believed to be a large encampment of Indians near the Little Bighorn River and so informed their commander. Custer, fearing that the Indians would disperse and run, did not view in advance either the encampment or the terrain around the encampment. Thus, completely blind as to the number of Sioux and Cheyenne encamped there— Custer thought that he was outnumbered only two-to-one—he decided to attack without waiting for Gibbon.

Custer, like Terry but without the general's numbers, divided his unit into three battalions[36] and devised a plan to cut off the fleeing Indians. One unit of 140 men would be led by Marcus Reno. A second, 125 men, would be led by Custer's old adversary Frederick Benteen, and the third, consisting of over 250 men, would be led by Custer himself. So instead of attacking with the 3,000 men of Terry, Crook and Gibbon, the attack would consist of some 500 men, and they would be attacking a village of some 7,000 Indians, although some historians place the number at between 10,000 and 12,000. Regardless, and most importantly, there were at least 2,000 warriors, armed and ready for combat.

Reno attacked first and succeeded only in infuriating the Sioux and Cheyenne, who boiled out of their encampment like hornets, chased him into and then out of a stand of cottonwood trees and, in a rout, up to an escarpment that would subsequently be anointed as Reno's Hill. There, his troops made a stand. Benteen came up, and he and Reno briefly followed Custer, but, seeing the swarm of Indians ahead, quickly returned to Reno's Hill. Custer had in the meantime taken his troops on an enveloping move to the north, where they, now alone, faced the fury of two thousand braves.

Custer stood in the middle of his troops wearing a blue blouse and buckskin pants. He had his hair cut short, and he and his troops made a stand worthy of the brave men they were. In a matter of minutes, however, the battle was over. Custer took a bullet in his head. Another struck him in his rib cage near his heart. Presumably, after his death, his adversaries cut off one of his fingers and stuck an arrow shaft into his penis. Little Bighorn and the loss of 263 men—210 of them in Custer's battalion alone—drove another arrow into his reputation, tarnishing what was otherwise an outstanding Civil War career.

Captain Benteen, who was a subordinate of Major Reno's, took command of the troops on Reno Hill, as Reno himself was mentally incapacitated by the day's action and his troops' harrowing escape. Whatever else Benteen's personality disorders were, he led his troops well as they fought off the Sioux and Cheyenne for twenty-four hours. The Indians left the battlefield late in the day on June 26, and Gibbon arrived on June 27. He advanced to the Little Bighorn, where his men choked in horror at the sight of their slaughtered, mutilated cavalry brothers. When they found Custer,

Benteen growled: "There he is, God damn him, he will never fight any-more."[37] They buried the dead there, but a year later, at Libbie's request and in accordance with Custer's wishes, the army exhumed what they believed to be his body and moved it to West Point, where it remains to this day.

Sheridan, in Philadelphia with Sherman for the Centennial Exposition, did not receive word of the massacre until July 4. At first, Sheridan refused to believe the reports, but he soon realized that the worst had happened, and that Custer, twenty officers and 263 men—out of his entire command—had been lost to the Sioux. Like Pickett's Charge, however, the Seventh Cavalry and the Battle of Little Bighorn would forever be immortal. Of the battle and Custer, Sheridan wrote, "Poor Custer, he was the embodiment of gallantry.... But I was always fearful that he would catch it if allowed a separate command.... He was too impetuous, without deliberation; he thought himself invincible and leading a charmed life. When I think of the many brave fellows who went down with him that day, it is sickening."[38] And it was. Grant, now at the end of his presidency, also addressed the disaster: "I regard Custer's massacre as a sacrifice of troops, brought on by Custer himself that was wholly unnecessary—wholly unnecessary."[39]

Libbie lived until 1933, a day short of her ninety-first birthday, wrote three books about the cavalry on the plains and maintained homes in New York City and Florida, where she spent the winter months. When Libbie died, she left an estate of some $100,000. President Theodore Roosevelt wrote to her that "Your husband is one of my heroes as you so well know." And she did know Autie as a hero.

But there was more to Custer than his "Last Stand." Thus, historian Jeffrey D. Wert wrote:

> He has perhaps been denied greatness, but not immortality. It came to him on a day in the Moon of the Ripe Juneberries on a nondescript hill in Montana. But the winds that fill the coulees and ravines and lap over the ridges along the Little Big Horn River eventually blow east to Gettysburg, Haw's Shop, Trevilian Station, Winchester, Cedar Creek, Waynesborough, and Appomattox. It is in all of those places, the hallowed grounds of Montana, but also of Pennsylvania and of Virginia, that the measure of George Armstrong Custer must be taken.[40]

George Henry Thomas

"Old Slow Trot," "Pap," "The Rock of Chickamauga," "Old Reliable," "The Hammer or the Sledge of Nashville"

George Henry Thomas was a native Virginian, born there in 1816. He attended West Point, graduating in 1840, twelfth in his class out of forty-two, behind his friend William Tecumseh Sherman, who finished sixth. He served in the Second Seminole War and, subsequently, in the Mexican War, where he performed with distinction and received three brevet promotions to major. After the Mexican War he returned to West Point as a tactics instructor[41] and then served in the famous Second Cavalry, which comprised an all-star lineup of future Confederate generals: Albert Sidney Johnston, Robert E. Lee, William J. Hardee, Earl Van Dorn, Kirby Smith, John Bell Hood, Fitzhugh Lee and J.E.B. Stuart.[42]

George Henry Thomas (1861–1865).

In a patrol against the Indians, Thomas received a serious wound. An arrow passed through his chin and lodged in his chest. It was a painful injury, but it was not particularly debilitating. A more serious injury occurred when he fell into a deep ravine while getting off a train in Virginia. He spent the better part of a year rehabilitating from the fall.[43]

As the war approached, Thomas decided to remain loyal to the United States, alienating his family—especially his two sisters, Judith and Fanny—and his two brothers.[44] His friends in Virginia regarded him as a traitor, and some of his comrades in the Union Army doubted his loyalty. At the outbreak of hostilities, Thomas received a promotion to lieutenant colonel and soon to brigadier general,[45] when he was sent west. There he would spend the remainder of the war. Subsequently, he assumed command of a five-brigade division in the Army of the Cumberland, then commanded by Don Carlos Buell.[46]

A master of detail and able to rely upon an efficient staff, Thomas always saw to it that his men were well-trained, well-led, well-fed and well-armed. He served on the front lines and thus always knew what was happening, where and when, which gave him a significant advantage over back-benchers like William Rosecrans, whose failure at Chickamauga resulted, at least in part, from his failure to command from the front lines. At that battle, after Rosecrans and his staff fled in the face of a savage attack by Longstreet and John Bell Hood, Thomas formed a defensive position on Horseshoe Ridge with two-fifths of Rosecrans's army and saved the other three-fifths of Rosecrans's army, which was in rapid retreat, as well as Thomas's own force. His stand on Horseshoe Ridge earned him the title of the "Rock of Chickamauga." Grant then took command of the western theater and gave Thomas command of the Army of Tennessee. Thomas held Chattanooga against the besieging Confederates, opened up a supply line and led the successful—against all odds—assault on the Confederate positions at Missionary Ridge. He emerged a hero.[47]

As commander of the Army of the Cumberland, Thomas now served under his old friend Sherman, and together, the two fought though Georgia. But Sherman criticized Thomas for being "slow" in his advance on Atlanta, and Thomas counseled against Sherman's foolhardy frontal assault at Kennesaw Mountain, which was later taken by a flanking maneuver, thus demonstrating that the massive Union losses at Kennesaw Mountain had been for naught and that Thomas had been correct in his advice to Sherman.[48]

Sherman dispatched Thomas and his army to Tennessee to deal with John Bell Hood, who had evacuated Atlanta and headed north to draw Sherman away. Sherman embarked on his "March to the Sea," and two of Thomas's corps under John Schofield mauled Hood at Franklin. Then, after a major delay that prompted criticism both in Washington and from Grant, Thomas finished Hood off at Nashville, where he was anointed the "Sledge of Nashville." But Grant again criticized Thomas for failing to pursue Hood's defeated army expeditiously as it headed south.[49] Nevertheless, Thomas received a promotion to major general in the regular army in recognition of his performance at Nashville, but for him, combat was effectively over. He remained in Tennessee for the rest of the war.[50]

Postwar

With the war over, performance appraisals of Union generals began to appear in newspapers, magazines and in speeches. Although Thomas would not appraise others, he was the subject of appraisals *from* others. Generals Oliver O. Howard and Willard Warner compared him to George Washington, and Howard thought him greater than Lee and Jackson. Others thought he was *the* outstanding general of the war, a man who had never lost a battle. General, and future president, James A. Garfield praised "the gravity and dignity of his character, the solidity of his judgment, the careful accuracy of all his transactions, his incorruptible integrity, and his extreme but unaffected modesty." Garfield thought him equal in ability to Washington, Zachary "Old Rough and Ready" Taylor and the Duke of Wellington.[51]

There were six major generals in the Union Army at the close of the war, and alone among them, Thomas did not receive appointment to head a military department, but instead received a division within a department. He was stunned. Upon reconsideration at Thomas's request, President Andrew Johnson modified the divisions to give Thomas Kentucky, Tennessee, Mississippi, Alabama and Georgia. His focus was on Black emancipation and fairness to the freed slaves, victims of an institution that he, as a Virginian, hated. Nevertheless, he believed that the legacy of slavery could not be corrected overnight. He therefore focused on "giving blacks the true dignity in practice they deserved," rather than focusing upon revenge on the white man.[52]

In 1867, there came a political opportunity: friends and supporters made an effort to draft Thomas as a Democratic Party candidate for president. He refused, stating that he was a soldier and not a politician. He said, "As a politician I would be lost. No, sir.... I want to die with a fair record, and this I will do if I can keep out of the sea of politics." In 1868, President Johnson attempted to use Thomas in a gambit to make him a lieutenant general with seniority over Grant, whom Johnson accurately saw as a future opponent for president. Thomas saw through the ruse and refused to be used as a pawn to humiliate Grant.[53]

After Grant's election in 1868, he sent Thomas to the Military Division of the Pacific in 1869 to replace Halleck.[54] Lukewarm on the move, Thomas, ever the good soldier, complied with Grant's orders and headed west for San Francisco with his wife and her sister, who was part of his household. Soon after his arrival, he embarked on a tour of his territories, including Arizona, Nevada, Southern California, Idaho, the Washington Territory and the coastal area of Alaska, where he was shocked by the random killing for entertainment of seals, otters and other animals by soldiers. He also warned presciently that a gold rush would come and that it would destroy the native Aleuts and their culture. Thomas was, unfortunately, correct.

On March 12, 1870, Thomas read an anonymous letter in the *New York Tribune* in which the writer posited that credit for the success of the Nashville campaign should be accorded to John M. Schofield and not Thomas. Moreover, the writer argued that Thomas was slow in pursuing John Bell Hood after the Battle of Nashville. A second letter, however, defended Thomas, who then began his own response to the first, denigrating letter. Later, in 1885, Grant in his *Memoirs* would also write that Thomas was "slow," reprising his earlier criticism, but Thomas would not be around to refute that charge.

While drafting his reply, a blood vessel burst near Thomas's brain, and he suffered a massive stroke. They laid him on a couch outside his office, and his wife and sister-in-law came. His wife leaned down to him, and he whispered something to her. Then he died.[55]

Sherman, now general-in-chief of the army, announced Thomas's death the next day, writing of his old friend whom he had known since West Point days when Thomas had protected him from hazing upperclassmen:

> In battle he never wavered, and never sought advancement of rank or honor at the expense of any one. Whatever he earned of these were his own, and no one disputes his fame. He was ... the very impersonation of honesty, integrity, and honor ... the *beau ideal* of the soldier and gentleman.[56]

They buried him out of St. Paul's Episcopal Church in Troy, New York, his wife's home, in Oak Wood Cemetery, on April 7, 1870. President Grant and Generals Sherman, Sheridan, Meade, Rosecrans, Schofield and Hooker were in attendance.[57] None of Thomas's family attended the funeral. There is some dispute about his Virginia sisters' position with respect to his interment. One account holds that they stated that for them, Thomas died when he joined the Union Army at the outset of the war and that they had then turned his picture to face the wall. Another source, however, contends that his sisters did not turn his picture to face the wall and, while they did not attend his funeral, they had not emotionally disowned him.[58]

His former comrades in the Army of the Cumberland placed an equestrian statue of him on what became Thomas Circle in Washington, D.C. For the dedication, Joseph Hooker wrote from his deathbed that Thomas was "'the most gifted soldier' America had ever known."[59] George McClellan wrote, praising Thomas, for "the magnificent self-possession with which [Thomas] disregarded the attempts of men ignorant of the circumstances, or incapable of appreciating them, to force him to give battle prematurely; but waited till 'the proper moment arrived.'" Sherman spoke of Thomas's "noble qualities," qualities that Sherman, Grant, Schofield and others did not themselves demonstrate in their snarky treatment of Thomas in their memoirs and in their correspondence, which had run on behind his back. Indeed, Grant, in his memoirs, wrote: "Thomas' dispositions were deliberately made and always good. He was not as good, however, in pursuit as in action. I do not believe he could ever have conducted Sherman's army from Chattanooga to Atlanta against the defense and the commander [Joseph Johnston] guarding that line in 1864,"[60]

To this day, the reviews of Thomas's wartime service remain mixed. Many historians are persuaded by the opinions of Grant, Sherman, Schofield, et al., that he was "slow."[61] Others, however, like Bruce Catton, argued that "Thomas was perhaps 'the best [general] of them all,'" and that "there was nothing slow about Thomas ... or primarily defensive.... Grant was wrong." Above all the controversy, however, remains Thomas's true legacy: he never lost a battle, and he was the Rock of Chickamauga and the Sledge of Nashville.[62] Nothing anyone has said about him can take that away.

George Crook

"Uncle George"

Born near Dayton, Ohio, in 1828, George Crook was the ninth of ten children. He grew up in a farm family, and his father, a prominent Whig, secured an appointment to West Point for George. At this point in time, he was described as "health good, body perfect, height five feet eight inches, and a good English scholar."[63] He entered there in 1852 and, a mediocre student, graduated in 1856, thirty-eighth out of forty-three. That class would furnish both sides many officers, including generals, in a war to come. Upon graduation from West Point, Crook received orders to the West Coast, where he participated in Indian Wars in Northern California, Oregon and Washington. He received an arrow wound in one of those engagements.[64]

Upon the outbreak of the Civil War, Crook returned east and took command of an Ohio regiment and, as did George McClellan, fought successfully in what was to become West Virginia. Subsequently he saw combat at South Mountain during Robert E. Lee's Maryland campaign and then at Antietam, where his brigade was involved in the fighting around "Burnside's Bridge."[65]

Crook fought at Chickamauga, where he covered General William S. Rosecrans's ignominious retreat into Chattanooga.[66] Then came ignominy to Crook: back in West Virginia he was captured in his hotel bed by a band of Confederate guerrillas who held him until he was exchanged two months later.[67] Humiliated, Crook lost his command and after briefly sitting out the war, joined Sheridan for his savage campaign in the Shenandoah Valley. There, Crook devised the strategy

George Crook (1870–1880).

that won the Battle of Fisher's Hill, but Sheridan, ever the egotist, stole that
credit from him, engendering a bitterness that would haunt the two men's
relationship for the rest of Crook's life. It was of Sheridan's grab for credit
at Cedar Creek that Crook said of Little Phil: the "adulations heaped on
him by a grateful nation for his supposed genius turned his head, which,
added to his natural disposition, caused him to bloat his little carcass with
debauchery and dissipation, which carried him off prematurely."[68] At the
end of the war Crook had command of the Army of the Potomac's cavalry and fought successfully at the battles leading up to Lee's surrender at
Appomattox.[69]

   With the war over, Crook remained in the army, first doing Reconstruction duty in North Carolina. He married Mary Dailey, the daughter of the hotel owner in whose hotel Crook had been captured. Crook
left Mary behind—the first of many times that he would do so—when
he received orders to the Oregon territory.[70] There, he employed unusual
practices in dealing with the Indians, using "friendly" Indians to help fight
their "unfriendly" brethren.[71]

   Crook enjoyed "striking success" in the Northwest, and then received
orders to serve on what was known in the army as a "benzene board,"
named for a cleaning agent. The purpose of the board was to reduce the
size of the army's officer corps concomitant with the force reductions
among enlisted personnel taking place throughout the country.[72]

   After his benzine board service in San Francisco, Crook received
orders to take command of the Arizona territory and there to get the
Apaches under control. In Arizona, he innovated and used pack mules
instead of wagons to pursue the Apaches. Successful, Crook received a
promotion to brigadier general and moved in 1873 to the High Plains,
where the Sioux were fighting tenaciously to preserve their Black Hills
territory.[73]

   In the Sioux War of 1876, Crook participated in General Alfred Terry's campaign against the Sioux in Wyoming and Montana. His mission was to bring up troops from the south and then combine his troops
with those of George Armstrong Custer and General John A. Gibbon in
an attack on a large Sioux encampment. Crook's force encountered Sioux
at Rosebud Creek in June, 1876, and, after that battle—a tactical victory
that nevertheless bloodied the nose of Crook's command—instead of continuing north to join Custer, Crook turned back. This highly controversial
move was a major contributing factor in Custer's defeat at Little Bighorn,
and it seriously damaged Crook's reputation.[74]

   Crook's views on the Indian problem softened, and he began advo-
cating a program of paternalistic treatment to bring them into the white
man's world. This policy engendered support for him in the East and

enhanced his reputation as a reformer with respect to the administration's Indian policy, but he was a rare individual in the West and not a popular one. Subsequently, in 1882, Crook returned to Arizona, where Geronimo's raids were causing havoc among the settlers. Crook's efforts in dealing fairly with the Apaches were unsuccessful, and he left Arizona bitter about the lack of support he had received from the army and the administration.[75]

In 1889, Crook visited in Lynchburg, Virginia, his old adversary from the Shenandoah Valley campaign, Jubal A. Early. He found Early an unreconstructed rebel, a proponent of the "Lost Cause" catechism, and a man willing to sit up late into the night and have a drink with a former enemy. Amused by Early's apocryphal tales of the war, Crook left Lynchburg amazed that "Lee's bad old man" could be so firmly embedded in the past.[76]

Crook remained until his death, however, an unabashed campaigner for human rights for the Indians, serving as commander of the Division of the Missouri until his death on March 21, 1890, in Chicago. He is interred in Oakland, Maryland, where his wife lived.[77]

Henry Wager Halleck

"Old Brains," "Old Wooden Head"

Henry Wager Halleck, another of the controversial generals on both sides of the conflict, was a native New Yorker from the lush lands of the Mohawk Valley. The first of thirteen children, his father expected him to farm. Henry, however, had other ideas and ran away from home when he was sixteen. His Wager grandfather intervened and sent Henry off to a private academy, then on to Union College where he was selected for Phi Beta Kappa but, in a portent of things to come, alienated his classmates with his contentious, abrasive personality.[78]

Henry Wager Halleck (1861).

From Union College, young Halleck matriculated at West Point in 1835. He was a quick study—the function of a very quick mind—which led one of his instructors to have Halleck teach tactics while still a student. He graduated in the class of 1839, third in his class, and taught French at the Academy for a year. The army then sent him to France to study military tactics, the result of that trip appearing in the form of a book, the first of a number that he would write.[79]

With the advent of the Mexican War in 1846, Halleck headed west by ship for California. There, with little to do, he studied Mexican and American law and eventually resigned from the army to start a law firm in San Francisco. This venture made him a wealthy man, and he was there when the Civil War started. Still famous for his book on tactics, Halleck received an immediate appointment as a major general and returned to the Midwest, where he took command of the Department of Missouri, which was in shambles due to the ineptitude of Halleck's predecessor, John C. Fremont. Halleck quickly imposed organization and discipline on his troops and trained them in the art of warfare. He planned and then oversaw Union victories under Grant and John Pope that opened the Mississippi River down to Vicksburg. Following Grant's near disaster at Shiloh, Halleck took command of Grant's army, while refusing to cashier him, and advanced ponderously from Shiloh to the Confederate railhead at Corinth. That desultory performance allowed P.G.T. Beauregard to escape and led Lincoln to bring Halleck east to Washington as general-in-chief of the army to help develop overall strategy instead of exercising field command.[80]

For the remainder of the war, Halleck did just that, although reviews on his performance are mixed. His personality, his bug-eyed looks and his inability to exercise command over his subordinates led most historians and the contemporary press to pan his performance. Lincoln came to regard him as a "clerk." Stanton saw him as "probably the greatest scoundrel and most bare-faced villain in America." George McClellan said of Halleck that he was "the most hopelessly stupid of all men in high position." Navy Secretary Gideon Welles wrote in his diary that Halleck "originates nothing, anticipates nothing ... takes no responsibility, plans nothing, suggests nothing, is good for nothing."[81] In recent years, however, revisionist historians have given him more credit for formulating the multifront strategy that brought the Confederacy to its knees.

Postwar

On April 16, 1865, Halleck received orders to report to Richmond, which lay smoldering in ruins and chaos.[82] His assignment was to restore order to the city and surrounding countryside and to facilitate the transition of Blacks from slavery to freedmen. In the latter regard, Halleck was somewhat of a conservative and did not feel the necessity to trample on the defeated Virginians, whom he saw as completely subjugated. Rather, he thought that his role was to assimilate them back into the Union, but despite this attitude, white Virginians were skeptical of his role in Richmond. Blacks were also skeptical, based on his performance early in the war in St. Louis, where he had prohibited fugitive slaves from entering army camps.[83]

Nevertheless, Halleck turned out to be a tonic for whites, treating them with courtesy and sympathy. He favored "gentle treatment" for former Confederate officers, speaking specifically of Robert E. Lee.[84] He also had the all–Black XXV Corps transferred away from Richmond, and he maintained Black freedmen in the subservient position they had occupied during slavery. He sought to install an economic system on this basis. "The army arrested thousands of rural blacks who came into Richmond looking for work, incarcerated them in the old slave pens, and then took them back to the plantations to labor."[85] He also sought, unsuccessfully, lenient treatment for the imprisoned Jefferson Davis. White Virginians were elated.

Finally, having had enough of Halleck, Blacks banded together and wrote to the *New York Tribune* of their shoddy treatment under Halleck's heavy hand. After only a few months in Richmond, Halleck received orders to take command of the Military Division of the Pacific, with his headquarters in San Francisco, where he had happily served before the war. He arrived there August 25, 1865, to find a prosperous city that had grown since his previous tour there and was unscathed by the war. Old Brains replaced General Irvin McDowell there, and his duties were purely administrative, work at which he excelled and that he enjoyed.

Unlike Grant and others, Halleck's attitude toward the Indians was not positive. He, in particular, loathed the troublesome Apaches, and he also loathed the corrupt Indian agents, who cheated the Indians and thus fomented "depredations" upon white settlers, which, in turn, led to harsh reprisals by U.S. troops. In 1867, Seward purchased Alaska from the Russians. Halleck read everything he could find about Alaska, but he did not, as his successor George H. Thomas would, visit the new territory. His territory was enormous: Alaska, Oregon, Washington, California, Nevada and Arizona, about a third of the United States. He commanded seven regiments and a large number of forts throughout the region, each usually manned by a company.

Halleck was plagued by health problems—facial neuralgia, sciatic nerve issues, lumbar disc disease, liver disease, heart disease and depression—but between those problems and his work, he had time to write a treatise on international law that Lippincott and Company of Philadelphia published in 1866. He and his wife, Elizabeth—the granddaughter of Alexander Hamilton[86]—enjoyed a highly active social life in San Francisco, although Halleck was ill at ease at social functions. Nevertheless, San Francisco gave Halleck time to spend with Elizabeth, and for the two of them, the city was good for and to them.[87]

In 1869, Halleck received orders to take command of the Department of the South, headquartered in Louisville, Kentucky, which he did on June 13.[88] That department included the states of Kentucky, Tennessee, West Virginia, Arkansas, Louisiana, Mississippi, Alabama, Georgia, Florida and the two Carolinas. By the next year, all of those states had been readmitted to the Union even though whites employed economic coercion and violence against Blacks. Consistent with his prior performance in Richmond, Halleck rejected all requests for action against whites, and remained an "armchair commander," unmoved by actual conditions on the ground within his department.[89]

The end came suddenly. "Around November 1, 1871, he had a hemorrhage in his bowels, together with what one reporter called 'dropsical symptoms.' He grew increasingly weaker, but in early January, 1872, seemed to rally, only to fall into a twenty-four-hour coma on January 8." He died on January 9, 1872, in Louisville.

Halleck was buried in Brooklyn, New York, and his interment drew little interest there. Indeed, the New York newspapers completely ignored his funeral. "A California newspaper mused that he was a cold, reserved man, not likely to win much affection except from intimate associates."[90] Halleck left Elizabeth well-off. The value of his estate was almost $431,000, an enormous sum that would be worth almost $10 million today. Elizabeth, only forty-one years old—seventeen years younger than Halleck—remarried in 1875 George W. Collum, sixty-six years old and twenty years older than she. Elizabeth apparently liked older men. She died in 1884 of cancer and is buried with Halleck.

So what, then, is Halleck's legacy? There is not much. He was a weak field commander, and as adviser to Lincoln—whom he saw as a military meddler and "bungler"—the reviews are mixed, at best. He had difficulty with interpersonal relations, difficulty in giving commands to his putative subordinate commanders, and myriad health and emotional issues that plagued him all of his life. His title "Old Wooden Head" is likely more apropos than the more complimentary "Old Brains." Uncelebrated during his life and at his death, he remains so today, for Henry Wager Halleck's melancholy life left behind an equally lugubrious legacy.

Irvin Mcdowell

"The Forgotten General," "The Hard Luck General"

Irvin McDowell was born in Columbus, Ohio, in 1818. He received his early education at the College of Troyes in France, where his family was living. McDowell entered West Point in 1834 at age sixteen and graduated there in 1838, finishing twenty-third in a class of forty-five. He received orders to the artillery and served until 1841 in a garrison on the Canadian border. McDowell next was ordered to West Point as an instructor of tactics, a position he held until 1844, when he joined the staff of General John E. Wood in Texas as aide-de-camp. This job posi-

Irvin McDowell (1860–1865).

tioned him for participation in the Mexican War, and he "fought with gallantry" at Buena Vista, which merited him a brevet promotion to captain. Subsequently he received orders to Washington, D.C., in the Adjutant General's department, from which, at the direction of his sponsor, General Winfield Scott, McDowell departed in 1858 for the study in Europe of "military establishments." When the Civil War began, McDowell was a major, having been promoted in 1856.[91]

McDowell would command troops in two Civil War battles, both battles at Bull Run, and both Union disasters. At the first Battle of Bull Run, he commanded a green, untrained and untested army of thirty-five thousand men. He had devised an excellent plan but, unfortunately, his army was unable to execute it. Moreover, to McDowell's detriment, Joseph Johnston escaped a Union Army in the Shenandoah Valley and, traveling by rail, arrived at Bull Run with an army of ten thousand men, thus bringing the number of Confederate troops almost even with McDowell's army, which fought well into the afternoon. Then a Confederate counterattack engineered by General P.G.T. Beauregard, McDowell's classmate, turned a retreat into a Union rout that, blocked by civilians on the road to Washington, engendered confusion among both the army and the onlookers, all mingling together in a race for safety. Many of both groups were captured. Writing six years later, General Sherman posited that the battle was lost not because of the absence of a good plan—he thought McDowell's plan excellent—or poor leadership, but because of the administration's failure to allow McDowell to train his troops, time for which both McDowell and Winfield Scott had begged. McDowell's troops blamed him, however, and many said in the aftermath of the crushing defeat that they would not fight for him again. Lincoln, hearing their cries, promptly relieved McDowell with George McClellan.[92]

The second battle at Bull Run took place about a year later. There, McDowell now commanded a corps, as opposed to an army, which, now christened the Army of Virginia, was under the command of General John Pope. That battle, too, was a Union disaster, and Pope blamed everyone except himself for the ignominious defeat, especially McDowell, whose men called him a "villain, traitor or scoundrel." McDowell demanded a court of inquiry into his performance at Second Bull Run, and that court exonerated him in February 1863.

After the Bull Run debacle, McDowell's Civil War was over, and he headed west to take over military command of the Department of the Pacific, where he saw action against Indians in Arizona and Oregon. That post was followed in 1865 by command of the Department of California. Incredibly, McDowell was promoted to be a regular army major general in November 1876. He served as commander of the Division of the South—where he replaced General George Meade—for four years, then returned to San Francisco to command the Department of the Pacific. He retired six years later in 1882 and lived thereafter in San Francisco, where he was buried after he died on May 4, 1885. Incredibly, his first name on the tombstone is inscribed as "Irwin." The hard luck general could not win, even in the end.[93]

John Pope

"The Miscreant General"

John Pope, the goat of the second battle of Bull Run who would work the rest of his life to redeem himself, got his nickname from no less a Civil War figure than Robert E. Lee.[94] The newly appointed commander of the Army of Northern Virginia assigned that appellation to Pope on the basis of a number of draconian orders applicable to Virginia civilians that Pope issued after he took command of the Union troops in northern Virginia on June 26, 1862. Pope, an arrogant, pompous man, was no more popular with his troops than with Virginia civilians and Lee. When he took command of the Army of Virginia, he told his troops that he was from the

West, where his soldiers were accustomed to seeing their enemies' backs, implying that this was not the case in the East. His officers and men were deeply offended, and Pope, who had the interpersonal skills of a Neanderthal, thus engendered deep resentment and consistent unpopularity among his soldiers.[95]

Pope was born in Louisville, Kentucky, on March 16, 1822, but was raised in Illinois. He was a member of a prominent family—he was collaterally descended from George Washington—and his father was a federal judge in whose court Abraham Lincoln had once practiced. His father and Lincoln had become friends.[96] His uncle was a Kentucky United States senator, and his father was territorial secretary before Illinois became a state. Pope was also connected to Mary Todd Lincoln's family by marriage, which gave him a second connection with Lincoln.[97]

After his father lost most of his money in land speculation, Pope, through his father's political connections, obtained an appointment to West Point, which he entered at age sixteen in 1838. Pope graduated in the storied West Point class of 1842—it produced seventeen general officers in the opposing armies of the great conflict to come[98]—and was first in his class in horsemanship and seventeenth overall out of fifty-six. His classmate James Longstreet, no mean horseman himself, described Pope as "a handsome, dashing fellow, a splendid cavalryman."[99]

John Pope (1860–1865).

Early on Pope established a habit of bolting the chain of command to communicate with superiors, in the beginning to complain about duty assignments that he did not like, and later about strategy, acts that constituted, in the army's eyes, gross insubordination. He did this in connection with his first two assignments until he finally got transferred to Maine, which is where he was when the Mexican War broke out. Pope served well in Mexico and received two brevet promotions. When the war was over, he joined other junior officers in the West, and by 1856, was a captain. Then the Civil War began, and Pope once again jumped the chain of command by writing to Lincoln with advice on how to deal with secession, recommending that Lincoln grant the secessionists no quarter, meaning executing them all.[100] In 1859, he married Clara Horton, the daughter of a congressman from a wealthy Ohio family.

Pope wheedled a brigadier's rank from the governor of Illinois, one of his father's friends, and then captured New Madrid, Missouri, and Island Number Ten in the Mississippi, opening the river to Memphis. He was promoted to major general, and he boasted to newspapers of his success, which he bloated, but the sensational press his boasting engendered led Lincoln to give him command of the Army of Virginia, a newly created entity whose mission was to place itself between Lee and the city of Washington and put pressure on Lee, who was in the process of driving McClellan from the Virginia peninsula.[101]

Lee, however, when he realized that McClellan was withdrawing his army and returning to Washington, wheeled and brought his two corps under Jackson and Longstreet north to take on Pope. Lee split his army and created a classic hammer and anvil situation, with Longstreet hammering Pope up against Jackson's anvil and then the two generals chasing Pope back to Washington.[102] Pope characteristically blamed everyone in his command for the debacle at Second Bull Run, but Lincoln was not buying what Pope was selling, and he relieved Pope and sent him to a backwater command in the northwest. Pope's Civil War participation was effectively over.

Pope's new headquarters, effective September 6, 1863, was in St. Paul, Minnesota, where whites were busy breaking treaties, and the Sioux were busy killing whites. Pope's charge was to defeat the Sioux and force them to return to the land that Minnesota state officials had reserved for them. The people of Minnesota, however, wanted a war of "extermination" to avenge the deaths of white settlers massacred by the Sioux. Under Pope's direction, troops from his command defeated the Sioux on September 26 at Wood Lake. The war against the Sioux continued through the autumn of 1862 into the spring of 1863 and, subsequently, throughout 1864. These campaigns were successful in bringing the Sioux to heel and driving them out of Minnesota and into the Dakotas.

Then followed commands in Fort Leavenworth and, subsequently, in the Pacific Northwest. Pope, however, wanted to return east. Accordingly, he applied and lobbied for the superintendent's job at West Point, which went to someone else. He then took command of Reconstruction in the Third Military District, consisting of Alabama, Georgia and Florida, with his headquarters in Montgomery and then in Atlanta. His attitude toward the South had hardened and, armed with the three Reconstruction Acts, which gave him plenary powers over the three states, Pope moved to bring those states into compliance with federal law. Andrew Johnson, a strident opponent of Congressional Reconstruction, soon replaced Pope with George Meade, and Pope moved north on February 1, 1868, to take command of the Department of the Lakes, with his headquarters in Detroit.

This was undemanding work, and only mild irritants like rumors of a Fenian invasion of Canada out of Michigan troubled him. Clara, whose health was now poor, and his two children—Lucretia and John Horton—joined him there. The monotony of this backwater command was broken only by his nomination as Michigan's vice president candidate.

On April 30, 1870, Pope received orders to take command of the Department of the Missouri, with his headquarters at Fort Leavenworth. There, he reported to Philip Sheridan, who commanded the Division of the Missouri, and the two quickly found themselves at odds over Sheridan's treatment of the Indians. Sheridan had just finished his savage winter campaign, and his philosophy was for the Indians to either conform or face extermination. Pope, on the other hand, believed in a more humane policy that would place the Indians on reservations, teach them to farm and raise livestock, and educate them. These principles were consistent with Grant's policies, and Grant was now president. In addition, Sheridan went to Europe to observe the Franco-Prussian War, so Pope was left a free hand to deal with the Indians.

He and Clara came to love Fort Leavenworth, at which Pope undertook a sea change, building new barracks and officers' quarters, instituting entertainment for the troops and building a race track with stands. He also oversaw construction and subsequent operation of the country's first military prison, which is still in operation. Finally, he built a new commanding officer's quarters featuring hot and cold running water, all-indoor plumbing "and before the end of the decade, a telephone."[103]

On October 26, 1882, Pope received a promotion to major general, "proving, if nothing else, that seniority in that era would win out over all imaginable obstacles."[104] He and Clara now had four children, and the oldest, Horton, was at Harvard. The following year, Pope received orders to take command of the Military Division of the Pacific with his headquarters at the Presidio in San Francisco. There, he and Clara became scions of San Francisco society. He began writing for *Century Magazine*'s "Battles and Leaders of the Civil War," with his first article on Second Bull Run. James Longstreet also wrote on that disastrous battle—for Pope and the North—giving the Southern perspective.

On March 16, 1886, Pope retired, and he and Clara returned to St. Louis, which Pope found to be "a city of money-grubbing philistines."[105] On February 18, 1887, he began a series of articles for the *National Tribune*, as well as other publications. The articles that he wrote dealt with Civil

War battles in which he had participated, as well as Civil War commanders, Mexican War battles in which he had also participated, a critique of the officer education system at West Point and the trip on which he had accompanied Lincoln from Springfield to Washington for his first inauguration. Unlike the articles and books of so many other Northern and Southern generals, Pope's articles were animated with goodwill and reconciliation rather than blame and negative criticism. He retired from the army in 1886.[106]

Pope died on September 23, 1892, and was buried beside his wife in St. Louis's Bellefontaine Cemetery.

Winfield Scott Hancock

"The Superb"

Winfield Scott and his twin brother, Hilary, were born on February 14, 1824, in Pennsylvania. Their father, Benjamin, was a lawyer and a "patriotic Democrat."[107] Hancock entered West Point at age fifteen and graduated eighteenth of twenty-five in 1844. His class standing placed him squarely in the infantry, as opposed to the Corps of Engineers, which was reserved for those who finished high in their class, like Robert E. Lee.[108]

After graduation, Hancock went west to Indian Territory, where he served two uneventful years. The Mexican War intervened, however, and Hancock received orders to Mexico, where he served with distinction alongside such future Confederate luminaries as James Longstreet, Lewis Armistead and

Winfield Scott Hancock (1863–1865).

George Pickett. As a result of his conduct at the Battle of Churubusco, Hancock was cited for "gallant and meritorious conduct" and received a brevet promotion to first lieutenant.[109] Hancock then served in St. Louis, where he met and married his wife, Allie, then in Florida fighting in the Third Seminole War. Next up was "Bleeding Kansas," where U.S. troops sought—largely unsuccessfully—to stop the fighting between pro-slavery and anti-slavery forces. Then came an expedition to Salt Lake City, where the so-called "Mormon revolution" raged, but that conflict had been settled peacefully with Brigham Young by the time U.S. troops, led by Albert Sidney Johnston, arrived. Hancock's final assignment prior to the Civil War was in California, where Allie and their two children joined him. He received a promotion to captain and served as chief quartermaster until the war took him back east. But prior to leaving California, Hancock formed deep friendships with officers who would serve in the Confederacy, especially Lewis Armistead, whose path would cross Hancock's at a critical point in the war to come.[110]

Promoted to brigadier general, Hancock took command of a brigade for George McClellan's ill-fated Peninsula Campaign, where, for his service at Williamsburg, he was termed "superb" by McClellan, thus giving rise to his nickname, "the Superb." He missed the Union debacle at Second Bull Run but served with distinction at the Antietam abattoir. With his superior officer dead, Hancock took command of a division and fought successfully to maintain the Union line in the face of heavy casualties. For his service there, Hancock received a brevet promotion to major general and a promotion to a permanent rank of major in the regular army.[111]

If Antietam was a slaughterhouse, Fredericksburg was murder. There, as noted, Burnside hurled his legions—including Hancock's division and contrary to Hancock's advice—against Lee's entrenched army behind a stone wall on the forward slope of Marye's Heights and against his larger force along the crest. Burnside's Army of the Potomac lost twelve thousand men, and Hancock's division suffered mightily. Nevertheless, it came closer to reaching the stone wall than any other Union unit. Hancock was wounded there.[112]

Next up was Fighting Joe Hooker's fiasco at Chancellorsville. After an exemplary maneuver to place himself on Lee's left flank at Chancellorsville with one hundred and thirty thousand men facing off against Lee's sixty thousand, Hooker frittered away his opportunity to launch a devastating and likely fatal attack on the Army of Northern Virginia. Lee then famously split his army and sent Stonewall Jackson on a flanking move around Hooker's right flank. Jackson attacked, and Chancellorsville came to constitute the high water mark of the Army of Northern Virginia and its commander, Lee. The Confederate victory was marred, however, by

Jackson's death resulting from friendly fire. As the debacle overwhelmed the Army of the Potomac, Hancock successfully covered Hooker's rear while that hapless officer retreated.[113]

Riding the crest of the Chancellorsville wave, Lee invaded Pennsylvania, and the fateful three-day battle at Gettysburg followed. George Gordon Meade placed Hancock in command of much of the line, and Hancock, recognizing the importance of the defensive position along the top of Cemetery Ridge, had his troops ready to fight from that position. He also saw the importance of Cemetery and Culp's Hills on the Union right flank and occupied those two defensive positions. The result was Fredericksburg in reverse, when Lee sent Pickett's doomed legion across the field and up the slopes of the ridge and into immortality.[114]

Hancock, however, was wounded in the groin, and his "old army" friend Lewis Armistead suffered what would turn out to be a fatal wound. Hancock was out of action until the spring of 1864 convalescing from his wound and returned to join what was now Grant's army for the Overland Campaign of 1864. He saw action at the Wilderness, Spotsylvania Courthouse and then during Grant's ill-advised assault on the Confederate lines at Cold Harbor, before which Hancock's men pinned pieces of paper bearing their names to their backs so that they could be identified, echoing D.H. Hill's description of Malvern Hill, which the Confederate general described as "murder." Hancock's corps lost over thirty-five hundred men at Cold Harbor.[115]

Grant flanked Lee after Cold Harbor, forcing him into a defensive position at Petersburg. There, Hancock's division, now containing a large number of green replacements, was routed at the Weldon Railroad, and for the first time, fled the battlefield. Hancock's wound opened up, and for him, the war was effectively over.

Postwar

John Wilkes Booth assassinated Abraham Lincoln, and Hancock, in charge of the military in Washington, D.C., was forced to oversee the executions of four of the conspirators, including that of Mary Surratt, whose execution he opposed as a matter of principle because she was a woman. He waited futilely for a stay of execution from President Johnson as the court proceedings ground along. Nothing, however, came of any of it, and Mrs. Surratt died on the gallows. Before her death, he said, "I have been in many a battle and have seen death, and mixed with it disaster and victory. I have been in a living hell of fire, and shell and grapeshot, and, by God, I'd sooner be there ten thousand times over than to give the order this day for the execution of that poor woman. But I am a soldier, sworn to obey, and obey I must."[116]

Hancock next took command of the Department of the Missouri, which ran from the Mississippi River west to the Rockies and south through New Mexico. Settlers, surveyors, miners and the railroad were all encroaching upon Indian lands, and friction was inevitable, punctuated by occasional violence. Hancock thus led a campaign against the Cheyenne that resulted in peace negotiations with the Indians, but when they fled during the negotiations, Hancock ordered their village burned and took his army back to its base. Critics said that his ineptitude in dealing with the Indians led directly to the Indian War of 1867.

George Armstrong Custer was also a problem. Ordered by Sherman to make a particular march, Custer force-marched his men until many of them deserted, and he then ordered that any deserters who were apprehended be shot. When he reached Fort Wallace, where Sherman had sent him, he abruptly left his command and went to see his wife, Libbie, at Fort Riley. Hancock ordered Custer arrested and court-martialed. Custer then wrote three articles for a New York magazine in which he accused Hancock of using the court-martial to cover up his "rashness and stupidity" in dealing with the Cheyenne. The court nonetheless found Custer guilty and suspended him from the army for one year.[117]

President Andrew Johnson then sent Hancock to New Orleans to take command of the Fifth Military District, encompassing Louisiana and Texas. For Hancock, the war was over, and he wanted to defer to the civil authorities in the two states. Hancock was a states' rights Democrat, and from the old army, he had many Southern friends—the dead Lewis Armistead, Albert Sidney Johnston and newspaper publisher Simon Bolivar Buckner, among others—and he was sympathetic to the South. He thus promulgated General Order Number Forty, which held that civilian rule was paramount and that civilians would enforce the laws and the rights of the people set forth in the Bill of Rights. That order set the tone for Hancock's New Orleans stay, in which he would continue to insist upon civilian rule in the courts and in elections. Those policies engendered popularity for Hancock in Louisiana and Texas but unleashed a storm of protest in the North. Finally, after continued controversy in the Fifth District, Grant relieved Hancock in February 1868, and Andrew Johnson ordered Hancock to Washington, where he would serve as commander of the Division of the Atlantic. His brief tenure as an agent of Reconstruction was over.

The year 1868 was an election year. The Republicans nominated Grant, but the Democrats were in disarray in coming up with a candidate to oppose America's war hero. Hancock, a confirmed Democrat and also a war hero, was a possibility. At the Democratic convention that summer, Hancock ran first after the sixteenth ballot among a number of candidates, and after eighteen ballots, was first among three. The convention adjourned for the night, and it appeared that Hancock had the nomination locked up. Then the politicians and schemers went to work, and by morning, the Democratic Party world had turned upside down. Hancock, the victim of overnight political chicanery of the first magnitude, eventually lost to Horace Seymour, who would, in turn, be swamped by Grant.

George Meade died in 1872, and Grant appointed Hancock commander of the Military District of the Atlantic, with responsibility for the military affairs of New England, the Middle Atlantic States, Washington, D.C., and the Great Lakes region. Hancock's headquarters would be on Governor's Island in New York. He moved his family there.

Hancock's daughter, Ada, died in 1875 at the age of eighteen. Hancock and Allie were devastated, but there would be more: their son, Russell, would die at the age of thirty-four, and Hancock's namesake grandson, Winfield Scott Hancock, also died. Those losses created holes in his heart that would never close.

Grant did not run again in 1876, and the Republican Rutherford B. Hayes was elected president in a controversial election that saw Hayes agree to pull federal troops out of the South in return for the electoral votes of South Carolina, Florida and Louisiana. The election, in a harbinger of things to come 144 years later, set off a furor. Democrats threatened to bring one hundred thousand protesters to Washington, and the threat of another civil war overhung the country. Republicans speculated that the Democrat Hancock would use his troops to engineer the election of the Democratic candidate, Samuel J. Tilden. They did not know Winfield Scott Hancock. He wrote to Sherman, general-in-chief of the army, that "'the army should have nothing to do with the selection or inauguration of Presidents.' The people, he said, elect the president, Congress declares the winner, and 'we of the army have only to obey his mandates.'" The crisis passed.

In July 1877, as companies cut wages in light of the continued recession that arose in 1873, strikes broke out all over the country by steelworkers, coal miners and railroad employees. The strikes led to violence, the violence led to deaths, and the deaths led to military intervention, supervised by Hancock. Intervention was antithetical to everything Hancock believed about the army, which, he contended, should protect the country only from *outside* enemies. Nevertheless, under direction of the president, the army intervened, restored the peace and, eventually, Hancock was able to withdraw them from the duty of strikebreaking.

Another election came in 1880, and his chief opponent was Samuel J. Tilden, who had lost the disputed election to Hayes in 1876. Machine politics notwithstanding, Hancock won the Democratic Party nomination for president. The Republicans nominated James A. Garfield. During the campaign that followed, Hancock shook off various attacks upon his record, but one in particular stung. Grant, in what he thought was an off-the-record interview that went public, said that Hancock was "ambitious, vain and weak."[118] There had been friction between Grant and Hancock before, primarily arising out of Hancock's leniency in New Orleans, and their relationship, in spite of an attempt at reconciliation, had remained chilly. This remark, however, completed the destruction of their friendship.

There were no major issues in the election of 1880 when the campaign started. Both parties embraced the same policies, and the candidates thus had little to talk about. A plank in the Democratic platform called for "a tariff for revenue only." It was the opening the Republicans needed. They seized upon these three words and screamed that the Democrats would, therefore, abolish tariffs that protected American industry, workers and prosperity. The Democrats let those attacks go unanswered, and in the end, that was enough. Hancock lost New York and lost the election, though the popular vote was extremely close. Garfield won it by seven thousand votes out of nine million votes cast. Garfield won the Electoral College, however, 214–155. If Hancock had carried New York—and he would have except for a weak local ticket—he would have won the Electoral College and the presidency, 190–179.

Hancock slept through the night of the election and awakened at five o'clock the morning after. He asked Allie what had happened. She replied that it had been "a complete Waterloo for you." "That is all right," he said. "I can stand it." Hancock then went back to sleep.[119]

Life now settled into a quiet routine for General Hancock. He and Allie lived on the small Governor's Island army base, this time interrupted by the specter of death that claimed Allie's mother, Hancock's old chief of staff, General William G. Mitchell, and Russell Hancock, which created another gaping emotional wound.

The years passed, and Hancock made fewer and fewer public appearances outside of his duty post on Governor's Island. A major appearance came in 1885 when he took command of the funeral arrangements for U.S. Grant. Hancock's organizational skills were exemplary, and the funeral went off without a hitch. Hancock led the funeral procession on a magnificent black horse in full military dress, gold braid flashing in the sun. The procession began on August 8 at nine that morning. It took four hours for Hancock to reach the site of Grant's temporary tomb on Riverside Drive, overlooking the Hudson.

Hancock's next appearance was at Gettysburg in November 1885. He went there to "clear up some matters of position and locale" that were the subject of debate among historians. On January 27, 1886, Hancock traveled to Washington, and felt ill. There was a carbuncle on the back of his neck, which he had lanced, but it continued to suppurate. Hancock declined rapidly after the procedure, and when he returned to Governor's Island, he became gravely ill, likely from the carbuncle, which had continued to grow, as well as diabetes. Hancock, the Superb, died February 9, 1886.[120]

Joseph Hooker

"Fighting Joe"

The fourth child of Joseph and Mary Hooker and the fifth male with the name Joseph, Joseph Hooker V was born November 13, 1814, in Hadley, Massachusetts. Joseph's progenitors had arrived in America in 1689, and the family had a military tradition dating back to the French and Indian War, which was fought from 1756 to 1763. The family was prosperous, but the War of 1812 devastated Joseph's father's business and sent him to work as a cattle buyer, at which he was never successful. The children then went to work at odd jobs to help support the family.

The younger Joseph entered West Point in 1833 and graduated in 1837, twenty-ninth out of a class of fifty.[121] His class included future Civil War generals John Sedgwick, Braxton Bragg, Jubal A. Early—who once kicked Hooker after a debate on slavery[122]—and William Walker. Also present at West Point during Hooker's stay there were Henry Halleck, William T. Sherman and George Thomas. Upon graduation, Hooker received his commission in the artillery and fought against the Seminoles in Florida.[123] He then served at West Point. "He was described by a fellow officer as a 'handsome fellow, polished in manner, the perfection of grace in every movement ... the courtesy of manner we attribute to old-time gentlemen.... He was simply elegant, and certainly one of the handsomest men the army ever produced.'" Hooker was also "ambitious and at times reckless and brash; he was also immodest and had a reputation for hard drinking and high living."[124] His recklessness would haunt him on future battlefields in a war to come.

Hooker participated with distinction in the Mexican War and was awarded three brevets, the third to lieutenant colonel.[125] After the war he served on the Pacific Coast, where he drank too much, gambled too much and chased the ladies too much. In the face of mounting gambling debts, Hooker took leave from the army, borrowing money on the way out from William T. Sherman and Henry Halleck. He never repaid those debts. Like his rashness, his failure to satisfy those debts would come back to haunt him.[126]

Subsequently, when his leave was up, he resigned from the army to farm near Sonoma, where he fell on hard financial times. Hooker would be out of the army until the war came in 1861. Lincoln personally promoted him to lieutenant colonel after Irvin McDowell's disaster at First Bull Run, and Hooker participated in McClellan's ill-fated Peninsula Campaign, distinguishing himself with hard fighting. The newspapers then gave him the name "Fighting Joe." He eventually received promotions through the officer ranks to major general of volunteers and command of a corps.[127] Hooker next participated in another Union disaster—Second Bull Run—this time under John Pope. Lincoln briefly considered Hooker to relieve Pope in com-

Joseph Hooker (1862).

mand of the Army of the Potomac but decided against him on the basis of his impetuosity and in the light of information with respect to his drinking. Hooker remained a corps commander and fought next at Antietam after Lee invaded Maryland. There he showed bravery and resourcefulness and almost broke through the Confederate lines, which would have destroyed Lee's Army of Northern Virginia.[128]

Next up was the Fredericksburg abattoir, where Hooker opposed the frontal assault plan of the newly appointed commander of the Army of the Potomac, Ambrose E. Burnside. After that slaughter and the desultory Mud March, Hooker then took command of the Army of the Potomac, and in a series of brilliant moves, placed his 135,000-man army in position to destroy Lee's army of half that size. At a critical juncture, however, Hooker lost his nerve, and instead of attacking, dug in, allowing Lee to split his army for the second time, and in an iconic move, he sent Jackson around Hooker's right flank and into immortality. The result was a rout, and Hooker, wounded in the head, retreated back across the Rappahannock. Halleck became disenchanted with Hooker, and as a result of Halleck going around him in the chain of command, Hooker resigned.

Lincoln then replaced him with George Meade, as Lee began his second invasion of the Union.[129]

Halleck sent Hooker west to join the Army of Tennessee, and Hooker fought well around Chattanooga following Rosecrans's ignominious defeat at Chickamauga. Hooker then served under Sherman in his drive on Atlanta, and Sherman insulted Hooker deeply "when he named Hooker's subordinate, Oliver O. Howard, to command of the Army of Tennessee."[130] Of Hooker, Grant said: "I ... regarded him as a dangerous man. He was not subordinate to his superior. He was ambitious to the extent of caring nothing for the rights of others. His disposition was, when engaged in battle, to get detached from the main body of the army and exercise a separate command, gathering to his standard all he could of his juniors." Sherman also castigated Hooker: "Hooker was a fool. Had he staid [sic] a couple of weeks he could have marched into Atlanta and claimed all the honors."[131]

Hooker resigned his command and returned to Washington. On September 28, 1864, Lincoln sent him to Columbus, Ohio, to the backwater command of the Northern Department. He moved his headquarters on October 6 to Cincinnati. With the war still raging, Hooker's primary responsibility was for conducting the draft in his region, a major comedown for a former commander of the Army of the Potomac. Nevertheless, there were raids into Indiana by guerrillas from Kentucky, which he stopped by assigning troops there. He overcame draft resistance and oversaw the prisoner-of-war camps located in his territory. Hooker also began the courtship of Olivia Groesbeck, a member of a prominent Cincinnati family.

The promotions of Sheridan, Sherman and Meade to major general in the regular army disturbed him. He asked rhetorically, "Would it not be far better to put military commissions in the market and dispose of them at public auction as any commodity?" He was particularly scornful of the mercurial Sherman, whom he thought to be insane and who had, Hooker contended, "no more judgment than a child." He also said that "it would have given me the greatest satisfaction to have broken my sabre over the head of Sherman."[132]

Hooker requested a hearing before the Congressional Committee on the Conduct of the War with respect to the Battle of Chancellorsville, and on March 4, the hearing commenced with testimony from Hooker, which, in the end, comprised sixty-seven pages of the hearing transcript. Amazingly, the committee found him blameless for the debacle even though it was Hooker's recalcitrance to attack that allowed Lee to split his army, send Jackson around Hooker's flank and then run Hooker back to Washington.

The war ended, and with the end came Lincoln's assassination. Now, back in Cincinnati, Hooker received orders to participate in Lincoln's funeral in Springfield. There, he led the funeral procession to the cemetery, followed by a coterie of senior military officers.[133]

Hooker received orders in late June 1865 to take command of the Military Department of the East, part of Meade's Division of the Atlantic. His new command consisted of New York, New Jersey and New England with headquarters in New York City. But there was one more item of business for him in Cincinnati, and he returned there to marry Olivia Groesbeck on October 3, 1865. Hooker was fifty years old. Neither of the parties to the marriage would enjoy good health in the days to come.

In November 1865, Hooker suffered a debilitating stroke[134] at a reception in New York City for Grant. He recovered sufficiently to accept a transfer to the Military Department of the Lakes, headquartered in Detroit; however, in early 1867, he suffered another stroke and took a leave of absence. Olivia's health had declined, but the two of them were able to take a trip to Europe, where they hoped to recover. Nonetheless, upon their return, she continued to decline and died on July 15, 1868. Shortly after his wife's death, Hooker resigned from the army.[135]

Olivia left him property in Cincinnati, and Hooker began participating in reunions of his wartime comrades and the dedication of monuments. His criticism of his fellow generals continued: "Grant, he said, had 'no more moral sense than a dog,' and Howard 'would command a prayer meeting with a good deal more ability than he would an army.'" And of Sherman, whose memoirs he read, Hooker said: "If I consider it to be my duty to go for him again I will not leave a grease spot of him. His ravings have become intolerable."[136]

Hooker was a diehard Democrat, and he reveled as that party took control of Congress. He supported Greeley against Grant and spoke warmly of the South. He entertained lavishly prominent Southern Civil war generals, one of whom was the "indomitable fighter, General John B. Gordon of Georgia."[137]

Hooker moved to Garden City, New York, on Long Island, from which he continued to travel to the battlefields of the war, moved back to Hadley, where he had been born, and then to his sister Mary's in Watertown, New York. He gained weight, and his hair turned gray, and he, in spite of his earlier stroke, enjoyed good health. Nevertheless, on October 31, he died suddenly. After a service in Garden City, his body lay in state in New York, where it was viewed by thousands. Hooker is buried in Spring Grove Cemetery in Cincinnati.[138]

Hooker's signal legacy is the term "hooker," which he unwittingly bequeathed to America and the English-speaking world. "Hooker," which denotes a prostitute, "is said to have derived from the class of females who frequented Ambrose's headquarters, to which it was said 'no gentleman cared to go and no lady could go.'"[139]

Joshua Lawrence Chamberlain

Medal of Honor Recipient

Joshua Lawrence Chamberlain was born September 8, 1828, in Brewer, Maine. From a long line of volunteer soldiers stretching back to colonial America, he attended Ellsworth Military Academy and then graduated from Bowdoin College in 1852. After three years at Bangor Theological Seminary, Chamberlain returned to Bowdoin as a professor of rhetoric and oratory.[140] He was teaching there when Lincoln's second call for volunteers issued, and he turned down a position as chairman of the Department of Modern Languages, with lifetime tenure and a two-year paid sabbatical in Europe, to serve his country.[141]

Chamberlain entered the service on August 8, 1862, as a lieutenant colonel in the 20th Maine,[142] soon to be one of the most storied infantry regiments in United States military history. Chamberlain had no military experience or training, but he was a born leader who did not ask his men to do anything that he would not himself do. He led them into battle twenty-four times and fought with them at the front, rather than sitting in the rear sending commands to his subordinate commanders. As a result he was wounded six times.[143]

Joshua Lawrence Chamberlain (1862–1866).

The 20th Maine joined the Army of the Potomac in September 1862, just in time for the Battle of Antietam, which, because they were "green," they missed, as they were held in reserve. The regiment's first combat occurred

December 13, 1862, at the Fredericksburg abattoir, when Burnside sent his legions up Marye's Heights against entrenched Confederates, who mowed the Union troops down like the cornstalks at Antietam. Chamberlain knew that the attack up the escarpment was a mistake, and he argued with his commander, Joseph Hooker, who disregarded his subordinate's warning, along with many others. It was, as history has recorded and Chamberlain had predicted, a disaster, and the 20th Maine suffered grievous losses. Chamberlain himself was wounded twice and spent a night huddled on the battlefield behind the bodies of dead and dying Union soldiers, whose pitiful moans rose into the cold night air.[144]

Because of smallpox, the regiment missed the Chancellorsville disaster, but in July 1863, it marched into the pantheon of iconic military units and Chamberlain into the pantheon of great American military commanders. There, at Gettysburg, the recently promoted Chamberlain, who had taken command of the 20th Maine, brought his men up on Little Round Top, which Confederate troops were about to take and thus enfilade the entire Union line on Cemetery Ridge. In vicious fighting, his troops ran out of ammunition as William Oates's Fifteenth Alabama regiment came on, threatening to rout his Maine boys and turn the Union left flank. At the head of the Maine line, Chamberlain ordered his men to fix bayonets and then led a wild charge into the startled Alabamians, instead routing them and saving Little Round Top. From this moment on, Chamberlain was the hero of Gettysburg.[145]

Many battles followed, as the 20th Maine fought with the Army of the Potomac through 1864 along Grant's famous summer "line" on into Petersburg. There Chamberlain received his sixth and most grievous wound, a bullet that tore through him from hip to hip and that would cause him major problems for the rest of his life.[146] Indeed, the wound was so serious that Union surgeons operated but pronounced the wound to their famous patient as mortal. Grant, recognizing what seemed to be inevitable, brevetted him to major general.[147] Two other surgeons were brought in that evening and worked through the night to perform what became known as a "miracle operation." They opened up his abdomen, "cut out dead tissue, tied off several blood vessels, removed the bullet, and inserted a urinary catheter, which enabled them to put the urethra back together." The catheter "preserved the anatomic integrity of the urethra and helped save Chamberlain's life, but the catheter was not the soft, flexible type used today; it was made of metal, and it was left in so long during Chamberlain's recovery that it caused a stricture of the urethra and, probably, the erosion that wore an opening [fistula] half an inch long in the penis just in front of the scrotum." The repairs necessitated five or six additional surgeries and caused pain and embarrassment to Chamberlain for the rest of his life. Eventually, complications arising out of the wound would kill him, but they would not do so for another fifty years.[148]

Chamberlain returned to duty—contrary to his wife Fanny's wishes—in time for the battles at Five Forks, Sayler's Creek and Appomattox. There, Grant designated him to receive the formal surrender of the fabled Army of Northern Virginia.[149] As General John Brown Gordon of Georgia, in command of the Confederate troops, marched his troops through the Union soldiers lined up along each side of the road, Chamberlain ordered his men to shoulder arms, a sign of respect for their defeated opponents. Gordon then turned his horse to face Chamberlain and executed a chivalric salute, rearing his horse and saluting Chamberlain with his sword, which he then lowered to his boot. Of Chamberlain, Gordon said that he was "that knightly soldier" and he marveled at the ceremony of which he had been part, saying, "No scene like it in any age was ever witnessed at the end of a long and bloody war."[150]

Chamberlain wrote of this famous moment, "Before us in proud humiliations stood the embodiment of manhood: men whom neither toils and sufferings, nor the fact of death, nor disaster, nor hopelessness could bend from their resolve; standing before us now, thin, worn and famished, but erect, and with eyes looking level into ours, waking memories that bound us together as no other bond:—was not such manhood to be welcomed back into a Union so tested and assured?"[151]

Chamberlain turned down a commission in the regular army and returned to Maine, where he was elected governor for four one-year terms beginning in 1866.[152] In his first term he was confronted by the nascent temperance movement that would ultimately culminate in the Eighteenth Amendment to the Constitution prohibiting the sale of alcohol. The Maine women who led that movement fomented legislation that would impose harsh criminal penalties upon those selling spirits. Chamberlain enjoyed a convivial drink. Indeed, at Appomattox, while Lee and Grant discussed and then signed the articles of surrender, Chamberlain and other officers of both armies stood in the McLean house yard and drank. He thus opposed the Maine legislation and, for his opposition, was pilloried by the prohibition proponents.[153]

Chamberlain's platform, which he successfully implemented, included the use of water power for manufacturing. Next was the "Swede" project, an effort to have Swedes immigrate to Maine. This, too, was successful, and some six hundred immigrated there and settled. Indeed, there is a large section of Maine even today populated by thousands of their decedents. Chamberlain, with his background in academia, was a proponent of a strong free public education program, and this program also came to fruition. Finally, he addressed the decline in Maine's shipbuilding industry, expanded training in agriculture and implemented measures to stop the flow of young people out of the state. In all, except for the temperance brouhaha, his years as governor were successful, and he remained popular with the people of Maine throughout his terms.

Chamberlain decided against a fifth term and returned to Bowdoin as president. There, for thirteen years he would provide the same strong leadership that he had as a major general in the Union Army. Bowdoin had produced distinguished alumni, including Franklin Pierce ('24), Henry Wadsworth Longfellow ('25) and Nathaniel Hawthorne ('25). In addition, it had awarded honorary degrees to Jefferson Davis—before the war—and U.S. Grant.[154] The college refused to abrogate Davis's degree after the war. It was a school of strong traditions, some so ossified that breaking them would require dynamite. Chamberlain took an explosive stick or two and went to work.[155]

The first move was the institution of a military drill program—a harbinger of the ROTC programs to come. Having seen the results of unprepared, undertrained officers and enlisted men in the war, Chamberlain believed that preparation for a future war was essential for avoidance of the myriad mistakes that haunted the Union armies in the first two and a half years of the Civil War. The program, within a year, engendered strident opposition from the students, and as opposition spread to the faculty, it forced Chamberlain to make the program voluntary. Within a decade, and after Chamberlain's departure, military drill was but a memory, and a bad one at that.[156]

Mandatory military participation was but one of his "reforms." He relaxed strictures upon his students, instead urging them to be adults and to be treated like adults, much as Robert E. Lee did at Washington College.[157] Chamberlain established a science curriculum, placed greater emphasis on modern languages and then created a master of arts degree. One part of his science program was a course of study in engineering.[158]

These years were the "Gilded Age," the age of Carnegie, Rockefeller, Alexander Graham Bell and Thomas Edison. Electricity, automobiles, steel mills, Standard Oil and the telephone roared to life. The age of small liberal arts colleges strait-jacketed in memorization and recitation was passing, and Bowdoin had to change. All of these changes met resistance among the faculty, but in time, the school grudgingly moved into the last, exciting half of the nineteenth century and implemented most of the changes Chamberlain had proposed.[159]

He enjoyed his personal life in Brunswick. Besides a house that he had lifted and under which he built a new first floor—that house is now a museum in his honor—he owned a twenty-six-foot sloop that he sailed on Casco Bay. He loved the wind on the bay and his family and the home, which had once been occupied by Longfellow. These were good years for Chamberlain, punctuated only by the discomfort of his wound and the need for further surgery from time to time.[160]

His wife, Fanny, was an artistic soul. She loved music and painting, but she also loved shopping and spending. She had been an independent spirit when she was young. During the War she would leave her two children—Grace and Wyllys—with relatives and travel to New York and Boston shopping for the latest fashions. Subsequently, however, Fanny began to lose her sight. She grew smaller and became reclusive, and travel became a thing of the past.[161]

In the early 1880s Chamberlain invested in a land development company in Florida and spent time in New York trying to raise capital.[162] His letterhead read:

> **The Florida West Coast Improvement Company**
> **Constructing and operating the**
> **Silver Springs, Ocala and Gulf Railroad**
> **Vice-Presidents Office**
> **56 Wall and 59 Pine Streets**
> **Joshua L. Chamberlain**
> **Vice President**

The business, forty or fifty years ahead of its time, failed.[163]

Chamberlain also filled his time with participation in civic and military organizations. At this point he was either a member of, or presided over, some twenty such organizations, including societies dedicated to "political science, genealogy, geography, Egyptian exploration, philosophy, history, religion, blindness, military and veterans affairs, [and] relief work," among many others. He attended Grant's funeral in 1885 in New York.[164]

Chamberlain was also president of another school, the Institute for Artists and Artisans; was president of *New England Magazine*; and was editor of a number of volumes titled *Universities and Their Sons*. He was commander of the Maine Department of the politically formidable and socially prominent Grand Army of the Republic and a member and Maine commander of the more exclusive Military Order of the Loyal Legion of the United States, known as "Mollus," which was open only to former officers and their descendants. Mollus, because of its hereditary aspect, is still extant and claims to be the country's oldest Civil War organization, having been chartered in 1865. Chamberlain was elected president of the Society of the Army of the Potomac at the twenty-fifth anniversary of the Battle of Gettysburg at Gettysburg in 1888.[165]

A success in the war and in academia, Chamberlain found the going rougher in the business world. When the Spanish-American War came along, the now seventy-year-old Chamberlain wrote to the secretary of war that he was ready to serve, and he proposed the creation of a New England organization of eight regiments from Maine, New Hampshire, Vermont, Massachusetts and Connecticut. Nothing came of this initiative, unlike the successful applications of Confederate generals Fitzhugh Lee and Joseph Wheeler, both of whom commanded troops in what Theodore Roosevelt termed a "bully little war."[166]

Although Chamberlain owned a significant home in Brunswick, "a considerable amount of real estate, a ten-ton schooner, and some good investments," he was cash poor and needed income. In late 1899, he thus applied for the collector of customs position in Portland, a position suitable for a former governor. He did not get the position, but he was appointed to the number two position, surveyor of customs, which paid $4,500 yearly.[167] The surveyor of customs job, however, was not a sinecure; rather it was a demanding position that required the former governor and major general to be out in the weather year-round, supervising "the force of inspectors, weighers, measurers, gaugers, and laborers." The job description read, "He takes charge of all vessels arriving from foreign ports and reports their cargoes and the lading of merchandise exported or transported in bond, or exported for the benefit of drawback. He ascertains and reports the quantity and proof of all imported spirits and of all spirits exported in bond. He has charge of the admeasurement of vessels for registry and for the adjustment of the tonnage tax." Chamberlain confided to close friends that for a man who had served as Maine's governor, a major general in the Union army and the president of a college, the position was demeaning.[168]

Chamberlain took leave later in 1900 and traveled to Italy, where he became gravely ill with complications of his old wound, and then on to Egypt, where in the warm weather he rallied and visited the pyramids, tombs, monasteries and ancient temples. He returned to find Fanny "increasingly depressed and reclusive."[169] In the summer of 1905, she fell and broke her hip. Fanny died later that year.

In May of 1913, Chamberlain attended the fiftieth anniversary of the Battle of Gettysburg. He was eighty-five years old, and that November, he became ill. A battler to the end, Chamberlain defied death for three months, but finally, on February 13, 1914, he died at his home in Portland.[170] He was buried at Pine Grove Cemetery in Brunswick.[171] Chamberlain had been out of the limelight for many years at his death, and his name faded quickly into the mists of history. In 1915, his book, *The Passing of the Armies*, was published posthumously. It remains one of the finest memoirs of the war.[172]

Obscurity, however, was not to be a permanent condition. In the 1920s and subsequently, articles began to appear that recognized Joshua

Lawrence Chamberlain as the hero of Gettysburg. Those writings culminated in the 1974 Michael Shaara book *The Killer Angels*, which was subsequently made into a movie. That combination propelled Chamberlain back into the public eye, which was reflected in, among other things, the large number of visitors to his home in Brunswick, Maine. Finally, the Ken Burns series on the Civil War completed Chamberlain's return to prominence, where he rightfully remains today, once again the Hero of Gettysburg.

William Starke Rosecrans

"Old Rosy"

William Starke Rosecrans, the chicken of Chickamauga, was born in Delaware County, Ohio, on September 6, 1819. The son of a War of 1812 veteran, Rosecrans entered West Point in 1838 and was a member of the star-studded class of 1842. It was at West Point that Rosecrans picked up the name "Old Rosy" and befriended a plebe named U.S. Grant, whom he protected from hazing. That friendship would not benefit him after his failure at Chickamauga and Grant's subsequent ascension to command of the Army of Tennessee. At West Point, Rosecrans also became friends with future Confederate general James Longstreet.

Old Rosy finished fifth in his class and, as a high-academic graduate, received a commission in the prestigious and much sought-after Corps of Engineers. Accordingly, he spent his early years in such desirable postings as Newport, Rhode Island, and the Washington Naval Yard. He sat out the Mexican War, missing the opportunity for brevet promotions.

Frustrated by the glacial pace of the peacetime army, by the slowness of promotions and by poor health, Rosecrans resigned his commission in 1854 and entered civilian life, focusing his engineering background on a career in mining and oil exploration. He spent some of that time in western Virginia, a place that would one day help launch his Civil War military career. It was during this era that he suffered a grievous injury from "an oil lamp explosion that left his face severely scarred and seemingly frozen in what his biographer called 'a permanent smirk.'"[173]

Rosecrans reentered the army with the outbreak of the Civil War, serving initially as an aide to General George B. McClellan, who commanded the Ohio state troops. Subsequently, Rosecrans took command of the Twenty-Third Ohio Infantry, two of whose members were future presidents, Rutherford B. Hayes and William McKinley. Rosecrans served with distinction in what was—with his help—to become West Virginia, eventually facing off with Robert E. Lee at Rich Mountain, where Rosecrans engineered a victory that drove Lee from West Virginia and led to the creation of that state, which remained loyal to the Union.

After West Virginia, now–Brigadier General Rosecrans moved west to join the Army of the Mississippi after Shiloh and then participated in Henry Halleck's "tortoise-like advance upon the railroad junction of Corinth."[174] Grant then relieved Halleck, and Rosecrans's one-time plebe took command over Old Rosy's troops. Rosecrans next received a promotion to major general, and on October 27, 1862, he took command of the new Army of the Cumberland in Kentucky, which then squared off with Braxton Bragg's Army of Tennessee. After a win at Stone's River, Rosecrans went inactive for six months before driving Bragg out of middle Tennessee and into Chattanooga. He drove Bragg out of Chattanooga, and his star was ascendant. The stage was now set for one of the great battles of the war.

William Starke Rosecrans (c. 1864).

Chickamauga was a creek whose name means "River of Death." It was that and then some, and for Rosecrans it was to be the death of his career. A crushing defeat, Rosecrans's army was saved at Chickamauga only by George H. Thomas's brilliant stand on Horseshoe Ridge, the stand that earned Thomas the sobriquet the "Rock of Chickamauga." Rosecrans, on the other hand, fled back into Chattanooga, allegedly in tears and revealed as a coward by his flight from the field.[175]

Bragg then besieged Rosecrans in Chattanooga, and Rosecrans did nothing to break the siege, thus prompting President Lincoln to call him "a duck hit on the head." Grant relieved Rosecrans, Rosecrans went to Missouri and, upon his relief there, his military career was effectively over. After moving to California, he resigned his commission two years later and left the army, this time for good. He purchased a sixteen-thousand-acre ranch in Southern California and a city block in San Diego, which he envisioned as the terminus of a railroad that would traverse the southern United States.[176]

A confirmed Democrat, Rosecrans received an appointment from President Andrew Johnson as a minister to Mexico and, once there, began working to build a cross-country railroad. He believed that it was in the United States' best interest for Mexico to be prosperous and safe, neither of which it was. Rosecrans, however, did not last long in his position. Grant assumed the presidency in 1869 and immediately sacked his old subordinate and West Point protector.

Rosecrans's political life was far from over, however. During the 1868 campaign for the presidency, Rosecrans traveled to White Sulphur Springs in West Virginia and met with a group of "prominent Southern leaders" who summered there. The result was what became known as the "White Sulphur Springs Manifesto," which read in part:

> Whatever opinions may have prevailed in the past with regard to African slavery or the right of a State to secede from the Union, we believe we express the almost unanimous judgment of the Southern people when we declare that they consider that these questions were decided by the war, and that it is their intention in good faith to abide by that decision.[177]

The purpose of the "Manifesto" was to blunt the Republican argument that a Democrat victory would eviscerate emancipation of Blacks in the South, although the statement fell notably short of urging full political rights for them. Indeed, the Manifesto stated that the authors opposed "a system of laws that would place the political power of the country in the hands of the negro race."[178] Instead, the paper argued for the full restoration of white—and states'—rights in the South. Signers of the document included Robert E. Lee, P.G.T. Beauregard, James Longstreet and Alexander Stephens. The paper had, however, little effect, and Grant won handily.

Finally, after declining a number of opportunities to run for office, Rosecrans relented and in 1882 ran for—and was elected—a congressman from California. As a congressman he was chairman of the Democratic Caucus and served as chairman of the powerful Military Affairs Committee. Not surprisingly, he opposed the Republican bill to give former President Grant—Rosecrans's old adversary—a military pension. Nevertheless, the bill passed, and President Chester A. Arthur signed it into law.

Rosecrans declined to run for a third term, but Democrat President Grover Cleveland appointed him Register of the Treasury, a position he held until 1893, when he resigned due to poor health and returned to California. Rosecrans became no stranger to death and loss. His son Adrian, a Paulist priest, died in New York City, and his daughter Mary Louise Rosecrans, a nun, died a year later. Then Rosecrans's Catholic bishop brother, Sylvester Rosecrans, also died. Finally, on Christmas Day, 1883, Rosecrans's wife died. Her family buried her in Mt. Oliver Cemetery in Washington, D.C. Rosecrans, when his time came, would not join her there. His losses were assuaged to some extent by the arrival of grandchildren, one of whom bore the name Rosecrans Toole.

In the meantime Rosecrans became involved in the Society of the Army of the Cumberland, attending a reunion and subsequently serving as president of that organization. He was also active in the formation of the Grand Army of the Republic, which was to become a political powerhouse, and he addressed a reunion of West Point graduates, as well as veterans of both armies present at the 1889 dedication of the park at Chickamauga. "His last public appearance for veterans was in 1892 at a Grand Army reunion. When the electric lights failed, President Hayes lit a match and held it close to his onetime commander's face so that the veterans could see him. A great roar of applause came from the assembled crowd."[179]

In 1893 he gave up the Treasury post and returned to Los Angeles, where he lived mostly at the Hotel Redondo with his daughter Anita, looking out over the Pacific. His son Carl and Carl's family lived nearby. It was a happy time for the old general. By 1898, he had become an invalid, however, and that same year he lost his grandson and namesake, Rosecrans Toole, to the croup. Two months later the general was dead at the age of seventy-nine and was buried in Rosewood Cemetery. Subsequently, his body was moved to Arlington National Cemetery, Robert E. Lee's old estate across the Potomac River from Washington. President Theodore Roosevelt attended his funeral, as did Confederate general James Longstreet.[180]

Rosecrans remains to this day a controversial general, his legacy darkened by the stain of the bloody defeat at Chickamauga, which overtook the West Virginia and Tennessee victories that preceded that shattering battle. Nevertheless, "he was admired by both his military comrades and foes. His strong religious faith, which in many ways was the defining mark of his personality, provided him with comfort and meaning for the vicissitudes of life. And of course he played a key, if not crucial, role in the war that preserved the United States of America as a unified country and emancipated a race. For that alone his name should be remembered."[181]

Lewis Wallace

Author of Ben Hur

Lewis "Lew" Wallace was born in Brookville, Indiana, in 1827.[182] His father, David, served as Indiana governor and moved his family to Indianapolis. Lew was a precocious youngster who was a disinterested student and who ran away from home to fight for Texas during the Texas war for independence from Mexico. Subsequently, he served in the First Indiana Infantry during the Mexican War but saw no action.[183]

After the Mexican War, Wallace gained admission to the Indiana bar and began practicing law. Elected to the state senate in 1856, Wallace became interested in military matters and formed a company of "guards." When the Civil War started, Wallace was ready and applied to the governor of Indiana for a commission in the Indiana volunteers. The governor instead appointed him the state's adjutant general.[184]

After organizing the state's initial quota of troops, he became commanding officer of a regiment and a colonel in the Indiana volunteers. After a brief tour in Virginia, the regiment moved to the western command of U.S. Grant and participated in the successful assaults on Forts Henry and Donelson, after which he received a promotion to major general—the youngest officer to hold that rank in the Union Army at that time—and command of a division. At Shiloh, however, he took his men on a confused march that precluded their participation in the battle on the first day. For that bungled movement, Wallace was the object of intense criticism and lost his command.[185]

After a tour in command of Union defenses around Cincinnati, Wallace received orders to take command of the Middle Department in Baltimore. From there he put together a ragtag outfit of regular and reserve troops and met a numerically superior Confederate force commanded by Jubal A. Early at what would become known as the Battle of Monocracy. Although eventually driven from the field, Wallace's stand there delayed Early's move on Washington by a day, which allowed Grant to shift two divisions into the city and thus thwart the attack.[186]

After the war, Wallace first went to Mexico to address the situation arising out of the installation of the Austrian archduke Ferdinand Maximilian as ruler of the country. Confederate troops had migrated there to work for Maximilian, and the government of Benito Juarez had been pushed from power. Wallace sought to neutralize Confederate troops and push Maximilian out of power, restoring Juarez. That mission failed.[187]

Next, Wallace received an appointment to a commission that was to investigate the Lincoln assassination. The commission's investigation was followed by a trial of eight of the alleged co-conspirators, during which Wallace sketched the commission members, the defendants and the spectators. Those drawings are still extant today. After the conclusion of weeks of testimony, the commission found all eight defendants guilty and sentenced four of them to death by hanging, including the owner of the boarding house where some of them had stayed, Mary Surratt.[188]

But Wallace's legal work was not complete. He next served as president of a military tribunal trying Henry Wirz, the commandant of

Andersonville Prison, for war crimes arising out the treatment of Union prisoners of war at that prison. The military court found Wirz guilty, and authorities hanged him on November 10, 1865.[189]

Wallace was not done with Mexico, however, and took a commission as a major general in the Mexican army to support Juarez's government against Maximilian, who eventually was abandoned by the French and was subsequently caught and executed by the Mexicans. Wallace would later be paid $15,000 for his services in support of the Mexican cause.[190]

He returned to Indiana to practice law, a vocation of which he said, "I never loved the profession. It was a drag. I worried at it, and it worried me. The routine was simply abominable—horrible."[191]

Lewis Wallace (1861–1865).

Following two unsuccessful runs for Congress, Wallace began writing and completed a novel, *The Fair God*, about the war between Montezuma's Aztec empire and its defeat by Spain. That book sold well, and its success encouraged Wallace to continue his writing. That work, however, had one drawback: his court opponents in trials always mentioned that he had written a novel, which invariably entertained the rural jurors and provoked ribald laughter. "I might as well have appeared in court dressed as a circus clown," Wallace later told novelist and young friend Booth Tarkington. To the people of Indiana, only women read novels.[192]

Although agnostic, Wallace next decided to write a novel about Jesus Christ and eventually decided to tell the story through a Jew named Judah Ben Hur. He wrote in his home at night under a tree in his yard during the afternoon. His writing was interrupted, however, by two events: first, he served on a commission appointed to resolve the election dispute between Democrat Samuel Tilden and Rutherford B. Hayes, the Republican, over who had won the election of 1876. The commission eventually resolved the election in favor of Hayes, who immediately pulled Union troops out of the South, ending Reconstruction.

Hayes accordingly offered Wallace the position of minister to Bolivia, but he turned it down, instead choosing to become territorial governor of New Mexico at half the salary because he did not want to leave his wife in Indiana. He traveled to Santa Fe to assume his position and found the town and the territory lawless and as rough as the roads he took to get there. While serving as territorial governor, Wallace became involved with William H. Bonney, who would subsequently become famous as "Billy the Kid." That relationship arose out of Bonney's involvement in several murders and testimony that he gave at Wallace's urging concerning another killing in which Bonney was not involved. That chain of events ended in Bonney's death at the hand of Sheriff Pat Garrett, and Billy the Kid passed into lore and legend.

Nights, Wallace continued to write *Ben Hur*, which he completed in March 1880. When it was presented to Harper and Brothers publishing company, Joseph Henry Harper looked at it and said, "This is the most beautiful manuscript that has ever come into this house. A bold experiment to make Christ a hero that has been often tried and always failed."[193] The book—two hundred thousand words long—came out later that year, and although it sold poorly initially and received poor reviews from critics, gradually it caught on with readers and became a smashing, worldwide success. Wallace sent the book to U.S. Grant at his New York home, and Grant read it straight through in a little over twenty-four hours. By 1889, the book had sold four hundred thousand copies, and it had been translated into a number of different languages. *Ben Hur* eventually sold over a million additional copies.

Wallace had one more significant experience in New Mexico: wars with Apaches, who were led by their stellar chieftain, Victorio. Wallace was impressed with the chief, who, after attacks on American settlements, would disappear into Mexico, out of the reach of the U.S. Cavalry. So impressed was Wallace that he later named a dog "Victorio." He gave the dog, an English mastiff, to the sultan of Turkey.

On March 1, 1881, Wallace resigned as territorial governor and with his wife, Susan, returned to Indiana. He was not to stay there, however, as President James Garfield, impressed by *Ben Hur*, appointed Wallace minister to Turkey. He and Susan would be in Turkey four years, during which they would visit the Holy Land, where Wallace would be amazed at how well he had captured in *Ben Hur* the land and its many moods.

After his tour in Turkey, Wallace again returned to Indiana, where he wrote his third novel, *The Prince of India*. It was a two-volume set, and it sold two hundred and fifty thousand copies in the first seven months after its release. It was not, however, another *Ben Hur* and sold mostly because of

Wallace's literary reputation arising out of *Ben Hur*. Wallace was much in demand as a speaker, and he wrote seven books in all. His last book was his autobiography, which his wife completed after his death in February 1905, from cancer, the result of smoking. His grave marker bears a quotation from *Ben Hur*: "I would not give one hour of life as a Soul for a thousand years of life as a man."[194] Wallace, in his later life, had become a devout Christian.

Worthy of further discussion is *Ben Hur*, which, in its 130 years of existence, has never been out of print. The book has been made into a play and three movies, the last in the 1950s, starring Charlton Heston as Judah Ben Hur. That movie version won eleven academy awards and earned more than $40 million. It also likely saved MGM from bankruptcy.

Finally, Indiana, honored its native son with a marble statue in Statuary Hall at the U.S. Capitol in Washington, D.C., where each state is permitted to honor two persons "known for their 'historic renown or for distinguished civic or military services.'" It is the only statue honoring a novelist in the hall and bears a poem written by "the Hoosier poet," James Whitcomb Riley, a fitting tribute to one of America's largely forgotten treasures.

David Dixon Porter

The Union's "Other Admiral"

Born to a naval warfare hero, David Porter, David Dixon Porter was slated for the navy from his birth. His contumacious father—he finally resigned from the navy rather than accept punishment for insubordination—had fought on the sea in every war from 1776 to 1824, and his son would be "every bit as daring, obstreperous, and opinionated as his father." The elder Porter accepted a commission in the Mexican navy after his resignation, and young David accompanied him.[195]

Young Porter went to sea with his father when he was ten as a midshipman—so-called because they lived in the middle of the ship—and, like his foster brother, David Farragut, moved up the ranks to become a naval officer. Thus followed numerous billets ashore and at sea, including a period of time during which he took leave from the navy to command various merchant ships, when he could not get command of navy vessels. It would take a war to pry his career loose from the hidebound navy bureaucracy and his twenty-year career as a lieutenant.[196]

At the outbreak of the Civil War, Porter received orders to take command of the *Powhatan* and relieve the besieged Fort Pickens near Pensacola.[197] Subsequently, after blockade duty, Porter finally received a promotion to commander.[198] His career was now moving, and his next charge was to assist his foster brother, Farragut, in taking New Orleans.[199] The story is well-known: Farragut ran the guns of the two forts guarding that city— while Porter's squadron bombarded them—and took New Orleans without firing a shot.[200]

Next up was Vicksburg, the "Citadel of the Confederacy" through which poured supplies for the Confederate states east of the Mississippi River. At Vicksburg, Porter first ran the guns going north and then did so again running south. His squadron ferried Grant's army across the Mississippi to Bruinsburg, from which Grant launched his invasion of Mississippi. Porter worked closely with Grant and Sherman in taking the city in the summer of 1863.[201] It was a classic coordinated army-navy operation that would portend operations to come in World War II. For his work at Vicksburg, Porter received the thanks of both generals and the thanks of Congress,[202] as well as a promotion "to rear admiral over eighty officers his senior in rank."[203]

After Vicksburg, Porter took command of a fleet that attacked Fort Fisher near Wilmington, North Carolina, and with the eventual help of the army, took the last Confederate stronghold on the coasts of the Confederacy. His final action in the Civil War came when he took his fleet up the James River and forced Confederate admiral Raphael Semmes to scuttle his squadron. For Porter, the war was over. He received three official "thanks" of Congress, which was unprecedented.[204]

His first postwar billet was superintendent of the nascent Naval Academy at Annapolis, which he held until 1869.[205] Some of his instructors were George Dewey, who would destroy the Spanish fleet at Manila Bay in 1898, and Winfield Scott Schley and William T. Sampson, both of whom would also emerge as Spanish-American War heroes. Porter's emphasis at the Academy, besides on steam-powered vessels, was on gunnery. He also emphasized social activities for the Academy's midshipmen, including monthly dances at which dance instructors prepared the midshipmen for the fleet. He also wheedled money out of a Congress intent on reducing America's military establishment for the purchase of additional land and buildings.[206]

While at the Academy, Porter received a promotion to vice admiral,[207] when his foster brother, Farragut, became admiral of the navy. Farragut died in 1870, and Porter succeeded him in that position. There, Porter oversaw the transition of the navy from sail to steam, modernized the Naval Academy's curriculum to focus on steam engines, and engaged in various verbal and written skirmishes with enemies he had made during the war, especially Benjamin Butler, who had failed to attack New Orleans and Fort Fisher by land and thus incurred Porter's wrath.

Building on the relationship they had established during the Civil

War, Porter and Grant became fast friends, with Porter—when Grant ran for president—volunteering his "absurd testimony" that Grant was a teetotaler. Once elected, Grant wanted Porter to be his secretary of the navy, but the president recognized that there was a significant element in Congress who wanted no military personnel in civilian positions, so he instead nominated and secured the position for Adolph E. Borie, "a wealthy Philadelphia merchant who knew nothing about the Navy—and assigned Porter to special duty in the Department as [his] mentor."[208]

David Dixon Porter (1861–1865).

When Grant took office, the war had been over almost four years, a time during which the navy had fallen into disrepair and ruin. Borie and Porter at once set out to revitalize the fleet, the oversight of which was lodged in myriad "bureaus," each operating independent of the others and largely independent of Borie and Porter, who immediately went to work bringing the navy's bureaucracy under control. The various bureaus were not without political connections, however, and Porter's aggressive approach engendered enemies in Congress.

Admiral Farragut died on August 14, 1870, and Grant immediately promoted Porter to full admiral.[209] But there was trouble for the two men on the horizon. During the war, Porter had written a letter critical of Grant for his nonfeasance with respect to the operations at Fort Fisher. The gravamen of Porter's complaint was that Grant was slow in supporting the naval operation. Porter's enemies now released the letter to the press, and Grant suffered egregiously from the words of his friend. Porter apologized publicly, but the damage was done, even though Grant said that he forgave Porter.

As "Lord High Admiral," the honorary title accorded Porter by his friend Sherman, the admiral took up residence at a large home in Washington. The house was only a five-minute walk from the Navy Department and had once housed the British embassy. It soon "became a mecca for politicians and naval officers." Porter maintained a well-stocked pantry of fine wines and whiskey, carefully inventoried and itemized. With Civil War prize money continuing to flow into his personal coffers, Porter was able to buy summer homes at Perth Amboy and in Newport, Rhode Island, a growing destination for America's wealthy.[210]

Porter then in his spare time became a writer, writing first his memoirs and then "a torrent of fiction" that included four novels, one of them a two-volume set.[211] One of the books even became a play, with its gala opening in New York attended not only by Admiral and Mrs. Porter, but by General Sherman as well. At intermission, "the audience cheered the venerable author."[212]

By now, Porter's attitude toward the South had become one of "sympathetic understanding." They had fought and fought well, and they had lost. It was time to heal the old wounds and bring the country together again.

The admiral then wrote *The Naval History of the Civil War*, in support of which he relied mostly on his memory rather than Navy Department official records. He was too impetuous to take the time to mine those records for factual material. The account was flawed from its inception, its factual basis in some cases nonexistent.

Porter's last social event was the celebration of his fiftieth wedding anniversary, held at his Washington home and attended by President Benjamin Harrison. Then, to celebrate the centennial of Washington's inauguration as president, Porter took command of all the naval vessels in New York harbor. It was his last command afloat.

In 1890 Porter summered in Newport and, against his physician's advice, took a long, strenuous walk, after which he suffered a heart attack. He survived and returned to Washington, where he hung on during the fall and winter of 1890 and 1891. Then, on February 13, 1891, Porter died at his home there.

At high noon two days later the ships of the Navy fired fifteen-minute guns. A marine stood watch at the door of 1710 H Street. President Harrison, Vice President Morton, cabinet members, Governors, Congressmen, ranking rear admirals of the Navy, generals of the Union and of the Confederacy passed through the doorway of the house. Lining the sidewalk opposite were commodores, captains, lieutenants of the Navy in full dress with swords. At seventeenth Street the Marine Band was formed. Behind them were sailors and marines—as many as had stormed the salient of Fort Fisher.

General Joseph Johnston of the Confederate Army was a pallbearer. They took the admiral to Arlington for interment. "The gala, four-starred flag of the second Admiral was lowered from the mainmast head."[213] The combative Porter had fought the last of many battles. His war was at last over.

Daniel Edgar Sickles

The Rogue General

Daniel Sickles, a larger-than-life Falstaff of a general, is likely the most colorful commander to fight on either side in the Civil War. His life's story reads like a biographical combination of Boss Tweed, Al Capone and W.C. Fields, an amalgam of wild women, murder, profligacy and flamboyance, as well as an unwillingness to take orders from anyone he did not like, including, when he was a boy, his own father.

Sickles was born in New York City on October 20, 1819,[214] the seventh generation of a family of Dutch patricians—the original name was Van Sicklen. His father was a prominent patent lawyer with whom the boy had many conflicts, after many of which he ran away from home. Eventually, after a

Daniel Edgar Sickles (1861–1865).

number of fits and starts, Sickles studied law at New York University and entered the legal profession. He soon began a career in politics grounded in the Democratic Party machinery of Tammany Hall.[215] Sickles moved rapidly through the New York State Assembly into the United States Congress, all the while favoring booze, women of ill repute, gambling and, in general, high living. He teetered on the razor's edge of penury, refused to pay his debts, was accused of embezzlement, and his father, a wealthy man, refused to subsidize his sybaritic lifestyle.[216]

Sickles's wife, Teresa, was nineteen years younger than him, and although he kept prostitutes on the side, she was required by the societal norms of the day to remain faithful to her husband. Teresa, however, had other ideas and took up with young Philip Barton Key, the son of Francis Scott Key, the author of "The Star-Spangled Banner." Sickles uncovered the sordid affair and killed Key. His lawyer, Edwin M. Stanton, soon to be Lincoln's secretary of war, entered a plea of not guilty by reason of temporary insanity, a defense that had never been used in the United States, and Stanton was successful in gaining an acquittal for his notorious client, thus establishing a new line of defense in criminal cases.[217] Sickles then took his wife back, precipitating another scandal, for 1850s society was unforgiving of unfaithful wives.[218] In Congress, Sickles was alone. Even Mary Chesnut, the erstwhile Southern diarist, commented upon his forlorn nature as he sat in Congress one day. She remarked that he sat alone as though he had smallpox.[219]

As a Democrat, Sickles usually voted with the Southern bloc, but as war approached, sensing an opportunity to reverse his political decline, he switched horses and began to rail against secession, especially secession by force. When the war began, Sickles raised a New York brigade and received a commission as a brigadier general, although he had no military experience and was of that class of commanders known euphemistically as "political generals," whom the regulars from the "old army" detested.[220]

Sickles's brigade—the Excelsior Brigade—proved to be an excellent fighting outfit and Sickles a fine combat commander. His brigade was a part of Joseph Hooker's corps, and the two roustabouts became fast friends, sharing a love of booze and prostitutes, both of which and whom were found in abundance in Hooker's headquarters. It was said that Hooker's headquarters was "a combination of barroom and brothel."[221] When Hooker took command of the Army of the Potomac, Sickles relieved him as commanding general of the Third Corps. In Sickles's own headquarters, "the Champaign and whiskey ran in streams," and Sickles had meals catered by Delmonico's in New York.[222]

At Chancellorsville, Sickles's men reported that Jackson was on the move at Hooker's right flank, but Sickles concluded that Jackson was retreating and prepared his men to give chase. The rest is well-known. Jackson slammed into General Oliver O. Howard's XI Corps, whose right flank was "in the air," and Hooker was routed at Chancellorsville. Meade, whom Sickles despised, then took Hooker's place.

At Gettysburg, Sickles engineered one of the most controversial moves of the war. Assigned a section of Meade's line along Cemetery Ridge that would have filled a gap and placed Sickles's left on the Round Tops, Sickles instead, inexplicably and contrary to Meade's direct orders, moved his corps forward into the Peach Orchard, where it created a salient with both sides exposed to enfilading artillery fire.[223] On the second day, Longstreet's corps savaged Sickles's corps, and Sickles left the field on a stretcher, sitting up and smoking a cigar,[224] after having his leg almost severed by artillery fire. Union surgeons afterward took it off. Undaunted by the disaster, Sickles would later claim that he saved Meade by advancing and dissipating the Confederate attack before it could overpower Meade's precarious position on Cemetery Ridge. Sickles also maintained that if he had not moved forward, Meade would have retreated on the second day. The bitter dispute between the two generals remains a point of controversy among historians to this day, although the weight of authority is that Sickles bungled the second-day battle and, by creating a gap in Meade's line, almost cost the Union its victory.[225]

With the loss of his leg, the bone from which was placed in a Washington museum—wags said it was the only thing about Sickles that was totally white—Sickles's Civil War career was over. He continued his battles against Meade, in the Congress, before the Committee on the Conduct of the War, and with anyone who would listen to his savage attacks on the hero of Gettysburg, or at least, *one* of the heroes of Gettysburg.[226]

Sickles campaigned for Grant in 1868 and received as his reward appointment as minister to Spain, where he quickly became involved in a busy social life, his usual philandering and, it was rumored, an affair with Queen Isabella II. Teresa having died in 1867, Sickles soon remarried an attendant in Isabella's court, but rumors had it that the marriage was merely a cloak for the continuing queenly affair. Finally, fed up with his personal life and frequent sorties into Spanish politics, the Spanish government requested the United States to recall him, which it did.[227]

Upon his return, Sickles held political sinecures in New York before gaining his ultimate revenge, reelection to Congress in 1892. Defeated in 1894, he still managed further revenge—this of a military nature—when he incredibly was awarded the Congressional Medal of Honor for his service at Gettysburg, a tribute as much to his political skill and connections as to his military prowess on that field of battle.[228]

Sickles's father died in 1887 and left him an estate of $5 million, an enormous sum in that day, worth over $165 million today. By the time of his death, in 1914, Dan was, however, broke, having squandered his estate on his usual pastimes: booze, women, high living and bogus business deals. He thought, and said, that dying rich would be a waste of good money.[229]

Sickles's lasting legacy was the military park at Gettysburg, which he visited many times in the years after the war. He met his old adversary, newly minted Republican—anathema to his former Confederate comrades—James Longstreet, and together they famously got roaring drunk at a dinner in Atlanta. The two were bound by more, however, than their love of good Irish whiskey: they were both branded goats for their performances at Gettysburg, Sickles for his foolhardy and costly salient and Longstreet for being "late" on the second day. Indeed, Longstreet, in 1902, wrote a widely published article in which he contended that Sickles's move into the Peach Orchard had saved the day for Meade.[230]

In his last days—he would live to be ninety-four—Sickles contented himself with visits to Gettysburg and with taking guests to see his leg at the Washington Medical Museum. Of that predilection, Mark Twain wrote, "I noticed that the general valued his lost leg way above the one that is left. I am perfectly sure that if he had to part with either of them, he would part with the one he has got."[231] Sickles' tibia remains on display to this day at the Army Medical Museum in Bethesda, Maryland.[232]

Major General Daniel Edgar Sickles died "irresponsible and cantankerous" on May 3, 1914, on the eve of another great war, and is buried in Arlington National Cemetery.[233]

Notes

Chapter One

1. Wakelyn, Jon L., "George Gordon Meade," in Ritter, Charles F., and Wakelyn, Jon L., Eds., *Leaders of the American Civil War*, 281.
2. Bache, Richard Meade, *Life of General George Gordon Meade*, 2–15, 563; Eicher and Eicher, *Civil War High Commands*, 364; Huntington, Tom, *Searching for George Gordon Meade*, 14–34; Jones, Wilmer L., *Generals in Blue and Gray*, Vol. 1, 285–287; Meade, Colonel George Gordon, *The Life and Letters of George Gordon Meade*, Vol. 1, 12–31, 222–23-, 281; Sauers, Richard A., "George Gordon Meade," 1295; Wakelyn, "Meade," 278–287; Warner, Ezra J., *Generals in Blue, Lives of the Union Commanders*, 315–316.
3. Jones, Wilmer L., *Generals*, Vol. 1, 288.
4. Huntington, *Searching*, 84–85.
5. Huntington, Id., 96; Meade, *Life*, 341–349.
6. Eicher and Eicher, *High Commands*, 385; Sauers, "Meade," 1295.
7. Huntington, *Searching*, 133.
8. Huntington, *Searching*, 206.
9. Huntington, *Searching*, 250; Meade, *Life*, 199.
10. Bache, *Life*, 419–420; Huntington, Id., 270; Jones, Wilmer L., *Generals*, Vol. 1, 296; Meade, *Life*, Vol. 2, 214.
11. Huntington, *Searching*, 294; Sauers, "Meade," 1296.
12. Huntington, Id., 294–295.
13. Id., 296.
14. Wakelyn, "Meade," 217.
15. Povall, Allie Stuart, *Rebels in Repose, Confederate Commanders After the War*, 175.

16. Huntington, *Searching*, 319–320; Meade, *Life*, Vol. 2. 246–247. 270, 272–272.
17. Huntington, Id., 346; Jones, Wilmer L., *Generals*, Vol. 2, 298; Lyman, *Headquarters*, 245–246.
18. Huntington, *Searching*, 357.
19. Id.
20. Meade, *Life and Letters*, Vol. 2, 315.
21. Sauers, "Meade," 1297.
22. Meade, *Life and Letters*, Vol. 2, 315.
23. Meade, *Life and Letters*, Vol. 2, 317–318.
24. Huntington, *Searching*, 359.
25. Green, Carl R., and Sanford, William R., *Union Generals of the Civil War*, 74; Huntington, Id., 359.
26. Jones, Wilmer L., *Generals*, Vol. 1, 298.
27. Huntington, *Searching*, 360.
28. Meade, *Life and Letters*, Vol. 2, 327–328.
29. Huntington, *Searching*, 362; Meade, Id., 328–329.
30. Meade, *Life and Letters*, Vol. 2, 332.
31. Huntington, *Searching*, 362–363; Jones, Wilmer L., *Generals*, Vol. 1, 298; Meade, Id., Vol. 2, 337.
32. Huntington, *Searching*, 362–363.
33. Huntington, *Searching*, 362–363.
34. Meade, *Life and Letters*, Vol. 2, 339.
35. Green and Sanford, *Generals*, 74.
36. Jones, Wilmer L., *Generals*, Vol. 2, 298.

Chapter Two

1. Beagle, Jonathon, M., "George Brinton McClellan," in Heidler, David S., and Jeanne T., Editors, *Encyclopedia of the*

American Civil War, 1273; Sears, Stephen W., *George B. McClellan, The Young Napoleon,* 2–3.
  2. Sears, *McClellan,* 3.
  3. Beagle, "McClellan," 1273; Green and Sanford, *Generals,* 59; Jones, Wilmer L., *Generals,* Vol. 1, 72; Rowland, Thomas J., "George Brinton McClellan," in Ritter and Wakelin, *Leaders,* 259; Warner, *Generals,* 290.
  4. Sears, *Young Napoleon,* 5–8.
  5. Sears, *Young Napoleon,* 5–8; Warner, *Generals,* 72.
  6. Jones, Wilmer L., *Generals,* Vol. 1, 75; Sears, Id., 47–48.
  7. Sears, Id., 63.
  8. Id., 58–59.
  9. Jones, Wilmer l., *McClellan,* Vol. 1, 78–79; Rowland, "McClellan," 263; Sears, *Young Napoleon,* 132–133.
  10. Beagle, "McClellan," 1273–1274; Green and Sanford, *Union Generals,* 81; Jones, Wilmer L., *Generals,* Vol. 1, 78; Rowland, "McClellan," 262–263.
  11. Sears, *Young Napoleon,* 199.
  12. Id., 202.
  13. Id., 276–277.
  14. Beagle, "McClellan," 1276; Eicher and Eicher, *High Commands,* 372; Jones, Wilmer L., *Generals,* Vol. 1, 85; Sears, Stephen W., "Lincoln and McClellan," in Borritt, Gabor S., Editor, *Lincoln's Generals,* 40–42; Rowland, "McClellan," 267–268.
  15. Sears, *Young Napoleon,* 344–345.
  16. Sears, *Young Napoleon,* 347.
  17. Sears, *Young Napoleon,* 356.
  18. Sears, *Young Napoleon,* 358–359.
  19. Sears, *Young Napoleon,* 361–362.
  20. Id., 363–364.
  21. Id., 366–367.
  22. Beagle, "McClellan," 1277; Sears, *Young Napoleon,* 369–386.
  23. Jones, Wilmer L., *Generals,* Vol. 1, 87; Sears, Id., 387–388.
  24. Sears, *Young Napoleon,* 388.
  25. Jones, Wilmer L., *Generals,* Vol. 1, 87; Sears, *Young Napoleon,* 391.
  26. Eicher and Eicher, *High Commands,* 372; Sears, Id., 393.
  27. Printed in *Harper's Weekly* as a series and subsequently as a book.
  28. Sears, *Young Napoleon,* 397–400.
  29. Sears, *Young Napoleon,* 401.
  30. Id.; Jones, Wilmer L., *Generals,* Vol. 1, 88.
  31. Beagle, *McClellan,* 1277.

Chapter Three

  1. Duffy, James P., *Lincoln's Admiral,* 2–4; Davis, Michael S., "David Glasgow Farragut," in Heidler and Heidler, Eds., *Encyclopedia,* 682.
  2. Eicher and Eicher, *High Commands,* 231.
  3. Davis, "Farragut," 683; Duffy, *Lincoln's Admiral,* 4; Hearn, Chester G., *Admiral David Glasgow Farragut,* xvi.
  4. Davis, "Farragut," 683, Duffy, *Admiral,* 4.
  5. Hearn, *Admiral,* xv.
  6. Davis, "Farragut," 683; Duffy, *Lincoln's Admiral,* 5.
  7. Hearn, *Admiral,* xix.
  8. Davis, "Farragut," 683; Duffy, *Lincoln's Admiral,* 30–31.
  9. Davis, "Farragut," 684; Duffy, *Lincoln's Admiral,* 33–36; Hearn, *Admiral,* 34–37.
  10. Davis, "Farragut," 684; Duffy, *Lincoln's Admiral,* 45–58; Eicher and Eicher, *High Commands,* 232; Hearn, *Admiral,* 42–51.
  11. Chesnut, Mary Boykin, *Mary Chesnut's Civil War,* Edited by C. Vann Woodward, 330.
  12. Duffy, *Lincoln's Admiral,* 116.
  13. Id., 203–219; Hearn, *Admiral,* 220–221; Lewis, *Farragut,* 183–197.
  14. Hearn, Id.
  15. Duffy, *Lincoln's Admiral,* 219.
  16. Id., 219–220.
  17. Hearn, *Admiral,* 222–223.
  18. Duffy, *Lincoln's Admiral,* 226–233; Hearn, *Admiral,* 227; Lewis, *Farragut,* 222.
  19. Davis, "Farragut," 684; Duffy, Id., 245–246 (states that the *Tecumseh* sank in thirty seconds); Hearn, Id., 245; Lewis, Id., 267.
  20. Hearn, Id., 263.
  21. Hearn, Id., 260–261, 263; Lewis, *Farragut,* 269.
  22. Hearn, *Admiral,* 263; Lewis, *Farragut,* 263–264.
  23. Davis, "Farragut," 684; Duffy, *Admiral,* 265.
  24. Hearn, *Admiral,* 263–265.
  25. Duffy, *Admiral,* 247.
  26. Lewis, *Farragut,* 269–270.
  27. Duffy, *Admiral,* 248.
  28. Hearn, *Admiral,* 290.
  29. Davis, "Farragut," 685; Duffy, *Lincoln's Admiral,* 256–257; Hearn, Id., 302; Lewis, *Farragut,* 298–303.

30. Eicher and Eicher, *High Commands,* 232.
31. Lewis, *Farragut,* 319.
32. Id., 322.
33. Lewis, *Farragut,* 323.
34. Lewis, *Farragut,* 324–325.
35. Id., 331.
36. Id., 330–331.
37. Hearn, *Admiral,* 303.
38. Lewis, *Farragut,* 331.
39. Davis, "Farragut," 685; Eicher and Eicher, *High Commands,* 232; Lewis, Id., 331.
40. Lewis, Id., 332.
41. Hearn, *Admiral,* 309.
42. Hearn, *Admiral,* 310.
43. Id., 311.
44. Lewis, *Farragut,* 317.
45. Hearn, *Admiral,* 311.
46. Duffy, *Admiral,* 258; Hearn, Id.
47. Hearn, *Admiral,* 311.
48. Lewis, *Farragut,* 345.
49. Hearn, *Admiral,* 313.
50. Hearn, *Admiral,* 314.
51. Hearn, *Admiral,* 316–317.
52. Id., 317.
53. Hearn, *Admiral,* 317–318.

Chapter Four

1. Fredricksen, John C., "Sheridan," *Encyclopedia,* 1760; Morris, *Terrible Swift Sword,* 2.
2. Sheridan, *Memoirs,* 2.
3. Morris *Sheridan,* 14.
4. Drake, *Little Phil,* 16.
5. Wheelan, *Terrible Swift Sword,* 194.
6. Id., 195.
7. Drake, *Little Phil,* 428.
8. Drake, *Little Phil,* 444–445; Ritter and Wakelyn, *Leaders,* 363; Sheridan, *Memoirs,* 402; Wheelan, *Terrible Swift Sword,* 209–212.
9. Drake, *Little Phil,* 448–458; Wheelan, *Terrible Swift Sword,* 212–216.
10. For a detailed account of the incident at Fort Pillow, see Heidler and Heidler, *Encyclopedia,* 745–746.
11. Fredriksen, "Sheridan," 1762; Wheelan, *Terrible Swift Sword,* 222–228.
12. Wheelan, Id., 228.
13. Wheelan, *Terrible Swift Sword,* 230.
14. Fredriksen, "Sheridan," 1762; Morris, *Sheridan,* 328; Wheelan, *Terrible Swift Sword,* 252.

15. Wheelan, *Terrible Swift Sword,* 250.
16. Id., 252.
17. Wheelan, *Terrible Swift Sword,* 253. See also Drake, *Little Phil,* 521–524 and Sheridan, *Memoirs,* 492.
18. Drake, *Little Phil,* 522.
19. Wheelan, *Terrible Swift Sword,* 257.
20. Drake, *Little Phil,* 525.
21. Povall, *Rebels,* 128.
22. Drake, *Little Phil,* 532; Wheelan, *Terrible Swift Sword,* 258–259.
23. Morris, *Sheridan,* 335–338.
24. Drake, *Little Phil,* 533; Wheelan, *Terrible Swift Sword,* 260.
25. Wheelan, Id.; Morris, *Sheridan,* 340–341.
26. Wheelan, *Terrible Swift Sword,* 261. See also Morris, *Sheridan,* 340.
27. Morris, Id., 342.
28. Morris, *Sheridan,* 344–345; Wheelan, *Terrible Swift Sword,* 264–265.
29. Wheelan, *Terrible Swift Sword,* 268. See Povall, *Rebels,* 137–138, for a discussion of Semmes and the *Somers.*
30. Drake, *Little Phil,* 553–556; Morris, *Sheridan,* 349–354; Wheelan, *Terrible Swift Sword,* 274–275.
31. Drake, Id., 556; Morris, Id., 355–356; Wheelan, Id., 273–274.
32. See pages 368–371 for a detailed discussion of the Battle of Little Bighorn.
33. Drake, *Little Phil,* 566–573; Morris, *Sheridan;* Wheelan, *Terrible Swift Sword,* 281.
34. Drake, *Little Phil,* 562–574; Morris, *Sheridan,* 361–364; Wheelan, *Terrible Swift Sword,* 276–277.
35. Drake, Id., 585–587.
36. Drake, *Little Phil,* 589.
37. Wheelan, *Terrible Swift Sword,* 287.
38. Drake, *Little Phil,* 598; Morris, *Sheridan,* 379; Wheelan, Id., 303–304.
39. Morris, *Sheridan,* 384.
40. Wheelan, *Terrible Swift Sword,* 292–299.
41. Wheelan, *Terrible Swift Sword,* 307.
42. Morris, *Sheridan,* 256.
43. Drake, *Little Phil,* 636; Wheelan, *Terrible Swift Sword,* 311.
44. Povall, *Rebels,* 205.
45. Drake, *Little Phil,* 636–637.
46. Povall, *Rebels,* 77–78.
47. Wheelan, *Terrible Swift Sword,* 311–313.
48. Wheelan, Id., 313–314.

Chapter Five

1. Marszalek, John F., "William Tecumseh Sherman," in Heidler and Heidler, *Encyclopedia*, 1764–1765; Sherman, William Tecumseh, *Memoirs*, 1–3.
2. Jones, Wilmer L. *Generals*, Vol. 1, 199–200; Marszalek, "William Tecumseh Sherman," in Ritter and Wakelyn, Editors, *Leaders*, 366–367; Sherman, Id.
3. Marszalek, "Sherman," 366; Sherman, Id.
4. Jones, Wilmer L., *Generals*, Vol. 1, 199–201; Sherman, *Memoirs*, 3.
5. Jones, Id.; Green and Sanford, *Generals*, 86–87; Sherman, Id., 4.
6. Warner, *Generals*, 442.
7. Sherman, *Memoirs*, 5.
8. Id., 8.
9. Id., 13.
10. Id., 48.
11. Povall, *Rebels*, 81–82.
12. Id, 87–88.
13. Sherman, *Memoirs*, 54–65.
14. Id., 68.
15. Jones, *Generals*, Vol. 1, 202.
16. Sherman, *Memoirs*, 71–80.
17. Marszalek, "Sherman," 1766.
18. Jones, Wilmer L., *Generals*, Vol. 1, 202.
19. Marszalek, "Sherman," 1766.
20. Fellman, Michael, "William Tecumseh Sherman," in Boritt, Gabor S., Editor, *Lincoln's Generals*, 135.
21. Id.
22. Green and Sanford, *Union Generals*, 88; Warner, *Generals*, 442.
23. Warner, Id.
24. Jones, Wilmer L., *Generals*, Vol. 1, 204; Marszalek, "Sherman," *Encyclopedia*, 368–369.
25. *See* Povall, *Rebels*, 8. 14–15, 58–59.
26. Green and Sanford, *Union Generals*, 88; Warner, *Generals*, 443.
27. Jones, Wilmer L., *Generals*, Vol. 1, 205.
28. Jones, Wilmer L., *Generals*, Vol. 1, 205.
29. McDonough, *William Tecumseh Sherman*, 380.
30. Marszalek, "Sherman," in Ritter and Wakelyn, *Leaders*, 371.
31. McDonough, *Sherman*, 382.
32. Id., 377.
33. Jones, Wilmer L., *Generals*, Vol. 1, 205; Marszalek, "Sherman," 1767;

Sherman, in Ritter and Wakelyn, *Leaders*, 370.
34. Marszalek, "Sherman," *Encyclopedia*, 1767; McDonough, *Sherman*, 423.
35. Warner, *Generals*, 443.
36. Jones, Wilmer L., *Generals*, Vol. 1, 206.
37. Povall, *Rebels*, 120–122.
38. McDonough, *Sherman*, 501–502.
39. Jones, Wilmer, *Generals*, 206. Povall, *Rebels*, 102.
40. Jones, Id.
41. Marszalek, *Sherman*, 1768; For the Confederate perspective, see, e.g., Povall, *Rebels*, 57–58, 101–102.
42. Marszalek, Id.
43. Jones, Wilmer L., *Generals*, Vol. 1, 208.
44. Id.
45. McDonough, *Sherman*, 594.
46. Hart, B. H. Liddell, *Sherman, Soldier, Realist, American*, 356.
47. Green and Sanford, *Union Generals*, 90.
48. Jones, Wilmer L., *Generals*, Vol. 1, 208.
49. Marszalek, "Sherman," 1768.
50. Flood, Charles Bracelen, *Grant and Sherman, The Friendship That Won the Civil War*, 331.
51. McDonough, *Sherman*, 625–630.
52. McDonough, *Sherman*, 625–630.; Sherman, *Memoirs*, Volume 2, 379.
53. Flood, *Grant and Sherman*, 346; Green and Sanford, *Generals*, 92; Marszalek, John F., *Sherman, A Soldier's Passion for Order*, 346.
54. Flood, *Grant and Sherman*, 339; Marszalek, "Sherman," 1768.
55. Flood, Id., 352; Marszalek, Id., 1768–1769.
56. Jones, Wilmer L., *Generals*, Vol. 1, 210.
57. Flood, *Grant and Sherman*, 352.
58. Id., 355, 389; Marszalek, *Passion*, 352, 353, 357.
59. Jones, Wilmer L., *Generals*, Vol. 1, 211; Marszalek, *Passion*, 358.
60. Jones, Id.
61. Marszalek, *Passion*, 361; McDonough, *Sherman*, 648.
62. O'Connell, Robert L., *Fierce Patriot, The Tangled Lives of William Tecumseh Sherman*, 310–314. See also, McDonough, *Sherman*, 648.
63. McDonough, Id., 651.

64. Marszalek, *Passion*, 361.
65. Id.
66. Marszalek. *Passion*, 362.
67. Hart, *Sherman*, 406.
68. O'Connell, *Fierce Patriot*, 313.
69. McDonough, *Sherman*, 650.
70. O'Connell, *Fierce Patriot*, 313.
71. Hart, *Sherman*, 407; Marszalek, *Passion*, 366.
72. Marszalek, "Sherman," 1769.
73. Marszalek, *Passion*, 365–369.
74. Hart, *Sherman*, 406–410.
75. Marszalek, *Passion*, 364; McDonough, *Sherman*, 662.
76. Jones, Wilmer L., *Generals*, Vol. 1, 211.
77. Marszalek, *Passion*, 381.
78. Id., 379.
79. Marszalek, Id., 380; McDonough, *Sherman*, 678.
80. McDonough, *Sherman*, 651.
81. Hart, *Sherman*, 404.
82. Id., 405.
83. McDonough, *Sherman*, 652.
84. O'Connell, *Fierce Patriot*, 319.
85. McDonough, *Sherman*, 654.
86. Id., 654–655.
87. McDonough, *Sherman*, 656.
88. McDonough, *Sherman*, 656.
89. Marszalek, *Passion*, 379.
90. McDonough, *Sherman*, 658.
91. Hart, *Sherman*, 411–412.
92. Marszalek, *Passion*, 384.
93. McDonough, *Sherman*, 665.
94. Id., 666.
95. McDonough, *Sherman*, 665–666.
96. McDonough, *Sherman*, 669.
97. Marszalek, *Passion*, 394.
98. Marszalek, *Passion*, 394–395; McDonough, *Sherman*, 669–672.
99. Marszalek, Id., 362–364.
100. Hart, *Sherman*, 414–416; O'Connell, *Fierce Patriot*, 319–320.
101. Marszalek, *Passion*, 387.
102. Id., 405–406; McDonough, *Sherman*, 679.
103. Marszalek, *Passion*, 418–419; O'Connell, *Fierce Patriot*, 327–330.
104. Hart, *Sherman*, 417.
105. Hart, *Sherman*, 417.
106. McDonough, *Sherman*, 709.
107. Hart, *Sherman*, 418; Jones, Wilmer L., *Generals*, Vol. 1, 213; O'Connell, *Fierce Patriot*, 322–323.
108. Jones, Wilmer L., *Generals*, Vol. 1, 213.

109. O'Connell, *Fierce Patriot*, 331–337.
110. Marszalek, *Passion*, 401.
111. Marszalek, *Passion*, 442–443; O'Connell, *Fierce Patriot*, 318–319.
112. Marszalek, Id., 437.
113. McDonough, *Sherman*, 687–688.
114. Marszalek, *Passion*, 398–399.
115. McDonough, *Passion*, 682.
116. Id., 682–683.
117. See, e.g., O'Connell, *Fierce Patriot*, 322–323.
118. Marszalek, *Passion*, 485; McDonough, *Sherman*, 688.
119. Marszalek, Id., 418–420; O'Connell, *Fierce Patriot*, 337–338.
120. Marszalek, *Passion*, 492.
121. McDonough, *Sherman*, 704
122. Jones, Wilmer L., *Generals*, Vol. 1, 212; Marszalek, *Passion*, 453; McDonough, Id., 705.
123. See Povall, *Rebels*, 149–206.
124. Marszalek, "Sherman," 1769; Marszalek, *Passion*, 420–421; Povall, Id., 154.
125. McDonough, *Sherman*, 706–707.
126. Hart, *Sherman*, 420–423.
127. McDonough, *Sherman*, 708.
128. McDonough, *Sherman*, 310–311.
129. Marszalek, *Passion*, 488–499.
130. McDonough, *Sherman*, 314.
131. Marszalek, *Passion*, 489.
132. O'Connell, *Fierce Patriot*, 345.
133. McDonough, *Sherman*, 319–320.
134. Marszalek, *Passion*, 499.
135. Jones, Wilmer L., *Generals*, Vol. 1, 213; Marszalek, Id., 490–492; McDonough, *Sherman*, 321.
136. Jones, Id., 213.
137. Marszalek, "Sherman," 374.
138. Id., 374–375.
139. Marszalek, "Sherman," 376.

Chapter Six

1. Grant, Ulysses S., *Memoirs*, 16.
2. See, e.g., Brand, *The Man Who Saved the Union, Ulysses Grant in War and Peace*, 16; Grant, Id., 16; Smith, Jean Edward, *Grant, A Biography*, 21. Quoted matter from Chernow, Ron, *Grant*, 5.
3. Brand, *The Man*, 7–8; Chernow, *Grant*, 4; Smith, Grant, 22; Waugh, Joan, *U.S. Grant, American Hero, American*

Myth, 13; White, Ronald C., *American Ulysses, A Life of Ulysses S. Grant*, 4.
4. Waugh, Id., 19; White, Id., 25.
5. Chernow, *Grant*, 18; Waugh, Id., 20.
6. McFeely, William S., *Grant*, 21; Smith, *Grant*, 26.
7. Waugh, *Grant*, 22; See also, McFeely, *Grant*, 20.
8. McFeely, Id., 16.
9. Brands, *The Man*, 18; Smith, *Grant*, 30; White, *American Ulysses*, 45, 51–52.
10. Grant, *Memoirs*, 29.
11. Chernow, *Grant*, 42.
12. Chernow, Id., 48; Grant, *Memoirs*, 57; White, *American Ulysses*, 84.
13. Chernow, *Grant*, 57–59; Grant, *Memoirs*, 80–81.
14. Grant, *Memoirs*, Vol. 1, 31; Smith, *Grant*, 35.
15. Brands, *The Man*, 70–72; Smith, *Grant*, 86–87.
16. Smith, Id., 90.
17. Chernow, *Grant*, 98; McFeely, *Grant*, 62; Smith, Id., 91.
18. Chernow, *Grant*, 135–137; McFeely, *Grant*, 75.
19. Chernow, Id., 146; McFeely, Id., 92.
20. Chernow, *Grant*, 164.
21. Grant, *Memoirs*, 51.
22. Grant, *Memoirs*, 165; Hubbell, John T., "Ulysses Simpson Grant," in Ritter and Wakelyn, *Leaders*, 157; McFeely, *Grant*, 115; Povall, *Rebels*, 14, 29.
23. Borritt, *Lincoln's Generals*, 179.
24. Jones, Wilmer L., *Generals*, Vol. 1, 165; Sommers, Richard J., "Ulysses Simpson Grant," in Heidler and Heidler, *Encyclopedia*, 868; Warner, *Generals*, 185; Waugh, *Grant*, 63–64.
25. Sommers, "Grant," 868.
26. Hubbell, *Grant*, 158; Jones, *Generals*, 172–173; Sommers, "Grant," 868; Waugh, *Grant*, 62–64; Warner, *Grant*, 185, White, *American Ulysses*, 270–286.
27. Eicher and Eicher, *High Commands*, 264.
28. Sommers, "Grant," 868; White, *American Ulysses*, 295.
29. White, *American Ulysses*, 284–285.
30. McFeely, *Grant*, 166–168; Sommers, "Grant," 869; Waugh, *Grant*, 84.
31. Waugh, Id., 86.
32. Grant, *Memoirs*, 353; Jones, *Generals*, 174; Sommers, "Grant," 869; Warner, *Generals*, 185; Waugh, *American Ulysses*, 85; White, *American Ulysses*, 360–361.

33. McFeely, *Grant*, 169.
34. Waugh, *Grant*, 89.
35. McFeely, *Grant*, 197.
36. Grant, *Memoirs*, 437; Smith, *Grant*, 402–438; Waugh, *Grant*, 99.
37. Grant, *Memoirs*, 442.
38. Grant, *Memoirs*, 443–447; White, *American Ulysses*, 412.
39. Grant, Id., 457–458; White, Id., 417.
40. Grant, *Memoirs*, 466.
41. Chernow, *Grant*, 561.
42. Id., 546.
43. McFeely, *Grant*, 237.
44. Chernow, *Grant*, 547.
45. Smith, *Grant*, 419; White, *American Ulysses*, 419.
46. Chernow, *Grant*, 551.
47. Brands, *The Man*, 383; Smith, *Grant*, 417–418; White, *American Ulysses*, 418.
48. White, *American Ulysses*, 419.
49. Chernow, *Grant*, 560.
50. Brands, *The Man*, 389; McFeely, *Grant*, 238–239; White, Id., 422.
51. Chernow, *Grant*, 563–565; McFeely, Id., 239.
52. Chernow, *Grant*, 570; McFeely, Id., 244.
53. Brands, *The Man*, 393; Smith, *Grant*, 422.
54. McFeely, *Grant*, 245; White, *American Ulysses*, 245.
55. Waugh, *Grant*, 115; White, *American Ulysses*, 434.
56. McFeely, *Grant*, 246; White, Id., 427–429.
57. Chernow, *Grant*, 573; Waugh, *Grant*, 113.
58. Waugh, Id., 117.
59. White, *American Ulysses*, 440.
60. Brands, *The Man*, 401; Chernow, *Grant*, 585; McFeely, *Grant*, 259–260; Waugh, *Grant*, 116.
61. Chernow, Id., 577–588; McFeely, *Grant*, 250–252.
62. White, *American Ulysses*, 435.
63. Chernow, *Grant*, 578.
64. Chernow, *Grant*, 582–583.
65. McFeely, *Grant*, 261–262.
66. White, *American Ulysses*, 447.
67. White, *American Ulysses*, 441.
68. Smith, *Grant*, 440–441.
69. Waugh, *Grant*, 118.
70. Chernow, *Grant*, 609.
71. Chernow, *Grant*, 608.
72. White, *American Ulysses*, 463.

73. Id.
74. McFeely, *Grant*, 264–265.
75. Brands, *The Man*, 416; White, *American Ulysses*, 463.
76. Brands, Id., 426.
77. McFeely, *Grant*, 289.
78. Brands, *The Man*, 426–427; McFeely, Id., 286–289; Smith, *Grant*, 459–466; Waugh, *Grant*, 122–124; White, *American Ulysses*, 471–472.
79. McFeely, Id., 289.
80. Brands, *The Man*, 429–433; McFeely, *Grant*, 291–302; Smith, *Grant*, 468–473; Waugh, *Grant*, 122–127; White *American Ulysses*, 473–475.
81. Smith, *Grant*, 472; Waugh, *Grant*, 126.
82. Smith, *Grant*, 474.
83. Id.
84. White, *American Ulysses*, 476–477.
85. Smith, *Grant*, 473.
86. McFeely, *Grant*, 304–305; Smith, *Grant*, 474–475.
87. McFeely, Id., 303; White, *American Ulysses*, 477.
88. McFeely, *Grant*, 305–311.
89. McFeely, Id., 305–318; Waugh, *Grant*, 132–134.
90. Brands, *The Man*, 436; White, *American Ulysses*, 478–479.
91. White, Id.
92. Brands, *The Man*, 437–440; McFeely, *Grant*, 321–331; White, *American Ulysses*, 478–485.
93. Brands, Id., 439–440.
94. McFeely, *Grant*, 328.
95. Brands, *The Man*, 445–446.
96. McFeely, *Grant*, 324, 328–329.
97. Brand, *The Man*, 449; McFeely, *Grant*, 332–355; Smith, *Grant*, 509–515; Waugh, *Grant*, 135–137; White, *American Ulysses*, 505–516.
98. Brand, *The Man*, 448–452; McFeely, *Grant*, 322–355; Smith, *Grant*, 493–499; White, *American Ulysses*, 505–507.
99. Brand, *The Man*, 452–462; McFeely, *Grant*, 342–352; Smith, *Grant*, 499–506; Waugh, *Grant*, 137; White, *American Ulysses*, 507–515.
100. McFeely, *Grant*, 329–331.
101. White, *American Ulysses*, 517.
102. McFeely, *Grant*, 370; Smith, *Grant*, 543.
103. White, *American Ulysses*, 523.
104. Smith, *Grant*, 542–544.
105. Brands, *The Man*, 469.
106. Smith, *Grant*, 544.
107. Waugh, *Grant*, 141.
108. McFeely, *Grant*, 372–373.
109. Waugh, *Grant*, 146–147.
110. Id.
111. Brands, *The Man*, 500–504.
112. White, *American Ulysses*, 529–530.
113. Id., 530.
114. Brands, *The Man*, 493; Smith, *Grant*, 547–549; Waugh, *Grant*, 530–532.
115. Smith, Id., 549; White, *American Ulysses*, 533.
116. Smith, *Grant*, 549; White, *American Ulysses*, 530–532.
117. Brands, *The Man*, 496; White, Id., 549.
118. Smith, *Grant*, 549.
119. White, *American Ulysses*, 534.
120. Brands, *The Man*, 505; White, *American Ulysses*, 536.
121. Brands, *The Man*, 483; Smith, *Grant*, 551; White, Id., 536.
122. Smith, *Grant*, 547; Waugh, *Grant*, 141.
123. White, *American Ulysses*, 539–540.
124. White, *American Ulysses*, 540.
125. McFeely, *Grant*, 385.
126. Smith, *Grant*, 557–558.
127. White, *Grant*, 545.
128. Waugh, *Grant*, 147–149.
129. McFeely, *Grant*, 401.
130. Smith, *Grant*, 573.
131. Brands, *The Man*, 517–530; McFeely, *Grant*, 393–397; Smith, *Grant*, 575–578; White, *American Ulysses*, 541–543.
132. McFeely, Id., 387–388; Smith, Id., 558–563.
133. McFeely, Id., 400–404; Smith, Id., 574; White, *American Ulysses*, 547.
134. McFeely, *Grant*, 530–531; Smith, *Grant*, 577–578.
135. Brands, *The Man*, 541; White, *American Ulysses*, 550.
136. White, *American Ulysses*, 550–551.
137. McFeely, *Grant*, 405–410; Smith, *Grant*, 583–584; White, *American Ulysses*, 564–567.
138. McFeely, *Grant*, 426–428.
139. Brands, *Grant*, 559–561; McFeely, *Grant*, 426–436; Smith, *Grant*, 594–596; White, *American Ulysses*, 564–567.
140. McFeely, Id., 430–432; Smith, Id., 586–587; White, Id., 558–560.
141. McFeely, *Grant*, 432.

142. Id.
143. White, *American Ulysses*, 562–563.
144. Smith, *Grant*, 584.
145. Brands, *The Man*, 561.
146. Brands, *The Man*, 565; McFeely, *Grant*, 438.
147. Brands, *The Man*, 567–577; McFeely, *Grant*, 441–447; Smith, *Grant*, 596–605; White, *American Ulysses*, 573–581.
148. Smith, Id., 605.
149. Brands, *The Man*, 579.
150. Smith, *Grant*, 607.
151. McFeely, *Grant*, 453; Smith, *Grant*, 606.
152. Brands, *The Man*, 579; Chernow, *Grant*, 863; McFeely, Id., *453;* Smith, Id., 607; Waugh, *Grant*, 156; White, *American Ulysses*, 590.
153. Waugh, *Grant*, 158.
154. Brands, *The Man*, 580–581; McFeely, *Grant*, 455–460; Smith, *Grant*, 608; Waugh, *Grant*, 158; White, *American Ulysses*, 591–592.
155. McFeely, Id., 458.
156. Brands, *The Man*, 585; McFeely, *Grant*, 470; White, *American Ulysses*, 602.
157. Brands, Id., 585; McFeely, Id., 469.
158. Brands, *The Man*, 585; McFeely, *Grant*, 468–469; White, *Grant*, 603.
159. Smith, *Grant*, 608; Waugh, *Grant*, 159.
160. White, *American Ulysses*, 602.
161. McFeely, *Grant*, 477.
162. Smith, *Grant*, 611; White, *American Ulysses*, 600.
163. McFeely, *Grant*, 472–473.
164. Brands, *The Man*, 590–591.
165. Smith, *Grant*, 612.
166. Smith, *Grant*, 612.
167. White, *American Ulysses*, 608–609.
168. Id., 605.
169. White, *American Ulysses*, 616.
170. Chernow, *Grant*, 882; McFeely, *Grant*, 476; Smith, *Grant*, 613; Waugh, *Grant*, 161; White, Id., 613–616.
171. Smith, *Grant*, 614; White, Id., 617.
172. White, *American Ulysses*, 617.
173. McFeely, *Grant*, 481.
174. Id., 483; Smith, *Grant*, 616; Waugh, *Grant*, 163.
175. White, *American Ulysses*, 619–621.
176. Smith, *Grant*, 618.
177. McFeely, *Grant*, 487; Id., 618–619.
178. Brand, *Grant*, 619.

179. McFeely, *Grant*, 489; Smith, *Grant*, 619; White, *American Ulysses*, 625–628.
180. Smith, *Grant*, 619.
181. Brands, *The Man*, 619–620; McFeely, *Grant*, 490; Smith, Id.
182. McFeely, *Grant*, 629; Smith, *Grant*, 620; White, *American Ulysses*, 629.
183. Brands, *The Man*, 620; White, Id., 629–630.
184. Brands, Id., 620–621; Smith, *Grant*, 620.
185. Smith, *Grant*, 620.
186. Brands, *The Man*, 620–621; Smith, *Grant*, 621; White, *American Ulysses*, 630.
187. Brands, Id, 622; Smith, Id., 622–623.
188. Smith, *Grant*, 621–622.
189. White, *American Ulysses*, 632,
190. Brands, *The Man*, 622; McFeely, *Grant*, 495; Smith, *Grant*, 622; Waugh, *Grant*, 171–172; White, Id., 634.
191. Chernow, *Grant*, 935; McFeely, *Grant*, 499–500; Smith, *Grant*, 602; Waugh, *Grant*, 182. Note: Some biographers say 75 percent of proceeds or net profits. See, e.g., Brands, *The Man*, 622.
192. Smith, Id., 624.
193. Waugh, *Grant*, 173.
194. Id., 193.
195. Brands, *The Man*, 622.
196. Smith, *Grant*, 625; White, *American Ulysses*, 641.
197. Brands, *The Man*, 627.
198. Waugh, *Grant*, 180.
199. Smith, *Grant*, 626.
200. White, *American Ulysses*, 659.
201. McFeely, *Grant*, 519.
202. Id., 521; White, *American Ulysses*, 658–659.
203. McFeely, Id., 520–521.
204. Brands, *The Man*, 633.
205. See Povall, *Rebels*, 53–54, 205–206.

Chapter Seven

1. Biographer Benjamin Perley Poore posits May 23 as the date of birth (Poore, *The Life and Public Service of Ambrose E. Burnside*, 26).
2. Jones, Wilmer L., *Generals*, Vol. 1, 152–153; Poore, Id., 26–35.
3. Eicher and Eicher, *High Commands*, 155; Jones, Wilmer L., *Generals*, Vol. 1, 152. Poore at 45 states that he finished eighteenth out of thirty graduating cadets.

4. Eicher and Eicher and Warner both state that his commission was in the Second Artillery.

5. Jones, Wilmer L., *Generals*, Vol. 1, 152; Poore, *Burnside*, 64.

6. Jones, Id., 153.

7. Poore, *Burnside*, 74.

8. Jones, Wilmer L., *Generals*, Vol. 1, 153; Poore, Id., 73, 76.

9. Poore, *Burnside*, 86–87.

10. Jones, Wilmer L., *Generals*, Vol. 1, 155; Poore, Id., 86–88; Sauers, Richard S., "Ambrose Everett Burnside," in Heidler and Heidler, *Encyclopedia*, 327, Warner, *Generals*, 57.

11. Poore, *Burnside*, 92–93.

12. Jones, Wilmer L., *Generals*, Vol. 1, 156.

13. Jones, Id.; Poore, *Burnside*, 122; Warner, *Generals*, 57.

14. Eicher and Eicher, *High Commands*, 155; Poore, *Burnside*, 124–153; Sauers, "Burnside," 328, Warner, *Generals*, 57.

15. Jones, Wilmer L., *Generals*, Vol. 1, 158; Sauers, "Burnside," 328; Warner, *Generals*, 57.

16. Jones, Wilmer L., *Generals*, Vol. 1, 158; Poore, *Burnside*, 169, 175; Sauers, "Burnside," 328; Warner, *Generals*, 57.

17. Jones, Wilmer L., *Generals*, Vol. 1, 159–160; Poore, *Burnside*, 182–191; Sauers, "Burnside," 328.

18. Eicher and Eicher, *Burnside*, 156; Jones, Id., 160; Sauers, Id., 328.

19. Eicher and Eicher, *Burnside*, 156; Jones, *Generals*, Vol. 1, 164–165; Poore, *Burnside*, 236–248; Sauers, Id., 329; Warner, *Burnside*, 58.

20. Eicher and Eicher, *High Commands*, 156; Jones, Wilmer L., *Generals*, Vol. 1, 165; Poore, *Burnside*, 299–397; Sauers, Burnside," 329; Warner, *Generals*, 58.

21. Urwin, Gregory J. W., "George Armstrong Custer," in Heidler and Heidler, *Encyclopedia*, 539; Warner, *Generals*, 108–109.

22. Povall, *Rebels*, 61.

23. Urwin, "Custer," 539.

24. Urwin, "Custer," 542; Warner, *Generals*, 109.

25. Wert, *Custer*, 224–225.

26. Wert, *Custer*, 246–248.

27. Urwin, "Custer," *Encyclopedia*, 541; Wert, *Custer*, 260–263.

28. Wert, Id., 265.

29. Urwin, "Custer," 541; Warner, *Generals*, 109.

30. Urwin, Id.; Wert, *Custer* 264.

31. Irwun, "Custer," 541, Wert, *Custer*, 268–288.

32. Wert, Id., 293.

33. Urwin, "Custer," 549.

34. Wert, *Custer*, 326–327.

35. Wert, *Custer*, 333.

36. Urwin, "Custer," 541.

37. Urwin, "Custer," 541; Warner, *Generals*, 109–110; Wert, *Custer*, 355.

38. Drake, *Little Phil*, 566–73; Wheelan, *Terrible Swift Sword*, 281.

39. Wert, *Custer*, 355.

40. Wert, *Custer*, 358.

41. Jones, Wilmer L., *Generals*, Vol. 1, 246.

42. Eicher and Eicher, *High Commands*, 527; Jones, Id., 244; Ritter, Charles F., "George Henry Thomas," in Ritter and Wakelyn, Eds., *Leaders of the American Civil War*, 416 .

43. Isemann, "Thomas," in Heidler and Heidler, *Encyclopedia*, 1940–1941; Ritter, "Thomas," 417–418.

44. Jones, Wilmer L., *Generals*, Vol. 1, 243; Ritter, "Thomas," 246.

45. Eicher and Eicher, *High Commands*, 527; Jones, Id., 246.

46. Isemann, "Thomas," 1942.

47. Eicher and Eicher, *High Commands*, 527–528; Isemann, "Thomas," 1942–1943; Jones, Wilmer L., *Generals*, Vol. 1, 251–252; Warner, *Generals*, 501.

48. Eicher and Eicher, Id., 527; Isemann, Id.; Jones, Id., 750–751.

49. Jones, Wilmer L., *Generals*, Vol. 1, 254.

50. Eicher and Eicher, *High Commands*, 527; Isemann, "Thomas," 1940–1944; Jones, Id., 253; Warner, *Generals*, 501.

51. Bobrick, Benson, *Master of War*, 316–317.

52. Bobrick, *Master*, 316–323.

53. Jones, *Generals*, 254; Warner, *Generals*, 501.

54. Eicher and Eicher, *High Commands*, 527; Jones, Wilmer L., *Generals*, Vol. 1, 254; Warner, Id., 502.

55. Eicher and Eicher, *High Commands*, 527.

56. Bobrick, *Master*, 331.

57. Jones, *Generals*, 254.

58. Id., 243.

59. Bobrick, *Master*, 334.

60. Ritter, "Thomas," *Leaders*, 422.
61. Id., 423.
62. Bobrick, *Master of War*, 336–337; Jones, *Generals*, 244.
63. Crook, *Autobiography*, xvii.
64. Id., xiv–xviii; Eicher and Eicher, *High Commands*, 191; Machoian, "George Crook," 526; Warner, *Generals*, 102.
65. Crook, *Autobiography*, 97–100; Machoian, Id.; Warner, Id., 103.
66. Crook, Id., 105–107.
67. Id., 135–136; Warner, Id.
68. Crook, *Autobiography*, 134, fn 7; Wittenburg, *Little Phil*, 84, 90, 107–108, 139–140, 171.
69. Machoian, 526.
70. Crook, 136–141; Id.
71. Crook, *Autobiography*, 144–160.
72. Id., 160.
73. Eicher and Eicher, *High Commands*, 192.
74. Crook, *Autobiography*, 189–195; Machoian, 526.
75. Machoian, "George Crook," 526; Warner, *Generals*, 103.
76. Povall, *Rebels*, 54.
77. Crook, *Autobiography*, 300–301.
78. Fredriksen, "Henry Wager Halleck," in Heidler and Heidler, *Encyclopedia*, 908; Jones, *Generals*, 138; Ritter, "Halleck," *Leaders*, 169; Warner, *Generals*, 195.
79. Jones, Wilmer L., *Generals*, 138; Ritter, "Halleck," 170.
80. Fredriksen, "Halleck," *Encyclopedia*, 909; Jones, Id., 138–141; Ritter, "Halleck," 170–171; Warner, *Generals*, 195.
81. Warner, *Generals*, 196.
82. Ritter, "Halleck," *Leaders*, 175.
83. Jones, Wilmer L., *Generals*, Vol. 1, 150.
84. Marszalek, *Commander*, 329.
85. Id., 330.
86. Fredriksen, "Halleck," 909.
87. Marszalek, *Commander*, 248.
88. Fredriksen, "Halleck," 910–911; Ritter, "Halleck," 176.
89. Marszalek, *Commander*, 247.
90. Id., 249.
91. Eicher and Eicher, *High Commands*, 378; Fredriksen, "Irvin McDowell," Heidler and Heidler, *Encyclopedia*, 1283; Jones, *Generals*, 47–48.
92. Fredriksen, "McDowell," 1283–1284; Jones, Wilmer L., *Generals*, Vol. 1, 50–51.

93. Eicher and Eicher, *High Commands*, 378; Fredriksen, "McDowell," *Encyclopedia*, 1284; Jones, Wilmer L., *Generals*, Vol. 1, 53–55; Simone and Schmiel, *Searching*, 233–234.
94. Jones, Id., 122.
95. Jones, Wilmer L., *Generals*, Vol. 1, 53–55.
96. Fredriksen, "John Pope," *Encyclopedia*, 1540; Jones, Wilmer L., *Generals*, Vol. 1, 120.
97. Warner, *Generals*, 376.
98. Id., Jones, Wilmer L., *Generals*, Vol. 1, 119.
99. Cozzens, *Pope*, 9.
100. Jones, Wilmer L., *Generals*, Vol. 1, 120.
101. Warner, *Generals*, 376.
102. Fredriksen, "Pope," 1541; Jones, Wilmer L., *Generals*, Vol. 1, 123; Warner, *Generals*, 377.
103. Cozzens, Peter, *General John Pope*, 310–311.
104. Warner, *Generals*, 377.
105. Cozzens, *Pope*, 338.
106. Eicher and Eicher, *High Commands*, 434.
107. Cruff, Mary Lynn, "Winfield Scott Hancock," in Heidler and Heidler, *Encyclopedia*, 922.
108. Eicher and Eicher, *High Commands*, 277; Warner, *Generals*, 202–203.
109. Eicher and Eicher, Id., 277; Jones, Wilmer L., *Generals*, Vol. 1, 310.
110. Cruff, "Hancock," 922; Eicher and Eicher, *High Commands*, 277; Warner, *Generals*, 203.
111. Warner, Id.
112. Eicher and Eicher, *High Commands*, 278.
113. Warner, *Generals*, 203.
114. Id.
115. Jones, Wilmer L., *Generals*, Vol. 1, 320.
116. Jones, Wilmer L., *Generals*, Vol. 1, 321; Jordan, *Hancock*, 176–181.
117. Jordan, *Hancock*, 182–199
118. Jordan, *Hancock*, 289.
119. Jordan, *Hancock*, 305.
120. Cuff, "Hancock," 922–923; Eicher and Eicher, *High Commands*, 277–278; Jones, *Generals*, 309–322; Jordan, *Hancock*, 176–315; Warner, *Generals*, 202–204.
121. Meredith, James A., "Joseph Hooker," in Heidler and Heidler, *Encyclopedia*, 999.

122. Povall, *Rebels*, 40.
123. Eicher and Eicher, *High Commands*, 303.
124. Jones, Wilmer L., *Generals*, Vol. 1, 229–232.
125. Eicher and Eicher, *High Commands*, 304; Meredith, "Joseph Hooker," 999; Warner, *Generals*, 233.
126. Jones, Wilmer L., *Generals*, Vol. 1, 233, Meredith, "Joseph Hooker," 999.
127. Eicher and Eicher, *High Commands*, 304; Meredith, Id., 2000.
128. Jones, Wilmer L., *Generals*, Vol. 1, 233; Meredith, Id.
129. Jones, Wilmer L., *Generals*, Vol. 1, 234–239.
130. Warner, *Generals*, 234.
131. Hebert, Walter H., *Fighting Joe Hooker*, 286.
132. Hebert, *Hooker*, 286.
133. Hebert, *Hooker*, 292.
134. Eicher and Eicher, *High Commands*, 304.
135. Id.
136. Hebert, *Fighting Joe Hooker*, 294.
137. Id., 295.
138. Jones, Wilmer L., *Generals*, Vol. 1 242.
139. Warner, *Generals*, 235.
140. Eicher and Eicher, *High Commands*, 168; Nivison, Kenneth, "Joshua Lawrence Chamberlain," in Ritter and Wakelyn, *Leaders*, 77; Warner, *Generals*, 76.
141. Nivison, Id.
142. Eicher and Eicher, *High Commands*, 168; Warner, *Generals*, 76.
143. Loosbrock, Richard D., "Joshua Lawrence Chamberlain," in Heidler and Heidler, *Encyclopedia*, 389; Warner, *Generals*, 77.
144. Eicher and Eicher, *High Commands*, 168; Warner, *Generals*, 76–77.
145. Warner, Id., 76.
146. Loosbrock, "Chamberlain," 390.
147. Eicher and Eicher, *High Commands*, 169.
148. Pullen, John J., *Joshua Chamberlain*, 15.
149. Eicher and Eicher, *High Commands*, 169; Warner, *Generals*, 77.
150. Pullen, *Chamberlain*, 9.
151. Id., 22.
152. Loosbrock, "Chamberlain," 390; Warner, *Generals*, 77.
153. Loosbrock, "Chamberlain," 80; Pullen, *Chamberlain*, 34.

154. Pullen, Id., 60.
155. Loosbrock, "Chamberlain," 390.
156. Id.
157. Povall, *Rebels*, 184–185.
158. Ritter and Wakelyn, *Leaders*, 81.
159. Id., 80–81.
160. Pullen, *Chamberlain*, 59, 109.
161. Id., 112.
162. Warner, *Generals*, 77.
163. Pullen, *Chamberlain*, 114.
164. Ritter and Wakelyn, *Leaders*, 81–82.
165. Pullen, *Chamberlain*, 114–128.
166. Povall, *Rebels*, 219, 230.
167. Warner, *Generals*, 78.
168. Pullen, *Chamberlain*, 155.
169. Id., 156.
170. Ritter and Wakelyn, *Leaders*, 82.
171. Warner, *Generals*, 75.
172. Eicher and Eicher, *High Commands*, 169; Loosbrock, "Chamberlain," 390; Warner, *Generals*, 78.
173. Eicher and Eicher, *Civil War High Commands*, 461; Feis, William B., "William Starke Rosecrans," in Heidler and Heidler, *Encyclopedia*, 1677.
174. Warner, *Generals*, 410.
175. Chernow, *Grant*, 364–365.
176. Moore, David G., *William S. Rosecrans and the Union Victory*, 1678; Warner, *Generals*, 411.
177. Moore, *Rosecrans*, 189.
178. Id., 190.
179. Moore, *Rosecrans*, 192.
180. Eicher and Eicher, *Civil War High Commands*, 462; Feis, "Rosecrans," 1678; Warner, *Generals*, 411; Moore, Id., 193.
181. Moore, Id., 194.
182. Eicher and Eicher, *High Commands*, 551.
183. Warner, *Generals*, 536.
184. Eicher and Eicher, *High Commands*, 551; Boomhower, Ray E., "Lewis Wallace," in Heidler and Heidler, *Encyclopedia*, 557; Warner, *Generals*, 536.
185. Eicher and Eicher, *High Commands*, 551; Boomhower, "Lewis Wallace," 2055–2056; Warner, *Generals*, 536.
186. Povall, *Rebels*, 47; Warner, *Generals*, 536.
187. Boomhower, "Lewis Wallace," 2055–2056.
188. Id., 2056; Warner, *Generals*, 536.
189. Id.
190. Boomhower, "Lewis Wallace," 2055–2056.

191. Boomhower, Ray E., *The Sword and the Pen, A Life of Lew Wallace*, 89.

192. Boomhower, *The Sword*, 91.

193. Boomhower, *The Sword*, 110.

194. Boomhower, *The Sword*, 133–134; Eicher and Eicher, *High Commands*, 557.

195. Cardoso, "David Dixon Porter," in Heidler and Heidler, *Encyclopedia*, 1552; Eicher and Eicher, *High Commands*, 434.

196. Ritter, Charles F., "David Dixon Porter," in Ritter and Wakelyn, *Leaders*, 321–323.

197. Eicher and Eicher, *High Commands*, 434; Ritter, Id., 323.

198. Ritter, Id., 324.

199. Id.

200. Ritter, "David Dixon Porter," 327–328.

201. Id., 325.

202. Eicher and Eicher, *High Commands*, 434.

203. Cardoso, "David Dixon Porter," 1553.

204. Ritter, "David Dixon Porter," 327–328.

205. Id., 328; Eicher and Eicher, *High Commands*, 434; West, Richard S., *A Life of David Dixon Porter*, 304.

206. West, Id., 312–313.

207. Eicher and Eicher, *High Commands*, 434.

208. West, *A Life*, 316.

209. Ritter, "David Dixon Porter," 328.

210. West, *A Life*, 334–337.

211. Eicher and Eicher, *High Commands*, 434; Ritter, "David Dixon Porter," 328–329.

212. West, *A Life*, 339.

213. West, *A Life*, 344–345.

214. Eicher and Eicher, *High Commands*, 488.

215. Warner, *Generals*, 466.

216. Beckman, "Daniel Edgar Sickles," in Heidler and Heidler, 1784; Eicher and Eicher, *High Commands*, 488.

217. Eicher and Eicher, *High Commands*, 488; Warner, *Generals*, 446.

218. Beckman, "Daniel Edgar Sickles," in Heidler and Heidler, *Encyclopedia*, 1784.

219. Jones, *Generals*, 189.

220. Eicher and Eicher, *High Commands*, 488.

221. Jones, *Generals*, 192.

222. Beckman, "Daniel Edgar Sickles," in Heidler and Heidler, *Encyclopedia*, 1784.

223. Beckman, Id., 1785–1786.

224. Eicher and Eicher, *High Commands*, 488.

225. Eicher and Eicher, *Encyclopedia*, 488; Jones, *Generals*, 193–194.

226. Jones, Id., 183.

227. Eicher and Eicher, *High Commands*, 488; Jones, Id., 196–197; Warner, *Generals*, 447.

228. Beckman, "Daniel Edgar Sickles," in Heidler and Heidler, *Encyclopedia*, 1786; Jones, *Generals*, 197.

229. Jones, Id.

230. Id., 197–198.

231. Jones, *Generals*, 198.

232. Eicher and Eicher, *Encyclopedia*, 488.

233. Warner, *Generals*, 447.

Bibliography

Anderson, Dwight, and Nancy, *The Generals: Ulysses S. Grant and Robert E. Lee,* New York: Alfred Knopf, 1988.

Bache, Richard Meade, *Life of General George Gordon Meade,* Philadelphia: Henry T. Coates, 1897.

Battles and Leaders of the American Civil War, four volumes, New York: Thomas Yoseloff, 1956. First published in *Century Magazine* as a series of articles from November 1884 to November 1887 and subsequently as a four-volume set in November 1887.

Beagle, Jonathon M., "George Brinton McClellan," in Heidler, David S., and Jeanne T., Editors, *Encyclopedia of the American Civil War,* New York: W.W. Norton, 2000.

Beckman, W. Robert, "Daniel Edgar Sickles," in Heidler, David S., and Jeanne T., Editors, *Encyclopedia of the American Civil War,* New York: W.W. Norton, 2000.

Bobrick, Benson, *Master of War: The Life of General George H. Thomas,* New York: Simon & Schuster, 2009.

Boomhower, Ray E., *The Sword and the Pen: A Life of Lew Wallace,* Indianapolis: Indiana Historical Society Press, 2011.

Bourke, John G., *On the Border with Crook,* New York: Skyhorse, 2014; originally published Omaha, 1891.

Brands, H.W., *The Man Who Saved the Union: Ulysses Grant in War and Peace,* New York: Doubleday, 2014.

Canon, Jill, *Civil War Heroes,* Santa Barbara: Bellerophon Books, 2002.

Cardoso, Jack J., "David Dixon Porter," in Heidler, David S., and Jeanne T., Editors, *Encyclopedia of the American Civil War,* New York: W.W. Norton, 2000.

Chernow, Ron, *Grant,* New York: Penguin, 2017.

Chesnut, Mary Boykin, *Mary Chesnut's Civil War,* edited by C. Vann Woodward, New Haven: Yale University Press, 1981.

Cluff, Mary Lynn, "Winfield Scott Hancock," in Heidler, David S., and Jeanne T., Editors, *Encyclopedia of the American Civil War,* New York: W.W. Norton, 2000.

Commager, Henry Steele, *The Blue and the Gray,* Indianapolis: Bobbs-Merrill, 1950.

Cozzens, Peter, *General John Pope: A Life for the Nation,* Urbana: University of Illinois Press, 2000.

Davis, Michael S., "David Glasgow Farragut," in Heidler, David S., and Jeanne T., Editors, *Encyclopedia of the American Civil War,* New York: W.W. Norton, 2000.

Davis, Steven, *Atlanta Will Fall: Sherman, Joe Johnston and the Heavy Battalions,* Wilmington, DE: Scholarly Resources, 2001.

Drake, William F., *Little Phil: The Story of General Philip Henry Sheridan,* Prospect, CT: Biographical Publishing Company, 2005.

Duffy, James P., *Lincoln's Admiral: The Civil War Campaigns of David Farragut,* Hoboken: Castle Books, with permission of James Wiley & Sons, 1997.

Eicher, John H., and David J., *Civil War High Commands,* Stanford: Stanford University Press, 2001.

Faulkner, William C., *Intruder in the Dust,* New York: Random House, 1948.

Feis, William B., "William Starke Rosecrans," in Heidler, David S., and Jeanne T., Editors, *Encyclopedia of the American Civil War*, New York: W.W. Norton, 2000.

Flood, Charles Bracelen, *Grant and Sherman: The Friendship That Won the Civil War*, New York: HarperCollins, 2006, first published by Farrar, Straus and Giroux, 2005.

Foote, Shelby, *The Civil War: A Narrative*, three volumes, New York: Random House, 1974.

Fredriksen, John C., "Henry Wager Halleck," in Heidler, David S., and Jeanne T., Editors, *Encyclopedia of the American Civil War*, New York: W.W. Norton, 2000.

Fredriksen, John C., "Irwin McDowell," in Heidler, David S. and Jeanne T., Editors, *Encyclopedia of the American Civil War*, New York: W.W. Norton, 2000.

Fredriksen, John C., "Philip Henry Sheridan, Union General," in Heidler, David S., and Jeanne T., Editors, *Encyclopedia of the American Civil War*, New York: W.W. Norton, 2000.

Garland, Hamlin, *Ulysses S. Grant, His Life and Character*, New York: Macmillan, 1920.

Gerson, Noel B., *Yankee Admiral: A Biography of David Dixon Porter*, Leeds: Sapere Books, 1968.

Grant, Ulysses S., *The Complete Personal Memoirs of Ulysses S. Grant*, first published New York, 1885; republished New York: ReadaClassic, 2010.

Green, Carl R., and Sanford, William R., *Union Generals of the Civil War*, Springfield, NJ: Enslow Publishing, 1998.

Hardin, David, *After the War*: Chicago: Ivan R. Dee, 2010.

Hart, B.H. Liddell, *Sherman: Soldier, Realist, American*, Boston: Da Capo, 1998.

Hassler, Warren W., Jr., *General George B. McClellan, Shield of the Union*, Westport, CT: Greenwood Press, 1974; first published Baton Rouge: Louisiana State University Press, 1957.

Hearn, Chester G., *Admiral David Glasgow Farragut*, Annapolis: Naval Institute Press, 1998.

Hebert, Walter H., *Fighting Joe Hooker*, Lincoln: University of Nebraska Press, 1999.

Heidler, David S., and Jeanne T., Editors, *Encyclopedia of the American Civil War*, New York: W.W. Norton, 2000.

Hess, Earl J., *Braxton Bragg: The Most Hated Man of the Confederacy*. Chapel Hill: University of North Carolina Press, 2016.

Hewett, Lawrence L., "Braxton Bragg," In *The Confederate General*, six volumes, edited by William C. Davis and Julie Hoffman, Harrisburg, PA: National Historical Society, 1991.

Hubbell, John T., "Ulysses Simpson Grant," in Ritter, Charles F., and Wakelyn, Jon L., Editors, *Leaders of the American Civil War*, Westport, CT: Greenwood Press, 1998.

Huntington, Tom, *Searching for George Gordon Meade*, Mechanicsburg, PA: Stackpole, 2015.

Isemann, James, "George Henry Thomas," in Heidler, David S., and Jeanne T., Editors, *Encyclopedia of the American Civil War*, New York: W.W. Norton, 2000.

Jones, Terry L., *Historical Dictionary of the American Civil War*, Lanham, MD: Scarecrow Press, 2002.

Jones, Wilmer L., *Generals in Blue and Gray*, Vol. 1, Mechanicsburg, PA: Stackpole, 2006.

Jordon, David M., *Winfield Scott Hancock: A Soldier's Life*, Bloomington: Indiana University Press, 1988.

Klunder, Willard Carl, "John Pope," in Heidler, David S., and Jeanne T., Editors, *Encyclopedia of the American Civil War*, New York: W.W. Norton, 2000.

Lash, Jeffrey N., *Destroyer of the Iron Horse*, Kent, OH: Kent State University Press, 1991.

Lewis, Charles Lee, *David Glasgow Farragut: Our First Admiral*, Annapolis: Naval Institute Press, 1943.

Loosbrock, Richard D., "Joshua Lawrence Chamberlain," in Heidler, David S., and Jeanne T., Editors, *Encyclopedia of the American Civil War*, New York, W.W. Norton, 2000.

Lyman, Theodore, *Meade's Headquarters, 1863–1865*, Boston: Massachusetts Historical Society, 1922.

Mahan, Alfred Thayer, *David Farragut*, New York: D. Appleton, 1911; reprinted New York: The Confucian Press, 1981.

Marszalek, John F., *Commander of All Lincoln's Armies: A Life of General Henry W. Halleck*, Cambridge,: The Belknap Press of Harvard University Press, 2004.

Marszalek, John F., *Sherman: A Soldier's Passion for Order,* New York: The Free Press, 1993.
Marszalek, John F., "William Tecumseh Sherman," in Ritter, Charles F., and Wakelyn, Jon L., Editors, *Leaders of the American Civil War,* Westport, CT: Greenwood Press, 1998.
Martin, Samuel J., *General Braxton Bragg, CSA,* Jefferson, NC: McFarland, 2011.
McClellan, George B., *McClellan's Own Story: The War for the Union,* Big Byte Books, 2014; first published in New York, 1887.
McDonough, James Lee, *William Tecumseh Sherman: In the Service of My Country: A Life,* New York: W.W. Norton, 2017.
McFeely, William S., *Grant,* New York: W.W. Norton, 1982.
McMurray, Richard M., *John Bell Hood and the War for Southern Independence,* Lincoln: University of Nebraska Press, 1992.
Meade, George, *The Life and Letters of George Gordon Meade,* two volumes, edited by Major General George Gordon Meade, originally published 1913; republished by Big Byte Books, 2014.
Meredith, James A., "Joseph Hooker," in Ritter, Charles F., and Wakelyn, Jon L., Editors, *Leaders of the American Civil War,* Westport, CT: Greenwood Press, 1998.
Moore, David G., *William S. Rosecrans and the Union Victory,* Jefferson: McFarland, 2004.
Morris, Roy, Jr., *Sheridan: The Life & Wars of General Phil Sheridan,* New York: Vintage, 1993.
Nivison, Kenneth, "Joshua Lawrence Chamberlain," in Ritter, Charles F., and Wakelyn, Jon L., Editors, *Leaders of the American Civil War,* Westport, CT: Greenwood Press, 1998.
O'Connell, Robert L., *Fierce Patriot: The Tangled Lives of William Tecumseh Sherman,* New York: Random House, 2014.
Poore, Benjamin Perley, *The Life and Public Services of Ambrose E. Burnside,* Providence, RI: J.A. and R.A. Reid, 1882.
Povall, Allie Stuart, *Rebels in Repose: Confederate Commanders After the War,* Charleston, SC: The History Press, 2019.
Pullen, John J., *Joshua Chamberlain: A Hero's Life & Legacy,* Mechanicsburg, PA: Stackpole, 1999.
Ritter, Charles F., "George Henry Thomas," in Ritter, Charles F., and Wakelyn, Jon L., Editors,, *Leaders of the American Civil War,* Westport, CT: Greenwood Press, 1998.
Rowland, Thomas J., "George Brinton McClellan," in Ritter, Charles F., and Wakelyn, Jon L., Editors, *Leaders of the American Civil War,* Westport, CT: Greenwood Press, 1998.
Sauers, Richard A., "Ambrose Everett Burnside," in Heidler, David S., and Jeanne T., Editors, *Encyclopedia of the American Civil War,* New York: W.W. Norton, 2000.
Sauers, Richard A., "George Gordon Meade," in Heidler, David S., and Jeanne T., Editors, *Encyclopedia of the American Civil War,* New York: W.W. Norton, 2000.
Sears, Stephen W., *George B. McClellan: The Young Napoleon,* Boston: Da Capo, 1999; first published New York: Ticknor & Fields, 1988.
Sears, Stephen W., "Lincoln and McClellan," in Boritt, Gabor S., Editor, *Lincoln's Generals,* New York: Oxford University Press, 1994.
Sheridan, Philip Henry, *The Personal Memoirs of P.H. Sheridan,* two volumes, originally published New York: C. L. Webster, 1888; republished Boston: Da Capo, 1992.
Sherman, William T., *Memoirs of General W. T. Sherman,* first published St. Louis, 1875; most recent publication, Renaissance Classics, 2012.
Sifakis, Stephen, *Who Was Who in the American Civil War,* New York: Facts on File, 1980.
Simione, Frank P., Jr., and Schmiel, Gene, *Searching for Irvin McDowell: Forgotten Civil War General,* Middletown, DE: Frank P. Simione, Jr., and Gene Schmiel, 2021.
Smith, Jean Edward, *Grant: A Biography,* Newtown, CT: American Political Biography Press by arrangement with Simon & Schuster, 2001.
Sommers, Richard J., "Ulysses Simpson Grant," in Heidler, David S., and Jeanne T., Editors, *Encyclopedia of the American Civil War,* New York: W.W. Norton, 2000.
Spencer, James, *Civil War Generals,* Westport, CT: Greenwood Press, 1937.
Symonds, Craig L., *Joseph E. Johnston: A Civil War Biography,* New York: W.W. Norton, 1992.
Urwin, Gregory J.W., "George Armstrong Custer," in Heidler, David S., and Jeanne T., Editors, *Encyclopedia of the American Civil War,* New York: W.W. Norton, 2000.

Wakelyn, Jon L., "George Gordon Meade," in Ritter, Charles F., and Wakelyn, Jon L., Editors, *Leaders of the American Civil War*, Westport, CT: Greenwood Press, 1998.

Wakelyn, Jon L., "Philip Henry Sheridan," in Ritter, Charles F., and Wakelyn, Jon L., Editors, *Leaders of the American Civil War*, Westport, CT, Greenwood Press, 1998.

Wakelyn, Jon L., "Ulysses Simpson Grant," in Ritter, Charles F., and Wakelyn, Jon L., Editors, *Leaders of the American Civil War*, Westport, CT: Greenwood Press, 1998.

Warner, Ezra J., *Generals in Blue: Lives of the Union Commanders*, Baton Rouge: Louisiana State University Press, 1964.

Waugh, Joan, *U.S. Grant: American Hero, American Myth*, Chapel Hill: University of North Carolina Press, 2009.

Wert, Jeffrey D., *Custer: The Controversial Life of George Armstrong Custer*, New York: Simon & Schuster, 2004.

Wert, Jeffrey D., *From Winchester to Cedar Hill: The Shenandoah Campaign of 1864*, New York: Simon & Schuster, 1987.

Wert, Jeffrey D., *General James Longstreet: The Confederacy's Most Controversial Soldier*, New York: Simon & Schuster, 1993.

West, Richard S., Jr., *The Second Admiral: A Life of David Dixon Porter*, New York: Coward-McCann, 1937.

Wheelan, Joseph, *Terrible Swift Sword–: The Life of General Philip H. Sheridan*, Boston: Da Capo, 2012.

White, Ronald C., *American Ulysses: A Life of Ulysses S. Grant*, New York: Random House, 2016.

Winik, Jay, *April 1865. The Month That Saved America*, New York: Harper Perennial, 2001.

Wittenberg, Eric J., *Little Phil: A Reassessment of the Civil War Leadership of General Philip H. Sheridan*, Dulles: Potomac, 2002.

Index

Numbers in **bold italics** indicate pages with illustrations